# To Seek Out New Worlds

# To Seek Out New Worlds

## Science Fiction and World Politics

*Edited by Jutta Weldes*

palgrave
macmillan

First published in 2003 by PALGRAVE MACMILLAN™
175 Fifth Avenue, New York, N.Y. 10010 and
Houndmills, Basingstoke, Hampshire, England RG21 6XS.
Companies and representatives throughout the world.

PALGRAVE MACMILLAN IS THE GLOBAL ACADEMIC IMPRINT OF THE
PALGRAVE MACMILLAN division of St. Martin's Press, LLC and of Palgrave
Macmillan Ltd. Macmillan® is a registered trademark in the United States,
United Kingdom and other countries. Palgrave is a registered trademark in
the European Union and other countries.

0-312-29557-x (hardback)
1-4039-6058-5 (paper)

Library of Congress Cataloging-in-Publication Data Available from the
Library of Congress

A catalogue record for this book is available from the British Library.

First Palgrave Macmillan edition: May 2003
10  9  8  7  6  5  4  3  2  1

Transferred to Digital Printing in 2012

*To Diana and Jennifer with love.*

# CONTENTS

# PART III

## FUTURE WORLDS, ALTERNATIVE IMAGININGS

# ACKNOWLEDGMENTS

This volume has been a labor of love. I must, first and foremost, thank the contributors, who have made this project supremely enjoyable. Naeem and Aida initially had the idea for a book on science fiction (SF) and world politics, and everyone has done their bit with enthusiasm. The contributors' combined knowledge of world politics and SF has made this enterprise "serious fun." Several other individuals deserve mention. Special thanks are due to Cindy Weber for her excellent comments at the 2001 International Studies Association (ISA) meeting in Chicago on initial incarnations of several of the chapters and on the project as a whole. They influenced the very structure of the volume. Thanks as well to Louiza Odysseos for her comments on several additional chapters at the 2002 ISA in New Orleans. I would also like to extend my appreciation to Richard Little for encouraging me to pursue a project on popular culture: few international relations scholars are as open-minded as he. A semester's study leave from the Department of Politics at the University of Bristol—an unusually supportive and intellectually vibrant environment—allowed me to finish this project while starting several others. Special thanks go to Iver Neumann for quick and insightful assistance when I most needed it. I am grateful to Toby Wahl for his support of this project and to all those at Palgrave who so efficiently shepherded this manuscript through the production process. Finally, Mark Laffey provided *constant* encouragement and read *lots and lots* of drafts of the introduction (and told me to add the italics). Sadie and Finian took advantage of my interest in SF to stay up late watching *Star Trek,* and occasionally *Buffy.*

# Chapter 1

## POPULAR CULTURE, SCIENCE FICTION, AND WORLD POLITICS

### Exploring Intertextual Relations

*Jutta Weldes*

Why examine science fiction if we are interested in world politics? On the face of it, there seems to be little relation between the two. World politics, common sense tells us, is first and foremost about life-and-death issues: war and peace, ethnic cleansing and genocide, the global spread of AIDS, refugees, natural disasters, nuclear proliferation, terrorism and counter-terrorism, global trafficking in arms, drugs, and human beings, famines, free trade, rapacious corporations, globalization. World politics is serious business; it is difficult policy choices and intractable differences of opinion in "a domain of hard truths, material realities, and irrepressible natural facts" (Ó Tuathail and Agnew, 1992: 192).

Science fiction, in contrast, is precisely fictional. It is make-believe, and we read it, watch it, argue about it, and poach on it for fun.[1] As everyone knows, science fiction (or SF) deals with imagined futures, alien landscapes, bizarre cityscapes, sleek ships for traveling through space, improbable machines for escaping time, encounters with fantastic creatures from other worlds or our own future, and radical transformations of societies and their inhabitants. Its hallmark, writes Darko Suvin, is "an imaginative framework alternative to the author's empirical environment" (1979: 9) that, through strategies like extrapolation and estrangement, helps us to transcend our mundane environment. So what is the connection to world politics?

The apparent great divide between the "hard truths" of world politics and the imagined worlds of SF is deceiving, however. The dividing line between world politics' material realities and natural facts and the fictional worlds and imaginative possibilities of SF is far from clear. For instance:

- NASA/*Star Trek:* As Constance Penley has shown, a pervasive connection exists between the discourse of the U.S. National Aeronautics and Space Administration (NASA) and that of *Star Trek* (1997: 4; see also Nichols, 1994). It is perhaps best illustrated in the naming of the first U.S. space shuttle. Initially to be called *The Constitution,* it was in fact christened *The Enterprise*—in honor of *Star Trek*'s flagship—after U.S. President Gerald Ford, in the wake of a letter-writing campaign by *Star Trek* fans, directed NASA to change the name (18–19). This same U.S. space shuttle *Enterprise* then found its way back to *Star Trek:* it appears in the succession of ships called *Enterprise* shown in the montage that opens each episode of the fifth *Star Trek* series, *Enterprise.*[2]
- SDI/*Star Wars:* On March 23, 1983, U.S. President Ronald Reagan delivered a nationwide television address calling for research into defenses that could "intercept and destroy strategic ballistic missiles before they reached our own soil or that of our allies," thus rendering "nuclear weapons impotent and obsolete" (Reagan, 1983). The next day, SDI critics in the U.S. Congress lampooned Reagan's vision of a defensive military umbrella, successfully relabeling it "Star Wars" after George Lucas's block-buster SF movie (1977) (Smith, nd.).
- Hiroshima/*Locksley Hall:* U.S. President Harry Truman's decision to drop the newly developed atomic bomb on Hiroshima and Nagasaki was apparently influenced by his belief that demonstrating the power of an "ultimate superweapon" could end the war. Truman had copied 10 lines from Tennyson's poem *Locksley Hall*—lines that depict "ultimate aerial superweapons for the future, waging a terrible climactic war in the skies" (Franklin, 1990a: 157)—and carried them in his wallet for 35 years. In July 1945, realizing that he was about to gain control over just such a superweapon, Truman "pulled that now faded slip of paper from his wallet, and recited those lines . . . to a reporter" (ibid.).[3]
- Globalization/*Spaceship Earth: The Economist* depicts liberal globalization using many SF references. In particular, the magazine is awash in images of "spaceship Earth." This ubiquitous trope constructs the increasingly globalized world as, on the one hand, "a sin-

gle totality, 'the global village,' making it appear easily accessible"
while, on the other hand, positioning it "out there" on "the final
frontier" of space (Hooper, 2000: 68). For *The Economist*, liberal
globalization is made sensible "through imagery which integrates science, technology, business, and images of globalisation into a kind
of entrepreneurial frontier masculinity, in which capitalism meets
science fiction" (65).

- The Revolution in Military Affairs/*future war fiction:* The so-called
  Revolution in Military Affairs (RMA) might better be called "military
  science fiction." This ideology of the technological fix, championed
  in both official military futurology (e.g., U.S. Army's *Army Vision
  2010* or U.S. Space Command's *Vision for 2020*) and in a broader
  corpus of think tank projections (e.g., Shukman, 1996; O'Hanlon,
  2000; Metz, 2000), aims to transform threat perceptions and the
  technological, doctrinal, and organizational basis of warfare. The
  RMA, however, tells us less about the future of warfare than about
  "contemporary cultural obsessions and the continuing influence of
  powerful historical concerns, pre-occupations, fixations, and desires"
  (Latham, 2001: 9). In fact, the RMA is better understood not as a rational response to objective changes in military technology or the
  geo-strategic environment but as a cultural artifact powerfully shaped
  by enduring SF fantasies of future war, such that official military futurology mirrors SF's characteristic "anxieties, desires, fears, fetishes,
  insecurities, and cognitive and affective predispositions" (10).
- Neo-liberal globalization/*Foundation:* The neo-liberal discourse of
  globalization dominating public discussion is a self-fulfilling
  prophecy (Hay and Marsh, 2000: 9) that rests on a well-rehearsed set
  of narratives and tropes, including an Enlightenment commitment to
  progress, the wholesome role of global markets, a rampant
  technophilia, the trope of the "global village," and the interrelated
  narratives of an increasingly global culture and an expanding pacific
  liberal politics. As I've argued elsewhere (Weldes, 2001), this discourse displays striking homologies to American techno-utopian SF
  (exemplified in Isaac Asimov's classic Foundation novels [1951, 1952,
  1953, 1982, 1986, 1988, 1993]). These homologies help to render
  neo-liberal globalization both sensible and seemingly "inexorable"
  (Gray, 1998: 206). Moreover, underlying Asimov's Foundation universe lies a barely concealed authoritarian politics that alerts us to the
  covertly, but nonetheless demonstrably, un-democratic character of
  globalization and contemporary global governance.

While some of the connections between world politics and SF illustrated here are superficial, others are more deeply rooted. For example, explicit references might be made from one domain to the other. NASA poaches from *Star Trek,* while SDI's critics attempt to dismiss it as *Star Wars* (but even these relations turn out to be more complex). In other cases, deeper relations exist. Globalization and claims to a "global village" are made commonsensical through space-based images of "Spaceship Earth" that, although they became practically possible only in 1966, when the first photographs taken in outer space showed "planet Earth as one location" (Scholte, 1997: 16–17), have long been a staple of SF. Similarly, in hoping that his new "superweapon" would bring an end to World War II, Truman was no different from many of his compatriots, "who had grown up in a cultural matrix bubbling with fantasies of ultimate weapons." Such fantasies, Franklin explains, profoundly shaped "the nation's conceptions of nuclear weapons and responses to them, decades before they materialized" (1990a: 157; 1988). A long history of fantastic enemies and sophisticated high-tech wars—from H. G. Wells' *The War of the Worlds* (1898), through Robert Heinlein's *Starship Troopers* (1959), to Roland Emmerich's film *Independence Day* (1996)—renders desirable a future of militarized security seemingly attainable through advanced weapons and information warfare.

Conversely, SF is rife with references to wars, empires, diplomatic intrigue, and so forth—the very stuff of world politics. The first chapter of the 1954 edition of Arthur C. Clarke's *Childhood's End,*[4] for instance, makes direct reference to contemporary politics. The context is explicitly the cold war, "the cleavage between East and West" (2). The U.S. carrier *James Forrestal* searches for Russian submarines off the Pacific island launch site of the *Columbus,* soon to be headed for Mars; the U.S. space program is spurred on by new intelligence that "the Russians are nearly level with us" (2); a Russian gloats that "In another month we will be on our way, and the Yankees will be choking themselves with rage" (3). Many works of SF begin with, make explicit reference to, and poach on politics, including historical and contemporary events, situations, and characters from world politics. The relations between SF and world politics, then, are more numerous and more complex than is generally assumed.

Curiously, although we live in a time when "the political and the cultural can no longer be decoupled" (Dean, 2000: 2), this intimate relationship has rarely been examined. This is especially true of scholars of world politics or "International Relations," who have generally devoted their attention to "high politics," eschewing both the depths of low politics and the shallows of a frivolous popular culture. As Cynthia Weber put it: "Whether by neglect, by design, or by displacement, the politics of the popular is among the most under-valued and therefore under-analyzed aspects of international politics" (2001: 134). If it is unusual for popular culture in general to be studied in connection with world politics, it is even more so for world politics and SF to be studied together.

## POPULAR CULTURE AND WORLD POLITICS

Cynthia Enloe has argued that, while much scholarship on world politics has been obsessed with power, it has simultaneously dramatically "*under-*estimat[ed] the amounts and varieties of power it takes to form and sustain" the contemporary global system (1996: 186). She criticizes in particular the tendency to focus on the powerful—powerful states or powerful statesmen, for instance—on the assumption that this will provide the most important insights into and explanations of world politics. Against this view, Enloe argues that if we focus on the "margins, silences and bottom rungs" (188) we can see the myriad forms and the astonishing amounts of power that are required for the contemporary global system, including states, to exist at all.

Some of the power that defines and sustains world politics does of course reside in the realm of what has traditionally been labeled "high politics"—the arena of diplomacy and security, war and peace (e.g., Kegley and Wittkopf, 1999: 14). Whether or not states brandish nuclear weapons and how and to what extent they deploy military forces, for instance, affects the structure, processes, and outcomes of world politics. That the United States alone accounted for 37 percent of global military expenditures in 2000—roughly $295 billion out of $798 billion (*SIPRI Yearbook,* 2001)—certainly contributes to the uni-polar character of contemporary world politics, as it does to the particular, and peculiar, characteristics of the "war on terrorism." But power resides as well in the depths of "low politics"—defined not only in terms of conventional categories like economics and demography, but also in the more neglected terms of gender, class, race, and colonial relations (e.g., Enloe, 2000; Pijl, 1984; Gilroy, 1993; Grovogui, 1996, respectively). In fact, as more critical scholars have long recognized, "high" and "low" politics are inextricably intertwined. Enloe put it well: "The bedroom's hierarchy is not unconnected to the hierarchies of the international coffee exchange or of the foreign ministry" (1996: 193). Gender relations and gendered divisions of labor, for instance, are at the heart of globalization, whether national-level processes of economic restructuring or the efficient and profitable internationalization of capital (e.g., Wichterich, 2000). Even more important for our purposes here, however, power is produced and reproduced culturally, even in a *popular* culture typically dismissed out of hand as frivolous and thus irrelevant. This volume's focus on popular culture is part of a wider attempt to "pluralize" world politics by multiplying "the sites and categories that 'count' as political" (Dean, 2000: 4).

Although the term "culture" is highly contested (Williams, 1983: 160), it is analytically fruitful to think of culture as "the context within which people give meaning to their actions and experiences and make sense of their lives" (Tomlinson, 1991: 7). Culture, in this sense, is less a set of artifacts—novels, plays, television programs, comics, for instance—than it is a process or a set of practices. These practices, including representations, language, and customs, are "concerned with the production and the exchange of meanings—the 'giving and taking of meaning'—between members of a society or group" (Hall, 1997a: 2). Understood in this way, culture encompasses the multiplicity of discourses[5] or "codes of intelligibility" (Hall, 1985: 105) through which meanings are constructed and practices produced. This multiplicity, in turn, implies that meanings can be contested. Culture is thus composed of potentially contested codes and representations; it designates a field on which battles over meaning are fought. In Stuart Hall's words, culture encompasses "the contradictory forms of 'common sense' which have taken root in and helped to shape popular life" (1986: 26). *Popular* culture[6] properly comprises one substantial element in this field of contestable and contradictory common sense meanings.

As the chapters in this volume demonstrate, the connections between popular culture, and specifically SF, and world politics are intimate, complex, and diverse. On the one hand, popular culture helps to create and sustain the conditions for contemporary world politics. As Michael Shapiro has argued, "with the exception of some resistant forms, music, theater, TV weather forecasts, and even cereal box scripts tend to endorse prevailing power structures by helping to reproduce the beliefs and allegiances necessary for their uncontested functioning" (1992: 1). U.S. popular culture in the mid 1980s, for instance, helped to "redeem Vietnam and Teheran" with such films as *Rambo: First Blood, Part II* (1985) and the "techno-twit novels" of Tom Clancy, such as *The Hunt for Red October* (1984) and *Red Storm Rising* (1986) (Lipschutz, 2001: 146). On the other hand, it is possible for popular culture to challenge the boundaries of common sense, to contest the taken-for-granted. While prevailing cultural and discursive practices constrain and oppress people, they simultaneously provide "resources to fight against those constraints" (Fiske, in Nelson, Treichler, and Grossberg, 1992: 5). The film *Dr. Strangelove* (1964) is a classic example, ridiculing, among other things, anti-communist paranoia and the convolutions of nuclear deterrence; *Canadian Bacon* (1995) is another, hilariously deriding jingoism and warmongering. Sometimes, perhaps even often, popular culture both supports and challenges the common sense of world politics. The film *Starship Troopers* (1997), for instance, while subverting conventional narratives of security by showing how knowledge of the enemy and the self is created and secured, nonetheless reproduces the very self/other distinction on which contemporary world politics is based (Whitehall, this volume). Whether a particular popular cultural text supports or undermines existing relations of power, or both at once, examining such texts helps us to highlight the workings of power.

To the extent that popular culture reproduces extant power relations, we can examine it for insights into the character and functioning of world politics. For instance, both state officials and publics explain and grasp the workings of states and world politics in largely common sense terms. As the earlier examples of the RMA and its belief in the technological fix or of Truman's and Reagan's belief in the pacific potential of ultimate super-weapons indicate, popular culture helps to define and represent, or to construct, world politics for state officials. Official representations thus depend on the cultural resources of a society. So too do the ways in which they are understood. The plausibility of official representations depends on the ways in which publics understand world politics and the location and role of their own and other states and actors in it. It matters very much that state officials are able to represent world politics, and thus their foreign policies, in ways that at least significant portions of their publics find plausible and persuasive. Plausibility comes, at least in part, from the structural congruence between official representations and peoples' everyday experiences. This explicitly implicates *popular* culture in providing a background of meanings that help to constitute public images of world politics and foreign policy. SDI becomes "Star Wars" for its detractors, and then also for its defenders. Popular culture, then, helps to construct the reality of world politics for elites and the public alike and, to the extent that it reproduces the content and structure of dominant foreign-policy discourses, it helps to produce consent to foreign policy and state action. Popular culture is thus implicated in the "production of consent" (Hall, 1982).

This is not to argue that resistance is futile. Popular culture also provides alternatives that challenge the status quo; we can examine it for modes of thinking that resist dominant constructions of world politics, that provide alternative visions of world politics, and that offer possibilities for transformation. Utopias are a case in point. Whether in its original form, meaning "no place," or its later form, as a good or better place, a utopia is "an imaginary place, a nowhere land, a realm . . . where dreams may flourish and desires be realized" (Lefanu, 1988: 53). For instance, it is often assumed (whether correctly or not is another story, as the chapters by Neumann, Inayatullah, and Whitehall make clear) that the *Star Trek* universe offers an alternative, liberal future that not only has eliminated poverty, racism, sexism, jingoism, and colonialism, but also challenges contemporary society to rectify such unacceptable states of affairs (e.g., Whitfield and Roddenberry, 1968). Feminist utopias, as a sub-genre of SF, also offer a set of generic themes critical of, and alternative to, dominant trends in contemporary world politics, including the lack of central, or even formal, government, the rejection of traditional notions of private ownership, concern for the environment and sustainable relations with nature, and the peripheral nature of war and violence (Lefanu, 1988: 54; see also Crawford, this volume). They allow us to imagine how we might better organize and structure local and global politics.

Whether popular culture supports or challenges status quo power relations, or does both at once, its analysis allows us to access the political. Popular culture, in expressing, enacting and producing discourses and their specific ideological effects,[7] participates in meaning production, and thus in politics. The studies in this volume examine the connections between popular culture and "larger structures, relations, processes, and assemblages of power" (Dean, 2000: 7) that characterize both the practices and the analysis of world politics. Perhaps surprisingly, as one analyst has put it, fiction, including SF, provides excellent "vehicles for disclosing assumptions" (Bartter, 1990: 173), including assumptions about global politics.

## WHY SCIENCE FICTION?

In this volume we seek to explore the relatively uncharted relations between SF and world politics. SF, like culture, is a contested term. As many commentators and analysts have noted, although we all know SF when we see it, there exists no standard, generally accepted definition of it (e.g., Roberts, 2000: 1–19; Kuhn, 1990: 1). SF is certainly "readily identifiable and regularly identified" by its readers, by publishers, and by book sellers (Shippey, 1991: 1; see also James, 1994: 3). Conversely, it can also be identified, as Shippey put it, "by ricochet" in that "its detractors may not know much about the genre, but they know what they don't like" (3). While scholars have argued for decades over the precise nature of this very popular genre,[8] the contributors to this volume approach SF common-sensically: they know it when they see it. They have chosen to examine mainly widely recognized SF texts—films, television shows, and novels—through which multiple relationships between SF and world politics can fruitfully be investigated.

Although SF is difficult to define with precision, at least one of its central generic characteristics is directly relevant to its relations to world politics. Central to the genre[9] is the process of estrangement (Shippey, 1991: 13). Estrangement or alienation is based on what Darko Suvin dubbed the novum—Latin for "new" or "new thing"—which sets the imagined world of a work of SF off from the mundane (Suvin, 1979: 63–84). Classic examples of nova include aliens, spaceships, time machines, robots, androids, cyborgs, advanced computing machines, and hyper-drives. When we pick up a work of fiction and encounter such a novum, we know we are reading SF. On the first page of Philip K. Dick's *The Penultimate Truth* (1964), for instance, we meet several nova that signal that this is a work of SF. We are introduced to a man named John Adams, whose library is described as "an Ozymandiasian[10] structure built from concrete chunks that had once in another age formed an entrance ramp to the Bayshore Freeway." Clearly we are far into the future, and presumably the Bayshore Freeway has crumbled or been dismantled. We discover that the marble top to Adams' desk "had been salvaged from a bombed-out house in the Russian Hill section of the former city of San Francisco." San Francisco no longer exists, and there seems to have been an extensive war. Other nova are added. Adams seats himself at his desk, and turns on his "rhetorizor." At the same time, a woman named Colleen "disappeared to search for a leady to fix her a drink." Until we read further, we can't know what a "rhetorizor" is, or a "leady." We've entered a strange world, "an imaginative framework alternative to the author's [and reader's] empirical environment" (Suvin, 1979: 9).

These nova provide "a door through which we step into a different way of looking at things" (Roberts, 2000: 20), but they are also always "grounded in a discourse of possibility, which is usually called science or technology, and which renders the difference a *material* one rather than just a conceptual or imaginative one" (7). This discourse of possibility, rendering the nova plausible on their own terms, in their own universe, and thus providing explanations, or pseudo-explanations, for their existence, distinguishes SF from other imaginative literature, such as magical realism. At the same time that the nova provide a point of discontinuity from the known world, SF allows us to confront that world by representing it through "metaphoric strategies and metonymic tactics" (Broderick, 1995: 155). Through such strategies and tactics, the imagined SF world "encodes a part of the real world" (Roberts, 2000: 12). In this sense, one might argue, with Roberts, that *Blade Runner*'s androids—whose existence is hollow because of their built-in four-year life spans—are "a metaphor for the alienated existence of contemporary life" (13; see also Lipschutz, this volume).

SF offers an exceptionally useful focus for analysis because it concerns itself quite self-consciously with political issues; it directly addresses issues like technological and social change, confronting contemporary verities with possible alternatives. For instance, SF often extrapolates into the future.[11] As a strategy, extrapolation is "based on the metonymical extension of the ends of reality" (Stockwell, 1996: 5). That is, it starts with the known and projects or expands some part of it into the unknown. SF texts, in this sense, "reflect where this present is heading, both in terms of how they envisage the future but also as cognitive spaces that help to shape and direct how people conceive and make the future" (Kitchin and Kneale, 2001: 32). Utopias, for instance, tell us something about what we hope the future will be, dystopias something about what we fear it might be. Dystopias, of course, extrapolate negatively from contemporary trends. As a result, they often provide themes directly critical of contemporary world politics. William Gibson's "Sprawl" series[12] is a good example. Rooted in a 1980s perception that the state was declining at the expense of multinational corporations (MNCs), it portrays a genuinely globalized future in which states have been eclipsed by cyberspace, global corporations, and global organized crime. The global market is dominated by the Yakuza and MNCs: "Power . . . meant corporate power. The zaibatsus, the multinationals that shaped the course of human history, had transcended old barriers. Viewed as organisms, they had attained a kind of immortality" (1984: 242). Both Yakuza and MNCs are "hives with cybernetic memories, vast single organisms, their DNA coded in silicon" (242). Technology has run rampant. This is a world of body and mind "invasion" (Sterling, 1986: xii); a world of prosthetic limbs (Gibson, 1984: 9); eyes—"sea-green Nikon transplants"—that are "vatgrown" (33); and a cyborg dolphin, "surplus from the last war" and a heroin addict (Gibson, 1981: 23). Through such dystopias, we can criticize the trends of contemporary politics. In Mike Davis's words: "William Gibson . . . has provided stunning examples of how realist, 'extrapolative' science fiction can operate as prefigurative social theory, as well as an anticipatory opposition politics to the cyber-fascism lurking over the horizon" (1992: 3).

More important, of course, SF tells us about the present. As Ronnie Lipschutz notes later in this volume, SF never really is about the future: "It is about us and the world in which we live." William Gibson agrees: "What's most important to me," he has explained, "is that it's about the present. . . . It's a way of trying to come to terms with the awe and terror inspired in me by the world in which we live" (in Kitchin and Kneale, 2001: 31). This is because SF "presents syntagmatically developed possible worlds, as models (more precisely as thought-experiments) or as totalizing and thematic metaphors" (Suvin, 1988: 198). These possible worlds allow us to explore elements of *contemporary* society in more or less estranged settings. SF of the 1950s and 1960s, for example, used myriad future scenarios to explore the consequences and possible ramifications of nuclear war. With its focus on alternative worlds, SF can "accommodate radical doubt and questioning" (Davies, 1990: 4), thus providing space to interrogate contemporary politics.

On the face of it, SF can help us to understand world politics because it offers clear and direct representations of themes central to it. We can examine the overt contents of SF for reflections of contemporary trends and attitudes. As does other fiction, SF mirrors "attitudes, trends, and changes in society (social preoccupations)" or expresses "the collective psyche of an era (social psychological preoccupations)" (Kuhn, 1990: 16). This reflectionist model for reading SF might lead us to investigate *Dr. Strangelove* as a mirror for nuclear anxieties and a critique of cold war paranoia. We might read William Gibson's Sprawl series, as I did above, as a reflection of the growing power of and threat from multi-national corporations. And we might interpret films like *The Thing from Another World* (1951), *It Came from Outer Space* (1953), and *Invasion of the Body Snatchers* (1956) as depicting cold war fears of communist infiltration and subversion from within (e.g., Biskind, 1983).[13] On this reflectionist approach, SF actually is about contemporary politics, and world politics, and in rather straightforward ways.

For instance, Tom Shippey's analysis of "The Cold War in Science Fiction" (1982) argues that American preoccupations in the early cold war—such as the security, or lack thereof, of nuclear secrets and the dangerous lunacies of McCarthyism—are reflected in SF stories and novels. Ronnie Lipschutz's *Cold War Fantasies* uses film and fiction, including SF, to "evoke" the world of the cold war (2001: xii) because they reflect the time and place of their production. And Bruce Franklin has argued that SF films of the 1970s were deeply pessimistic, offering a "doomsday imagination" (1990b:19) with "despairing visions of the future" that "mirror the profound social decay" of a declining U.S. empire (31). A few analysts have even used SF to illustrate concepts central to theories of world politics. In their *International Relations through Science Fiction,* Martin Greenberg and Joseph Olander offered Arthur C. Clarke's short story "Superiority" to illustrate the concept of national power (1978: 16–27) and Frank Herbert's "Committee of the Whole" to illustrate the balance of power (28–45). Robert Gregg's more recent *International Relations on Film* (1998) uses film, as Greenberg and Olander used short stories, to explain and elucidate conventional concepts and theories of world politics, treating each popular cultural text as an unproblematic "window on the world" (2).

This approach, while certainly providing fascinating and useful analyses, is also in an important respect limited. Specifically, it assumes that world politics exists *apart from* the practices of popular culture. It assumes that representations and the "real world" are distinct from one another and that the representations reflect "the real" more or less transparently, in an unmediated fashion. In this way, we can read the real off of the representations. This approach can, unwittingly or not, take both theories and practices of world politics for granted, as directly accessible, and as unproblematic. The "balance of power" just *is* a central aspect of world politics—this remains unquestioned and so is rendered unquestionable—and Frank Herbert's "Committee of the Whole" shows us how it works. From such a reflectionist perspective, Gregg invites us "to study IR while we enjoy the derring do of spies, the heroism of soldiers in battle, and the agonizing of statesman as they grapple with the latest foreign policy crisis" (1998: 23).

But this is at best a partial understanding of the relationship between representation and "the real." The realities we know—the meanings they have for us—are discursive products.[14] "Because the real is never wholly present to us—how it is real for us is always mediated through some representational practice—we lose something when we think of representation as mimetic" (Shapiro, 1988: xii). SF is not just a "window" onto an already pre-existing world. Rather, SF texts are part of the processes of world politics themselves: they are implicated in producing and reproducing the phenomena that Gregg and others assume they merely reflect.[15] Instead of reading these texts as simple reflections of the real, we can read "the real"—in our case world politics—as itself a social and cultural product. "[T]o read the 'real' as a text that has been produced (written) is to disclose an aspect of human conduct that is fugitive in approaches that collapse the process of inscription into a static reality" (ibid.). For instance, through its overtly liberal ideology and mechanisms like the Prime Directive—which forbids interference by the United Federation of Planets in the normal internal development of technologically less developed societies— *Star Trek* helps to produce U.S. foreign policy as non-interventionary and benign (Weldes, 1999: 124–127). World politics, then, is itself a cultural product. Based as they are on such assumptions, our analyses have more in common with Cynthia Weber's use of popular film to "access what IR theory says, how it plots its story, and how all this *together* gives us a particular vision of the world" (2001: 132, emphasis added).

## SF/WORLD POLITICS INTERTEXT

In this volume we view SF as a generic discourse or system of meaning-producing codes, a "semiotic site for the production and negotiation of representations, meanings and identities" (Gledhill, 1997: 355). We also view it as a constitutive part of a SF/world politics intertext.[16] The notion of intertextuality draws our attention to the fact that texts, whether SF or world politics, are never read in isolation. They wouldn't make sense if they were. Instead, "any one text is necessarily read in relationship to others and . . . a range of textual knowledges is brought to bear upon it" (Fiske, 1987: 108). To use a slightly different terminology, all signs are multi-accentual: their meaning depends on how they are articulated to other signs and sign systems, and how they are articulated to social relations (Vološinov, 1986: 23; Hall, 1988). To poach from Bakhtin, we might say that each text "tastes of the . . . contexts in which it has lived its socially charged life" (1981: 293).

A prominent meaning-producing context is the genre itself: genres depend on intertextuality. SF texts repeat and rework generic conventions, and readers bring knowledge of those conventions, their generic expectations, to their consumption and appreciation of any particular text. SF texts also explicitly refer to earlier SF texts. As Kuhn notes, the SF comedy *Android* (1982) refers explicitly to Fritz Lang's *Metropolis* (1926) in "a scene in which a beautiful female robot is brought to life by a mad scientist" (1990: 177). Intertextuality also crosses genres: *Alien* (1979) is a "generic hybrid" of SF and horror, while *Blade Runner* (1982) combines conventions from SF and film noir (Kuhn, 1990: 178).

Most important, for our purposes, are the intertextual relations between SF and world politics. There are often striking similarities in the

way SF tells stories, the way world politics is officially and popularly narrated, and the way analysts of world politics represent "international relations." So, as I argued earlier, texts like *The Economist* and its descriptions
and promotions of globalization are read in relation to other texts, including SF and its futuristic images of "spaceship Earth." Broad intertextual
knowledges—the culture's "image bank," including generic SF narratives
and conventional SF tropes—"pre-orient" readers, guiding them to make
meanings in some ways rather than in others (Fiske, 1987: 108). *The Economist*'s discourse of globalization, for example, read in light of techno-
utopian SF, might look not only plausible—we are entering a glorious
high-tech future—but benign and downright praiseworthy—this future
promises benefits for everyone; indeed, it is only by embracing globalization that poor states can benefit (e.g., Ruggiero, 1996; Barshefsky, 1997;
IMF, 2000). But like all signs, "globalization" is multi-accentual. The same
pro-globalization text, read in light of techno-dystopic SF, might produce
an alternative reading, one in which globalization brings with it rule by
transnational corporations and organized crime, rampant violence, shocking squalor, and vast inequalities in wealth and life chances. In either case,
"studying a text's intertextual relations can provide us with valuable clues
to the readings that a particular culture or subculture is likely to produce
from it" (Fiske, 1987: 108), which readings are likely to be considered
plausible, and even which political contestations are likely to arise. By examining the relations between the discourses of SF and of world politics—
the SF/world politics intertext—we can unravel some of the conventions
through which world politics is made meaningful, as we also investigate
practices of global politics.

A striking example of the intertextual character of SF and world politics is found in the ways in which SF scenarios are actively being implemented. *Star Trek,* for instance, inspired NASA engineers and would-be
astronauts (Penley, 1997: Nichols, 1994). Future war fiction provides scenarios and nova—such as cyborgs—now actively being implemented in
the technophilic Revolution in Military Affairs (e.g., De Landa, 1991).
And cyberpunk has helped to shape the development of "information society" (e.g., Tomas, 1991). Allucquere Stone has suggested that Gibson's
*Neuromancer* "provided . . . the imaginal public sphere and reconfigured
discursive community that established the grounding for the possibility of
a new kind of interaction" (1991: 95). In shaping technological development, cyberpunk has helped to articulate "new geographical imaginations
of emerging spaces like the Internet" (Kitchin and Kneale, 2001: 23;
2002). But the attempt to put fictional visions into practice is not always

straightforward. Although William Gibson portrays the future as dark and violent, a despotic future ruled by massive MNCs, some analysts and politicians have actively drawn on Gibson "to justify investment in information and communications technologies" (Kitchin and Kneale, 2001: 24). Gibson notes the irony:

> I was delighted when scientists and corporate technicians started to read me, but I soon realized that all the critical pessimistic left-wing stuff just goes over their heads. The social and political naiveté of modern corporate boffins is frightening, they read me and just take bits, all the cute technology, and miss about fifteen levels of irony. (in ibid.)

Similarly, at a public lecture series on art in Los Angeles in 1990, "three out of five leading urban planners agreed that they hoped someday Los Angeles would look like the film *Blade Runner*. . . . It has become a paradigm for the future of cities, for artists across the disciplines" (M. N. Klein, in ibid.: 25). This despite the fact that Dick's Los Angeles is bleak, full of kipple and inequalities, highly stratified, and quite frighteningly violent.[17] "Fiction is becoming reality" (Kitchin and Kneale, 2001: 20), but in mediated, and sometimes unexpected, ways.

Crucial here is not only the reproduction, across the SF/world politics intertext, of similar images—whether of cyberspace, the post-modern city, or spaceship Earth.[18] These are the easiest relations to illustrate but, although central to the production of common sense, they are not ultimately the most significant aspect of the SF/world politics intertext. Instead, what renders this intertext so crucial to our understanding of world politics is the deep metaphysical—epistemological and ontological—overlap across its constituent texts. Their structural homologies, in other words, extend to their most basic assumptions: the nature of Self and Other, the character of knowledge, the possibilities of knowing the Self, or the Other, the nature of and relations between good and evil, the possibilities for community. The language of "inter-text" subtly implies that different texts are produced in different spaces/times/cultures. These different texts then have an interface: they meet and relate to one another. But if these texts already overlap at such fundamental metaphysical levels, then the notion of an "intertext" relies too heavily on an ontology of difference. Quite different texts—the constituent elements of the SF/world politics intertext—do get produced, but they share deeply rooted assumptions. Both SF texts and the texts of world politics are grounded in the same reservoir of cultural meanings. The SF/world politics intertext—as the

RMA or cyberspace shows—has no clear beginning or end. Instead, there is an endless circulation of meanings from world politics to SF, from SF to world politics, and back again. The analyses in this volume, then, highlight aspects of a world that is already fully present, never really new.

## OUTLINE OF THE VOLUME

The contributors to this volume, most of whom find their primary intellectual homes in the inter-discipline of International Relations, reject the "high culture" characterization of SF as "merely popular" that reduces it to political insignificance (although it is of course very popular). Each reads his or her SF texts from multiple perspectives, combining reflectionist readings with intertextual and, indeed, metaphysical ones. Each treats his or her respective SF/world politics intertext (sometimes intertexts) as revealing complex and sophisticated kinds of relations that highlight and allow us to explore key issues in world politics.

The first section, "World Politics in Outer Space," deals with the encounter, a central issue for both SF and world politics. As Roberts argues, "the key symbolic function of the SF novum is precisely the representation of the encounter with difference, Otherness, alterity" (2000: 25). It might indeed be fair to say that the very "root" of SF lies in "the fantasy of the alien encounter . . . the meeting of self with other" (McCracken, 1998: 102). In world politics, diplomacy is one means of encountering otherness, imperialism another. In "'To know him was to love him. Not to know him was to love him from afar': Diplomacy in *Star Trek*," Iver Neumann explores the nature of diplomatic relations in general—with whom can one communicate, in what ways, on what grounds, under what conditions?—through an investigation into the "interdiscursivity" between *Star Trek* and U.S. diplomacies. Neumann shows that *Star Trek* reflects the bifurcated understanding of diplomacy characteristic of the United States—a rejected "old world" version characterized by mutual suspicion and war contests with a new practice in which "American diplomats speak for mankind in general" on the basis of a universal rationality. But in U.S./Federation practice, it turns out, this new diplomacy, despite its benign focus on the "rights of man"/Prime Directive, ultimately leaves no room for dialogue across difference. While *Star Trek*'s encounters with various liminal others highlight many of the complexities of diplomacy, they ultimately reproduce a vision of encounter that is necessarily uni-linear rather than dialogic and so entails the assimilation of the other to this universal rationality. Beginning with the contemporary resurgence of a seemingly irresistible colonial drive, Naeem Inayatullah's "Bumpy Space: Imperialism and Resistance in *Star Trek: The Next Generation*" investigates imperialism through the problem of communication during "first contact." *Star Trek's* record, again, is mixed. Several *Next Generation* episodes offer surprising encounters in which problems of communication across difference are recognized and genuine respect for difference emerges. Nonetheless, through the nearly ubiquitous device of the "universal translator," which assumes that language merely mirrors a given, universal reality, *Star Trek* more often flattens difference, absorbing and assimilating diversity. The encounter remains imperialist; like Western relations with the "third world," "alien differences are [seen as] degenerate forms of a singular unity that must be reconverted to their original either through the pedagogy of force or the force of pedagogy."

The second section, "Aliens Among Us," follows up this theme of encounter by focusing more minutely on the nature of the Self and the Other. The encounters discussed here are internal to society rather than external. Highlighting the production of alien/ation and the effects of liminality and hybridity, they tell us a good deal about the alienating nature of global capitalism, about sovereignty and the construction of community, and about different visions of the international system and their attendant political subjectivities. Ronnie Lipschutz examines the films *Blade Runner, Falling Down,* and *The Matrix* in "Aliens, Alien Nations, and Alienation in American Political Economy and Popular Culture." Aliens are omnipresent in American politics and popular culture, their liminality demarcating borders not to be crossed. Although aliens are typically seen as threats, likely to consume or subvert, and thus radically destabilize, the body politic, Lipschutz argues the reverse: the social destabilization resulting from post-modern capitalism produces aliens and alien threats. The three films he investigates, each depicting the alienation of its major character from the post-modern capitalist societies in which he (appears to) live, locate the genesis of aliens, alienation, and alien spaces in the contradictions of a post-modern capitalism associated with the rise of globalization. Sovereignty and the moral boundaries of social space are the main themes of Patricia Molloy's "Demon Diasporas: Confronting the Other and the Other-Worldly in *Buffy the Vampire Slayer* and *Angel*." Molloy investigates the production of sovereignty and moral social space through the gradual transformation of the hierarchies of killing—who can and cannot legitimately kill and be killed—developed over the several seasons of *Buffy* and *Angel*. Traditional sovereign communities (such as those definitive of world politics) are maintained through the eradication of undesirable elements, of the Other. But *Buffy* and *Angel* call this violent notion of sovereignty into question: as the boundaries of good and evil become increasingly blurred, as the worldly and other-worldly become indistinguishable, sovereignty is revealed as a form of biopower. However, as Molloy shows, radical hybridity and a decentering of the Self in response to the Other, as demonstrated in *Buffy* and *Angel,* make possible a community "that refuses to ban the outlaw and invent the bandit." Aida Hozic examines the Soviet film *Stalker* in "Forbidden Places, Tempting Spaces, and the Politics of Desire: On *Stalker* and Beyond." In this film—about the journey of three men (Writer, Scientist, and Stalker, the guide) who are traveling through The Zone in search of The Room where deepest desires are fulfilled—Hozic finds a complex story about law, desire, and sovereignty. In her view, The Zone is a metaphor for the "state of exception," the extra-juridical space constructed and policed by the state where law is suspended so that sovereign power can be sustained. Hozic's analysis of the characters' different relations toward The Zone highlights different visions of the international system and different political subjectivities that accompany these visions. She concludes by investigating the sublime and sublime love and, through the character of Stalker's wife, the only one who never enters The Zone, charts an alternative subject position, one that rejects the materialism and cynicism of our age and is both self-sufficient and selfless.

The third section, "Future Worlds, Alternative Imaginings," addresses various forms of imaginative encounters with alternative or future worlds. Each in different ways highlights the politics and power, and the difficulties, of practices of representation. In "Representation is Futile? American Anti-Collectivism and the Borg," Patrick Jackson and Daniel Nexon investigate the suppression of the very possibility of collectivism in both American politics and popular culture through an analysis of the dramatic evolution of *Star Trek*'s representation of the Borg. The Borg, a cyborg race, first appears as the absolute Other of the liberal Federation, a single, undifferentiated collective entity with which no communication is possible; by its final appearance it has been radically decomposed, becoming hive-like, ruled by a despotic Queen and populated by oppressed drones. Examining the constraints that the narrative universe, the audience, and production techniques imposed on *Star Trek*'s representation of the collective, Jackson and Nexon simultaneously highlight the constraints and opportunities that its fundamental liberal individualist commitments have on U.S. foreign policy, particularly its relentless personalization of "the enemy." For Geoffrey Whitehall, "The Problem of the 'World and

Beyond': Encountering 'the Other' in Science Fiction" represents a crisis: our contemporary representations of world politics are inadequate for grasping pervasive indeterminacy, contingency, and change. The result is frantic, yet failed attempts to contain movement, deny change, and ignore difference. Whitehall examines *Star Trek, Starship Troopers,* and Ray Bradbury's *The Martian Chronicles* to investigate different representations of the encounter with Otherness. *Star Trek,* he argues, only manages the beyond; in attempting to secure modernity, it reproduces the dominant political response, disciplining both Self and Other. *Starship Troopers* offers somewhat more: through irony it mobilizes the beyond, rendering visible processes of representation and exposing seemingly self-evident identities, although ultimately it too reproduces the fundamental distinction between world/beyond, self/other. In *The Martian Chronicles,* Whitehall discerns an alternative: here world politics can be "wrestled from the modern political imagination" and imagined alternatively as a temporal practice of encounter that allows for the radical possibility of becoming Other. Finally, Neta Crawford concludes the volume on an expressly hopeful note. In "Feminist Futures: Science Fiction, Utopia, and the Art of Possibilities in World Politics," she challenges the traditional political rejection of utopia as "castles in the air," as "unrealistic" projections of unattainable states of perfection, and enjoins us instead to draw on utopian SF, and especially feminist utopian SF, to stimulate new perspectives and fresh insights into the processes and possibilities of world politics. Discussing a series of feminist SF's typical characteristics and concerns—its anti-realism, its conception of the political, its validation of emotion, its emphasis on non-violence, its alternative institutions—she advocates utopian SF for its ability to destabilize our present and to make room for holistic reconstruction. Feminist utopian SF, she concludes, challenges us "to be more ambitious" in our understanding and critique of world politics.

## NOTES

1. Fascinating studies of SF fandom are offered by Jenkins (1992), Bernardi (1998: Chapter 5), Bacon-Smith (2000).
2. Thanks to Patrick Jackson for this lovely point.
3. Although Franklin does not specify, the lines in question must have included the following: "Pilots of the purple twilight dropping down with costly bales; / Heard the heavens fill with shouting, and there rain'd a ghastly dew / . . . / Till the war drum throbb'd no longer, and the battle flags were furl'd" (Tennyson, 1842).

work offers a curious double example. The first chapter of the 1990 edi-
(published as an appendix to the 2000 edition, the 1954 version having
restored) similarly harkens back to world politics, but an updated, postwar world politics designed to catch up with 40 years of change.

term "discourse" is being used here to mean a set of capabilities—a set
ocio-cultural resources used by people in the construction of meaning
it their world and their activities" (Ó Tuathail and Agnew, 1992: pp.
-193)—and a structure of meaning-in-use—"a language or system of
:sentation that has developed socially in order to make and circulate a
rent set of meanings" (Fiske, 1987: 14).

ommon usage, the terms "popular" culture and "mass" culture are in-
angeable although they should perhaps be distinguished. For exam-
"popular culture" is sometimes reserved for those cultural artifacts
illy produced by "the people," and specifically by subordinated
es. In contrast, "mass culture" designates those texts and practices
while consumed by "the people," are not produced by them. We are
is sense dealing with "mass culture." Bennett (1986) provides a use-
iscussion of some of the problems in defining popular culture.

e the relationship between discourse and ideology is neither simple
iettled, it is useful to see discourse as enabling a process of making
iing and ideology as an effect of that process (Purvis and Hunt, 1993:
. A discourse thus has ideological effects in that it, for instance, priv-
i certain groups and interests over others, and is always implicated in
roduction and reproduction of power relations.

immensely popular, at least in the West, and especially in the United
s. According to Scott McCracken, one in ten books sold in the
:d Kingdom is SF, and the ratio is as high as one in four in the United
s (1998: 102). SF has, at least recently, been very popular in film as
In 1997, for instance, four of the top ten "worldwide" box office
- The Lost World: Jurassic Park, Men in Black, Star Wars, and The Fifth
nt—were SF (cited in Lacey, 2000: 168).

nre I mean simply the "patterns/forms/styles/structures which tran-
individual art products, and which supervise both their construction
e artist and their reading by audiences" (Ryall, in Lacey, 2000: 132).
re provides conventions for the production of individual texts—e.g.,
g, character, narrative, style, iconography (137)—and the attendant
tations for their consumption (Gledhill, 1997: 351).

eference is to Percy Bysshe Shelley's poem Ozymandias (1818), in
King Ozymandias claims: "Nothing beside remains. Round the
/ Of that colossal wreck, boundless and bare / The lone and level
stretch far away."

ts makes the interesting point that space travel and rockets to the
, classic SF nova and extrapolations into the future, have now be-
historical: "'going to the moon' was something our ancestors did,
imething we do today or are going to do in the future" (2000: 33).

The film *Apollo 13* (1996) makes this very clear. It is a historical film with a plot that mirrors such SF classics as *2001: A Space Odyssey* (1968) and *Dark Star* (1974). In general, Roberts argues, if not quite convincingly, "SF is a *historiographic* mode, a means of symbolically writing about history" (36) and its "chief mode . . . is not prophecy but *nostalgia*" (33, emphasis in the original). Of course, a revitalized program for travel to Mars, as planned in NASA's Project Prometheus, would render space travel topical once again (Berger and David, 2003).

12. The Sprawl series—which refers to "BAMA, the Sprawl, the Boston-Atlanta Metropolitan Axis" (1984: 57)—includes the novels *Neuromancer* (1984), *Count Zero* (1986a), and *Mona Lisa Overdrive* (1988), as well as related short stories, such as "Johnny Mnemonic," "New Rose Hotel," and "Burning Chrome" (1986b).

13. Reflections of global threats and anxieties abound in SF: other examples include the physical, biological, and environmental dangers facing the planet (*No Blade of Grass* [1956], *The Late Great Planet Earth* [1970], *The Omega Man* [1971], *Waterworld* [1995], *Deep Impact* [1998]); nuclear anxieties (*Godzilla* [1956], *The Day After* [1983], *Testament* [1983]); the creation of world governments (*Star Trek* [1967-], *1984* [1949]); the history of colonialism, ethnic and race relations, and in general problems of dealing with difference and cultural encounters (*Forbidden Planet* [1956], *Planet of the Apes* [1968], *Close Encounters of the Third Kind* [1977], *Ender's Game* [1985], *Alien Nation* [1988]); the consequences of technological development (*THX 1138* [1971], *Logan's Run* [1976], *Blade Runner* [1982]) and genetic engineering (*Gattica* [1997]); and scenarios for future war (*War of the Worlds, Starship Troopers, Independence Day, Space: Above and Beyond* [1995–96], *Babylon 5* [1993–98]).

14. As Ernesto Laclau and Chantal Mouffe have argued, "the entire development of contemporary epistemology has established that there is no fact which allows its meaning to be read transparently" (1987: 84). This insight, which underpins diverse contemporary social theories (for overviews see Shapiro, 1981; Gibbons, 1987), renders it implausible to continue to assume an empiricist relationship between representation and reality.

15. Examples that take popular culture as more firmly constitutive of world politics include Dorfman and Mattelart (1975); Corber (1993); Lutz and Collins (1993); and Kaplan and Pease (1993).

16. Kristeva (1980) first introduced the notion of intertextuality. See also Bennett and Woollacott (1987); Fox (1995); Hall (1997b: 233–4). Hooper (2001) offers an example directly relevant to the study of world politics.

17. Philip K. Dick coined the term "kipple" in *Do Androids Dream of Electric Sheep?* to describe the ever-accumulating detritus of modern life: "Kipple is useless objects, like junk mail or match folders after you use the last match or gum wrappers or yesterday's homeopape. When nobody's around, kipple reproduces itself. . . ." (1968: 56).

18. I thank Naeem Inayatullah for most of the arguments in this paragraph.

## BIBLIOGRAPHY

Asimov, Isaac. 1951. *Foundation,* New York: Del Rey.
Asimov, Isaac. 1952. *Foundation and Empire,* New York: Del Rey.
Asimov, Isaac. 1953. *Second Foundation,* New York: Del Rey.
Asimov, Isaac. 1982. *Foundation's Edge,* New York: Del Rey.
Asimov, Isaac. 1986. *Foundation and Earth,* New York: Del Rey.
Asimov, Isaac. 1988. *Prelude to Foundation,* New York: Bantam Books.
Asimov, Issac. 1993. *Forward the Foundation,* New York: Bantam Books.
Bacon-Smith, Camille. 2000. *Science Fiction Culture,* Philadelphia: University of Pennsylvania Press.
Bakhtin, Mikhail. 1981. *The Dialogic Imagination: Four Essays by M. M. Bakhtin,* edited by Michael Holmquist, Austin, TX: University of Texas Press.
Barshefsky, Charlene. 1997. Testimony before the Subcommittee on Trade of the House Committee on Ways and Means, Hearing on U.S. Trade with Sub-Saharan Africa, April 29. Online at http://waysandmeans.house.gov/trade/105cong/4-29-97/4-29bars.htm [July 3, 2001].
Bartter, Martha A. 1990. "Normative Fiction," in Philip John Davies, ed., *Science Fiction, Social Conflict and War,* New York and Manchester: Manchester University Press, pp. 169–185.
Bennett, Tony. 1986. "The Politics of 'the Popular' and Popular Culture," in Tony Bennett, Colin Mercer, and Janet Woollacott, eds., *Popular Culture and Social Relations,* Milton Keynes, UK: Open University Press, pp. 1–21.
Bennett, Tony, and Janet Woollacott. 1987. *Bond and Beyond: The Political Career of a Popular Hero,* London: Methuen.
Berger, Brian, and Leonard David. 2003. "White House Go Ahead on NASA Nuclear Prometheus Project," January 17. Online at http://www.space.com/business technology/technology/nuclear_power_030117.html (January 23, 2003).
Bernardi, Daniel Leonard. 1998. *Star Trek and History: Race-ing Toward a White Future,* New Brunswick, NJ: Rutgers University Press.
Biskind, Peter. 1983. *Seeing is Believing: How Hollywood Taught Us to Stop Worrying and Love the Fifties,* New York: Pantheon Books.
Broderick, Damien. 1995. *Reading by Starlight: Postmodern Science Fiction,* London and New York: Routledge.
Clancy, Tom. 1984. *The Hunt for Red October,* Annapolis, MD: Naval Institute Press.
Clancy, Tom. 1986. *Red Storm Rising,* New York: Putnam's Sons.
Clarke, Arthur C. 2000 [1954]. *Childhood's End,* Basingstoke: Pan Books, Macmillan.
Corber, Robert J. 1993. *In the Name of National Security: Hitchcock, Homophobia, and the Political Construction of Gender and Postwar America,* Durham, NC: Duke University Press.
Davies, Philip John, ed. 1990. *Science Fiction, Social Conflict and War,* New York and Manchester: Manchester University Press.

Davis, Mike. 1992. "Beyond *Blade Runner:* Urban Control, the Ecology of Fear." http://www.mediamatic.nl/magazine/8_2/Davis-Urban.html [June 30, 2002].

De Landa, Manuel. 1991. *War in the Age of the Intelligent Machine,* New York: Swerve Editions.

Dean, Jodi. 2000. *Political Theory and Cultural Studies,* Ithaca, NY: Cornell University Press.

Dick, Philip K. 1964. *The Penultimate Truth,* New York: Belmont Books.

Dick, Philip K. 1968. *Do Androids Dream of Electric Sheep?* New York: New American Library.

Dorfman, Ariel, and Armand Mattelart. 1975. *How to Read Donald Duck: Imperialist Ideology in the Disney Comic,* New York: International General.

Enloe, Cynthia. 1996. "Margins, Silences and Bottom Rungs: How to Overcome the Underestimation of Power in the Study of International Relations," in Steve Smith, Ken Booth, and Marysia Zalewski, eds., *International Theory: Positivism and Beyond,* Cambridge: Cambridge University Press, pp. 186–202.

Enloe, Cynthia. 2000. *Bananas, Beaches and Bases: A Feminist Introduction to International Relations,* Berkeley: University of California Press.

Fiske, John. 1987. *Television Culture,* London: Routledge.

Fox, Nicolas. 1995. "Intertextuality and the Writing of Social Research," *Electronic Journal of Sociology,* 1(2). Online at http://www.icaap.org/iuicode?100.1.2.1 [July 5, 2002].

Franklin, H. Bruce. 1988. *War Stars: The Superweapon and the American Imagination,* New York and Oxford: Oxford University Press.

Franklin, H. Bruce. 1990a. "Eternally Safe for Democracy: The Final Solution for American Science Fiction," in Philip John Davies, ed., *Science Fiction, Social Conflict and War,* New York and Manchester: Manchester University Press, pp. 151–168.

Franklin, H. Bruce. 1990b. "Visions of the Future," in Annette Kuhn, ed., *Alien Zone: Cultural Theory and Contemporary Science Fiction Cinema,* London: Verso, pp. 19–31.

Gibbons, Michael J. 1987. *Interpreting Politics,* New York: New York University Press.

Gibson, William. 1984. *Neuromancer,* New York: HarperCollins Publishers.

Gibson, William. 1986a. *Count Zero,* New York: HarperCollins Publishers.

Gibson, William. 1986b. *Burning Chrome and Other Stories,* New York: HarperCollins Publishers.

Gibson, William. 1988. *Mona Lisa Overdrive,* New York: Bantam Books.

Gilroy, Paul. 1993. *The Black Atlantic: Modernity and Double Consciousness,* London: Verso.

Gledhill, Christine. 1997. "Genre and Gender: The Case of Soap Opera," in Stuart Hall, ed., *Representation: Cultural Representations and Signifying Practices,* London: Sage, pp. 337–384.

Gray, John. 1998. *False Dawn: The Delusions of Global Capitalism,* London: New Press.

Greenberg, Martin Harry, and Joseph D. Olander, eds. 1978. *International Relations through Science Fiction*, New York: New Viewpoints.

Gregg, Robert W. 1998. *International Relations on Film*, Boulder, CO: Lynne Rienner.

Grovogui, Siba N. 1996. *Sovereigns, Quasi Sovereigns, and Africans*, Minneapolis: University of Minnesota Press.

Hall, Stuart. 1982. "The Rediscovery of 'Ideology': Return of the Repressed in Media Studies," in Michael Gurevitch, Tony Bennett, James Curran, and Janet Woollacott, eds., *Culture, Society and Media*, London: Methuen, pp. 56–90.

Hall, Stuart. 1985. "Signification, Representation, Ideology: Althusser and the Post-Structuralist Debates," *Critical Studies in Mass Communication*, 2(2): 91–114.

Hall, Stuart. 1986. "Gramsci's Relevance for the Study of Race and Ethnicity," *Journal of Communication Inquiry*, 10(2): 5–27.

Hall, Stuart. 1988. "The Toad in the Garden: Thatcherism Among the Theorists," in Cary Nelson and Lawrence Grossberg, eds., *Marxism and the Interpretation of Culture*, Urbana: University of Illinois Press, pp. 35–73.

Hall, Stuart. 1997a. "Introduction," in Stuart Hall, ed., *Representation: Cultural Representations and Signifying Practices*, London: Sage, pp. 1–11.

Hall, Stuart. 1997b. "The Spectacle of the Other," in Stuart Hall, ed., *Representation: Cultural Representations and Signifying Practices*, London: Sage, pp. 223–290.

Hay, Colin, and David Marsh. 2000. *Demystifying Globalization*, London: Palgrave.

Heinlein, Robert A. 1959. *Starship Troopers*, New York: Berkley Pub. Corp.

Hooper, Charlotte. 2000. "Masculinities in Transition: The Case of Globalization," in Marianne H. Marchand and Anne Sisson Runyan, eds., *Gender and Global Restructuring: Sightings, Sites and Resistances*, London and New York: Routledge, pp. 59–73.

Hooper, Charlotte. 2001. *Manly States: Masculinities, International Relations and Gender Politics*, New York: Columbia University Press.

IMF staff. 2000. 'Globalization: Threat or Opportunity?' April 12. Online at http://www.imf.org/external/np/exr/ib/2000/041200.htm [June 18, 2001]

James, Edward. 1994. *Science Fiction in the Twentieth Century*, Oxford: Oxford University Press.

Jenkins, Henry. 1992. *Textual Poachers*, New York: Routledge.

Kaplan, Amy, and Donald E. Pease, eds. 1993. *Cultures of United States Imperialism*, Durham, NC: Duke University Press.

Kegley, Charles W., Jr., and Eugene R. Wittkopf. 1999. *World Politics: Trend and Transformation*, 7th edition, Boston: Bedford; New York: St. Martin's Press.

Kitchin, Rob, and James Kneale. 2001. "Science Fiction or Future Fact? Exploring Imaginative Geographies of the New Millennium," *Progress in Human Geography*, 25(1): 19–35.

Kitchin, Rob, and James Kneale, eds. 2002. *Lost in Space: Geographies of Science Fiction*, London and New York: Continuum.

Kristeva, Julia. 1980. *Desire in Language: A Semiotic Approach to Literature and Art*, New York: Columbia University Press.

Kuhn, Annette, ed. 1990. *Alien Zone: Cultural Theory and Contemporary Science Fiction Cinema*, London: Verso.

Lacey, Nick. 2000. *Narrative and Genre: Key Concepts in Media Studies*, London: Macmillan.

Laclau, Ernesto, and Chantal Mouffe. 1987. "Postmarxism Without Apologies," *New Left Review*, 166: 79–106.

Latham, Andrew. 2001. "Fantasies of Future War: Official Military Future as Science Fiction," paper presented at the annual meeting of the International Studies Association, Chicago, February.

Lefanu, Sarah. 1988. *In the Chinks of the World Machine: Feminism and Science Fiction*, London: The Women's Press.

Lipchutz, Ronnie D. 2001. *Film, Fiction, and the Cold War—Popular Culture and Foreign Policy During America's Half-Century*, Boulder, CO: Rowman & Littlefield.

Lutz, Catherine A., and Jane L. Collins. 1993. *Reading National Geographic*, Chicago: University of Chicago Press.

McCracken, Scott. 1998. *Pulp: Reading Popular Fiction*, Manchester: Manchester University Press.

Metz, Steven. 2000. *Armed Conflict in the 21st Century: The Information Revolution and Post-Modern Warfare*, Carlisle, PA: Strategic Studies Institute, U.S. Army War College.

Nelson, Cary, Paula A. Treichler, and Lawrence Grossberg. 1992. "Cultural Studies: An Introduction," in Lawrence Grossberg, Cary Nelson, and Paula Treichler, eds., *Cultural Studies*, New York: Routledge, pp. 1–22.

Nichols, Nichelle. 1994. *Beyond Uhura: Star Trek and Other Memories*, New York: G. P. Putnam's.

O'Hanlon, Michael E. 2000. *Technological Change and the Future of Warfare*, Washington, DC: Brookings Institutions Press.

Ó Tuathail, Gearóid, and John Agnew. 1992. "Geopolitics and Discourse: Practical Geopolitical Reasoning in American Foreign Policy," *Political Geography*, 11(2): 190–204.

Penley, Constance. 1997. *NASA/Trek: Popular Science and Sex in America*, London: Verso.

Pijl, Kees van der. 1984. *The Making of an Atlantic Ruling Class*, London: Verso.

Purvis, Trevor, and Alan Hunt. 1993. "Discourse, Ideology, Discourse, Ideology, Discourse, Ideology . . . ," *British Journal of Sociology*, 44(3): 474–499.

Reagan, Ronald. 1983. "Address to the Nation on National Security," March 23. Online at http://www.fas.org/spp/starwars/offdocs/rrspch.htm [June 19, 2002].

Roberts, Adam. 2000. *Science Fiction*, London: Routledge.

Ruggiero, Renato. 1996. "Managing a World of Free Trade and Deep Interdependence," Address to the Argentinean Council on Foreign Relations, Buenos Aires, September 10. Online at http://www.wto.org/wto/english/news_e/pres96_e/pr055_e.htm [June 15, 2001].

Scholte, Jan Aart. 1997. "The Globalization of World Politics," in John Baylis and Steve Smith, eds., *The Globalization of World Politics: An Introduction to International Relations,* Oxford: Oxford University Press, pp. 13–30.

Shapiro, Michael J. 1981. *Language and Political Understanding: The Politics of Discursive Practices,* New Haven, CT: Yale University Press.

Shapiro, Michael J. 1988. *The Politics of Representation: Writing Practices in Biography, Photography, and Policy Analysis,* Madison: University of Wisconsin Press.

Shapiro, Michael J. 1992. *Reading the Postmodern Polity: Political Theory as Textual Practice,* Minneapolis: University of Minnesota Press.

Shelley, Percy Bysshe. 1818. "Ozymandias." Online at http://yoga.com/raw/readings/Ozymandias.html [July 5, 2002].

Shippey, Tom. 1982. "The Cold War in Science Fiction, 1940–1960," in Bernard Waites, et al., eds., *Popular Culture: Past and Present,* London: Croom Helm, pp. 308–322.

Shippey, Tom, ed. 1991. *Fictional Space: Essays on Contemporary Science Fiction,* Oxford: Basil Blackwell.

Shukman, David. 1996. *Tomorrow's War: The Threat of High Technology Weapons,* San Diego: Harcourt Brace.

*SIPRI Yearbook.* 2001. Online at http://editors.sipri.se/pubs.yb01/ch4.html [June 30, 2002].

Smith, Daniel, Colonel. Nd. "Chronology of the U.S. National Missile Defense Programs," Center for Defense Information. Online at http://www.cdi.org/hotspots/issuebrief/ch9/ [May 22, 2002].

Sterling, Bruce. 1986. "Preface," to Bruce Sterling, ed., *Mirrorshades: The Cyberpunk Anthology,* New York: Ace Books, pp. ix-xvi.

Stockwell, Peter. 1996. "Introduction," in Derek Littlewood and Peter Stockwell, eds., *Impossibility Fiction: Alternativity—Extrapolation—Speculation,* Amsterdam: Rodopi, pp. 3–9.

Stone, Allucquere Rosanne. 1991. "Will the Real Body Please Stand Up? Boundary Stories about Virtual Cultures," in Michael Benedikt, ed., *Cyberspace: First Steps,* Cambridge, MA: MIT Press, pp. 81–118.

Suvin, Darko. 1979. *Metamorphoses of Science Fiction: On the Poetics and History of a Literary Genre,* New Haven, CT: Yale University Press.

Suvin, Darko. 1988. *Positions and Presuppositions in Science Fiction,* Kent, OH: Kent State University Press.

Tennyson, Alfred Lord. 1842. "Locksley Hall." Online at http://www.library.utoronto.ca/utel/rp/poems/tennyson11.html [May 1, 2001].

Tomas, David. 1991. "Old Rituals for New Space: Rites de Passage and William Gibson's Cultural Model of Cyberspace," in Michael Benedikt, ed., *Cyberspace: First Steps,* Cambridge, MA: MIT Press, pp. 31–48.

Tomlinson, John. 1991. *Cultural Imperialism: An Introduction,* Baltimore: Johns Hopkins University Press.

United States. Department of the Army. 1997. *Army Vision 2010.* Online at http://www.army.mil/2010/ [June 20, 2002].

United States. Space Command. 1997. *Vision for 2020.* Online at http://www. spacecom.mil/visbook.pdf [June 20, 2002].

Vološinov, V. N. 1986 [1929]. *Marxism and the Philosophy of Language,* Cambridge, MA: Harvard University Press.

Weber, Cynthia. 2001. *International Relations Theory: A Critical Introduction,* London: Routledge.

Weldes, Jutta. 1999. "Going Cultural: *Star Trek,* State Action, and Popular Culture," Millennium, 28(1): 117–134.

Weldes, Jutta. 2001. "Globalization is Science Fiction," *Millennium,* 30(3): 647–667.

Wells, H. G. 1961. [1898]. *The War of the Worlds, and The Time Machine,* Garden City, NY: Doubleday.

Whitfield, Stephen, and Gene Roddenberry. 1968. *The Making of Star Trek,* New York: Ballentine Books.

Wichterich, Christa. 2000. *The Globalized Woman: Reports from a Future of Inequality,* London: Zed Books.

Williams, Raymond. 1983. *Keywords,* London: Fontana.

# Part I

*World Politics in Outer Space*

# Chapter 2

## "TO KNOW HIM WAS TO LOVE HIM. NOT TO KNOW HIM WAS TO LOVE HIM FROM AFAR"

### Diplomacy in *Star Trek*[1]

### *Iver B. Neumann*

### INTRODUCTION

Traditionally, investigations of popular artifacts such as *Star Trek* tend to have three different focal points: production, content, and reception. In this chapter, the focus will be on how one precondition of reception, namely the history of diplomacy, relates to content, namely the representations of diplomacy in *Star Trek*. One point on production is, however, apposite where circulation is concerned. It concerns how the writing process is ordered. In 1989, "the producers decided to make *Star Trek* the only show on network television willing to consider unsolicited, or 'spec', scripts [spec is short for speculation]. What this means is that any of the program's far-flung fans—from Cyndi Lauper to the Dalai Lama— can pitch ideas to the producers and dream of seeing their names in lights" (Greenwald, 1996: 1). As a result of this decision, the studio receives well over 1,000 spec scripts a year. The point here is not to privilege authorship. On the contrary, it is to play up the scope of the collaborative effort behind one of the intital parts of production, namely writing. As a medium, TV appears at around the same time as the death of the author.

Television at its inception acquired wholesale a series of values from radio in which the "writer" is privileged above any of the "technical" tasks such as direction and production. Yet in spite of this willingness to found its more "serious" productions on the idea of authorship, this has proved a relatively intractable task. For the average consumer, television is virtually an anonymous medium. The bulk of its output—news, documentaries, soap operas, serials, advertisements, come to us without any obvious "organizing consciousness" (Coward, 2000: 10).

As all who write know, however, for the author, there is a life after death. The sovereign author may be dead, but authors are still very much alive. An interview with Bryan Fuller (2000) demonstrates both how "spec" writers are being attached to the show, and how the writing process unfolds. Fuller, who was a story editor of the fourth season of *Voyager,* and subsequently went on to be executive story editor and then co-producer, gives the following account of the writing process:

> I met an agent who used to represent none other than Ronald D. Moore of TNG [*The Next Generation*] and DS9 [*Deep Space Nine*] fame. She sent me to a "Writing for *Star Trek*" seminar hosted by Ron and Brannon Braga. After the seminar, I wrote a spec script for *Deep Space Nine.* Once my agent submitted it through the proper channels, I was invited in to pitch and sold the story from my spec script and another story shortly after that. I had been pitching to *Voyager,* as well, and Brannon told me that Kes was going to be leaving the show and it might behoove me to come up with a few different ways to kill her off. . . . Generally speaking, a writer will have an idea and compose a story document, which usually takes about a week and anywhere from a few days to another week to rewrite and do notes. From that point we sit down and break it as a writing staff, which takes about another week. Once the story is broken and by that I mean it's "broken down" into a five-act structure, it takes about two weeks for the writer to go off and write the first draft. Then another week for notes from the head writer, in this case Ken Biller. From that point we distribute the script and have a pre-production meeting with all the department heads. Rick Berman gives another round of notes, and depending on how extensive they are, another week to churn out a final draft. At that point, we have our production meeting and the show's on the stage.

The point I want to make is a simple one. When the interface between society and TV is wider than it is for a number of other media, it is not only due to the number of viewers (a broad reception), and to the instantaneous feedback that hails from the fact that shows that receive low ratings lose advertisers and so may be taken off at the end of the season, but also to the specific writing practices that hold sway in this medium. And when the interface between society and *Star Trek* is particularly broad, it is not only due to all the re-runs, the production of best-selling novels based on each episode, the franchise products, or even the existence of a heavily institutionalized fandom holding large-scale conventions and editing a number of fanzines, but also because of the spec writing. The circulation of ideas between producers and spectators is enhanced by this particular production practice. In most other respects, including the existence of an official guide for potential writers ("the Bible") and the shooting regimen, production routines are fairly similar to other TV shows (cf. Silj, 1988: 12–20).

One scholar of literature in particular made his name during the final decades of the last century by grappling with the circulation between text and public. Steven Greenblatt (1988: 5) refers to the "study of the collective making of distinct cultural practices and inquiry into the relations among these practices" as a poetics of culture, and uses the concept of "social energies" to investigate this. The focal point of Greenblatt's investigations is more often than not Shakespeare. He asks what it was (and is) in his plays that fascinated the audience—which energies circulating between the play and the public gave the text the force to come alive. His answer is that there are parallels between the form and subject matter of the dramas, and the form and subject matter of political life at the time. Tensions of everyday life are played out (he does not deny an element of mimesis and a possible effect of catharsis), and Shakespeare makes this happen in such a way that the lines between the stage and everyday life are blurred. The social energies of everyday life circulate with the production of reality on stage. The play in turn fascinates and animates the public.

For Greenblatt, as a literary scholar, the main point is to demonstrate how this circulation may account for the power of the plays. For a social scientist, the main point will be how the representations offered in plays, novels, television series, and the like contribute to the constitution of the social. The first half of Constance Penley's (1997) *NASA/Trek* begins to take such a turn by teasing out the interdiscursivity between American space travel and *Star Trek*. I will try to do this where *Star Trek* and U.S. diplomacies are concerned.

## AMERICAN REPRESENTATIONS OF DIPLOMACY

In 1779, when the war with Britain was at its peak, Benjamin Franklin sent the following directive to the commanders of all armed ships acting by commission from the Congress of the United States:

Gentlemen, a ship was fitted out from England before the commencement of this war to make discoveries in unknown seas under the conduct of that most celebrated Navigator and Discoverer, Captain Cook. This is an undertaking truly laudable in itself, because the increase of geographical knowledge facilitates the communication between distant nations and the exchange of useful products and manufactures, extends the arts, and science of other kinds is increased to the benefit of mankind in general. This, then, is to recommend to you that should the said Ship fall into your hands, you would not consider her as an enemy, not suffer any plunder to be made of the efforts contained in her, nor obstruct her immediate return to England. (quoted in Killian, 1964: 63)

Benjamin Franklin was shortly to become one of the first envoys to represent the United States of America abroad. His was not a smooth transition to the diplomatic culture of the day. For example, he refused to dress the part when appearing at the Court of St. James, and only took to wearing court uniform upon the express order of the King. Even then, it was not a standard diplomatic uniform, but a rather dour affair of his own design.

Franklin's gesture to Captain Cook and to worldwide progress and his opposition to diplomatic ways were but two examples of how, seen from the United States, diplomacy was a particularly offensive old world practice. As Thomas Paine put it in 1792 (and making one of the first recorded uses of the term "diplomatic" for an envoy in doing so), American diplomacy should be a new diplomacy:

The situation of Dr Franklin, as Minister from America to France, should be taken into the chain of circumstances. The diplomatic character is of itself the narrowest sphere of society that man can act in. It forbids intercourse by the reciprocity of suspicion; and a diplomatic is a sort of unconnected atom, continually repelling and repelled. But this was not the case with Dr Franklin. He was not the diplomatic of a Court, but of MAN. (quoted in Der Derian, 1987: 172)

Old world diplomats are the suspicious spokesmen of specifics, whereas American diplomats speak for mankind in general. This attitude did not wear off during American diplomacy's ninetheenth-century hibernation, but stayed with the United States when they reappeared at the world scene toward the end of the century. As summed up by an insider like McGeorge Bundy in a 1962 lecture, "At the time of Woodrow Wilson, it was the articulate major premise of our democracy, and the inarticulate major premise of our new diplomacy, that people are not deeply different from one another. It followed that one could and should think of making the world safe for democracy by ways and means drawn directly from the American political tradition" (1964: 3). In the foreword to American diplomat Charles W. Thayer's autobiographical account published around the same time, Harold Nicolson writes that it is "the first comprehensive report written by a professional United States diplomatist and from the American point of view" (1960: ix). Thayer himself concurs when he writes that "Only in the generation since World War I has ordinary diplomacy been practiced by the United States, and then only spasmodically" (1960: xii) and insists that "there were no such things" (69) as career diplomats in the United States as late as in 1919 (but cf. Ilchman, 1961). A final quote brings out how key American politicians still explicitly privilege one of these representations of diplomacy over the other. As Congress mainstay Jesse Helms recently wrote, "It is a fanciful notion that free peoples need to seek the approval of an international body (a quarter of whose members are totalitarian dictatorships . . .) to lend support to nations struggling to break the chains of tyranny. The United Nations has no power to grant or decline legitimacy to such actions. They are inherently legitimate" (2000/2001: 31). One U.S. permanent representative to the UN once famously described it as a "sewer" (Jeane Kirkpatrick, quoted in Cronin, 2001: 115). Reviewing this tradition, John Ruggie (1994) makes two points that are pertinent to the present analysis. First, he points out that American discourse on diplomacy is embedded in a liberal discourse in which individuals as well as states, freed of old world chains, have to fend for themselves. This is a point of departure that could easily lead to seeing diplomacy as inevitable, for in an atomized social setting there must necessarily exist a functional need for rules that can mediate the interaction of the discrete entities. However, Ruggie's second point leads in another direction. Since liberal discourse also insists that any action should be universally defensible (witness Franklin's tip of the hat to Captain Cook), there must exist a universal rationality to guide actions. To Ruggie, the hallmark of American diplomacy lies exactly here, in its insistence on grounding diplomacy in an overall principle that dictates that specific structures must be accessible to all comers. To Ruggie, this principle of multi-lateralism is embedded in American diplomacy.

Ruggie sees the logic of American diplomacy as pushing toward the universal, in the sense that the pre-condition for any possible diplomacy should be that any institutionalized pattern of interaction should be open to newcomers. In political terms, this universal rationality is tied up with the existence of a republic that guarantees the possibility of an orderly life.

In Anne Norton's psychoanalytically informed phrasing, "The citizen seeks to complete himself in politics. Conscious of his incompletion, he surrenders himself to a more comprehensive identity, thereafter regarding his individuality as a shameful partiality only partly overcome. Split in the ambivalence of subject and Sovereign, the citizen acquires not an unambiguous unity, but the capacity to govern himself" (1988: 34). The sovereign individual and the sovereign political entity may thus be presented as not only existing together, but as co-constitutive phenomena.

We may go further. If there exists a universal rationality, and if the United States makes a point of living up to it by being a republic with universal significance, then the United States is a model to the world. Indeed, it is a microcosm. But if that is the case, then there exists no basis for diplomacy understood as a dialogue across cultural dividing lines. History is depicted as a movement whereby the microcosm—the United States—gets into contact with ever new entities. This contact must follow a rationality that necessarily changes the other entities in question, but that leaves the United States intact. It follows that prospective meetings are imagined as making the rest of the world conform to universal rationality—as they are already revealed and incorporated in the diplomacy of the United States (witness Franklin as the "diplomatic of MAN"). The problem with this vision is that it is not dialogical. It does not envision contact as the interaction of two or more parties, both of which may be transformed by it. Rather, it envisions contact as a uni-linear process whereby the microcosm of the United States makes more and more of the macrocosmos similar to itself. Another term for the process of making similar is assimilation.

In overall and necessarily overly homogenizing terms, then, there seem to be two American representations of diplomacy. First, diplomacy is represented as an old world practice of mutual suspicion. It does, as it were, play itself out in sewers. This kind of diplomacy is morally abominable, because it is read as an old world practice closely akin to or even leading to war. The latter element, that there is a gray zone where diplomacy involves the extention of threats that, if they are acted upon, may lead to war, is also tentatively present in the definition given in the entry for diplomacy in *The Oxford Companion to Politics of the World:*

> Above and before all else, diplomacy is a system of communication between strangers. It is the formal means by which the self-identity of the sovereign state is constituted and articulated through external relations with other states. Like the dialogue from which it is constructed, diplomacy requires and seeks to mediate otherness through the use of persuasion and force,

promises and threats, codes and symbols. It is also, according to American humorist Will Rogers, "the art of saying 'Nice doggie' until you can find a rock." (Der Derian, 1993: 244)

A second American representation of diplomacy, which is universalistic and thus ultimately anti-diplomatic, is of reaching out to the universe at large, inviting it to partake in the community of mankind by entering into the dialogue out of which diplomacy is eventually constructed.

## *STAR TREK* REPRESENTATIONS OF DIPLOMACY

In *Star Trek,* diplomacy is ruled out as a formal mode of interaction with pre-warp civilizations, that is, worlds that are not capable of interstellar flight. This is a logical consequence of the Prime Directive, which prohibits the representatives of the United Federation of Planets (hereafter the Federation) to interfere in the "natural development" of other cultures (see Weldes, 1999: 124). There is a central tension in the series between the explicit goal of seeking out "new life and new civilizations," on the one hand, and adhering to the Prime Directive, which forbids the representatives of the Federation to interfere in the "natural development" of other cultures, on the other. Due to flukes, accidents, and subterfuge, there are a number of occasions in which the Federation interacts with such cultures. These occasions are all narrated in similar ways. The narration centers on how the other world represents the Federation. Two basic representations frame these interactions. Either the Federation is seen as god-like, or indeed as consisting of or being led by gods. In a *Star Trek* setting, a (fully fledged) god is an immortal and omnipotent being, omnipotence meaning that it can take up any viewpoint along the time/space continuum in the universe. Alternatively, the Federation is seen as a technologically more advanced world. The binary set of concepts of religion/science thus frames the relationship. A major narrative in *Star Trek* is how these two narratives vie with one another. The domination of the representations on a certain world is always chronologically ordered, so that the religious representation gives way to the scientific one. A world's embrace of a scientific representation of human progress is framed as part of that world's progress. A major drama of these episodes concerns how the Federation on the one hand protests its disinterestedness in this question (cultural relativism), and on the other is loathe to see religion rather than science frame the worldview of other worlds.

In his definition of diplomacy given above, James Der Derian stresses that diplomacy is a formalization of dialogue. To repeat, "Like the dialogue from which it is constructed, diplomacy requires and seeks to mediate otherness through the use of persuasion and force, promises and threats, codes and symbols." Although diplomacy is ruled out as a formal mode of interaction between pre-warp worlds and the Federation, the dialogues between them nonetheless exibit certain regularities. Religious codes and symbols compete with scientific ones for the framing of that dialogue in terms of their respective root metaphors. To sum up, qualifying for diplomacy in *Star Trek* involves re-presenting the Other from God to life form. There is a clear parallel to *Trek* that Der Derian (1987) traces in his genealogy of diplomacy, from an originary mytho-diplomacy to what he calls proto-diplomacy.

The "new civilizations" that the Federation is supposed to seek out are thus limited to warp-capable worlds. One episode that holds special interest in this regard is *TNG*'s "Darmok," which details an encounter between the *Enterprise* and a ship manned by a people calling themselves "the Children of Tama." Uncharacteristically, Tamarian culture is warp capable, but at the same time has evolved a language whose metaphors are so tied up with the specific myths of the culture that it is, at the outset of the episode, impenetrable to Captain Picard and the Federation. Also uncharacteristically, myth is seen here as hampering rather than helping bring about interworld communication, for as pointed out by Thomas Richards, in general "*Star Trek* sees myth as performing a vital and under-appreciated function: as the central means of communication between races, and as the very basis of language itself" (1997: 127). Darmok/komrad, the captain of the Tamarian ship, sets out to establish relations with the Federation, and, at the cost of his life, he is indeed able to establish the possibility of contact.The importance of this episode to the topic of diplomacy is that, at what the series clearly presents as the threshold of the possibility of diplomacy, myth is the language available for contact, and this language has a grammar that is not necessarily immediately available. Myth is presented as a necessary but inherently problematic starting point of communication, and ultimately as something that has to be overcome for diplomacy to blossom. Diplomacy begins where specific myths give way to language, which avails itself of a grammar that the universal translator can make sense of (see Inayatullah's chapter in this volume).

Due to the nature of first contacts, incommensurability must be the major theme. The incommensurability cannot be absolute—then there would be only one story to tell, namely how a party fails to make contact (but see Whitehall's chapter in this volume). Although this failure may be narrated in a number of different ways, the topic has definite limits in a genre where holding viewer attention is a sine qua non. However, a major plot in *Star Trek* concerns how first contact is, painfully, reached across a wide linguistic and cultural abyss. These plots are invariably limited to only one episode, and they tend to concern contacts with worlds or species that are more technologically advanced, or think themselves more advanced, than the Federation. For example, in the episode "The Squire of Gothos" from the original *Star Trek* series, the crew of the *Enterprise* is caught in a simulation of eighteenth-century England. It transpires that the simulation is the creation of a child from a species about which we can know no more than that they are technologically vastly capable, and that they are non-corporeal. The comic climax of the episode has the parents of the wayward son scolding him for making life hard for lesser species and apologizing for his behavior. No further contact ensues. In a number of episodes, technologically advanced species perform more or less menacing and damaging tests on members of the Federation. These episodes invariably end with the Federation officers managing somehow to put an end to the experiments to which they are subjected. Crucially, however, the species in question neither seek nor desire further contact (characteristically, one species, which addresses the crew of the *Enterprise* as "ugly bags of mostly water," also states that it does not find them "advanced" enough for further contact to be worthwhile). No further contact ensues, which means that diplomacy is excluded as a mode of interaction.

We may now establish two thresholds beyond which diplomacy is not framed as existing in *Star Trek*. On the one hand, relations with pre-warp civilizations are mytho- or proto-diplomatic. They involve dialogue, and that dialogue is framed either in religious terms or in scientific terms. In either case, however, diplomatic relations are not allowed to ensue, either because the other party's all-pervasive religious worldview precludes it by representing the Federation as god-like, or because the other party's level of scientific progress is seen by the Federation as too low to warrant or allow diplomatic involvement. On the other hand, relations with technologically much more advanced species—who tend to have left corporeality behind and to exist as pure energy—is also out of the question. In this case as well, the reason is that the gap in technological prowess is perceived to be too large—but now it is the other party who finds the Federation wanting. The upshot is a certain technological determinism where the possibility of structured dialogue and the development of diplomacy is concerned. For there to be diplomatic relations, or even a promise of possible diplomatic relations, worlds must fall roughly within the same bracket of technological prowess.

Like all categorizations, *Star Trek*'s technically determined framing of the bandwidth for possible diplomatic relations leaves borderline cases or liminars. On the one hand, there are the species that are framed as almost too technologically advanced for diplomatic contact, and on the other, those who are framed as just about ready for it. "Darmok" is an example of how the show explicitly acknowledges this (and the liminality of the Children of Tama as possible diplomatic partners is further underlined in that it is actually the second stab at first contact—that is, second contact).

There are two species of the former type in the *Star Trek* universe—the Founders (in *DS9*), and the Borg (in *TNG* and *Voyager*). It is hardly coincidental that they are not only liminar where the possibility of diplomacy is concerned, but that a member of the species also fills the liminar subject position—to the humanoid species as such—first formulated for Data in *TNG* (see Hanley, 1997). In *DS9,* this position is taken up by the Founder security chief Odo, a shape-shifter, and in *Voyager* by Seven of Nine, a former Borg drone.[2] The drama of what degree of inter-species similarity it takes for two species to enter into diplomatic contact with one another is paralleled by the drama of what it takes to be human(oid). Where collective identities are concerned, recognition is made a question of developing diplomatic relations. Individual identity is framed as an isomorphic question, where recognition is made a question of going through a process of socialization thoroughly enough to fit into life aboard a starship.

Whereas the species that are too advanced for diplomatic contact with the Federation tend to be energetic, the Founders in *DS9* exist primarily in a liquid state—that is, somewhere in-between body matter and pure, ethereal soul. Whereas the claims by energetic lifeforms are presented as statements of fact, when a Founder by the name of Laas claims that his species has reached "the next stage" of development relative to humans, his human interlocutors scoff at him. Complete non-corporeality seems to be a condition for claims of clear-cut technological superiority to be accepted by Federation officers. The liminality of the Founders is a dual matter. It is not only presented as a matter of nature and substance, but also as one of culture and history. We are explicitly informed by a leading Founder that they used to be explorers of the universe, but that they were hounded and suppressed due to their metamorphic nature. Their response was twofold. They retreated from exploration—that is, they stopped searching out new worlds and new civilizations. Furthermore, they embarked on a new career as empire builders—that is, they colonized other worlds in order, we are told, to "bring order to chaos." The Founders see the rest of the world as something it is up to them to order in their own image, something to bring under direct imperial control. The specificity of the other worlds may be maintained, but that specificity cannot be ordered according to the political principle of sovereignty, only of suzereignty (see Wight, 1977).

The Borg are post-diplomatic in a rather more thoroughgoing sense than are the Founders. Their goal is "to reach perfection"—to reach a state of absolute order. Their way of doing this, however, is not to establish suzereign relations with other worlds, but, as they put it on the eve of their assimilation of other species, to "add your biomatter to our own." As we learn in *TNG*'s "The Best of Both Worlds," "They identify what is useful to them, then consume it." Their goal is to make the non-Borg world into more of the Borg same. Within that same, no externality can be left to explore, and where there is no externality, there can be no space of communication to traverse. Indeed, Borg communication is totally internal—the image presented to the viewer is that of "a hive mind," where thought is collective and rapport instantaneous.

When the Founders and the Borg are nonetheless liminars of diplomacy, and not simply alien to the concept, it is because they recognize the value of communication in certain senses and in certain situations. For example, when the Borg plan an invasion of Earth in order to "add new biomatter to their own," they abduct Captain Picard and enhance him genetically to fit into their collective. But they let him maintain enough of his individuality to allow him to present himself not as "We are the Borg," but as "I am Locutus of Borg." Locutus is Latin for "the one who addresses," and addressing one collective on behalf of another is a typical diplomatic function. Furthermore, when the Borg fails to assimilate what they refer to as "species 8472" and that species retaliates by launching a potentially devastating attack against the Borg, Captain Janeway of the starship *Voyager* is actually able to forge an alliance with them. The forging of alliances is another typical diplomatic function, and in *Star Trek* it is explicitly treated as such (see below). The Founders are also seen to forge alliances with other species (notably the Cardassians), and they orchestrate a wide variety of relations with a number of other political entities from their position as imperial center.

If the Founders and the Borg have a corporeality that sets them apart from humanoids, the other kind of diplomatic liminars are corporally distinct in an opposite direction: their physique is without exception strikingly sturdy. Physical sturdiness goes with war-like ways and an adherence to particularly strict codes of conduct. One example of this kind of liminar are the Hirogen, who capture *Voyager* and force its crew to act out, on the ship's holodeck, the role of World War II allies to the Hirogens' own Nazis. The Hirogen/Nazi infatuation with purity of blood and body is matched by their categorization of other species as prey to be hunted down and killed for sport. One does not communicate with one's prey in other modes than through the hunt. Diplomacy is therefore ruled out as a mode of communication. Characteristically, the climax of the relationship between the Federation and the Hirogen is reached when Captain Janeway is able to present and have them accept a gift. The bearing of gifts is a standard diplomatic practice. As stressed by historians of diplomacy, as late as in the 1600s meting out the quality and value of gifts to be presented to diplomatic representatives of other states was a key work of recognition, and gift-exchange continues to play a role in diplomacy.[3] As demonstrated in a classic study by Marcel Mauss (1990), receiving a gift involves accepting the bearer of the gift as an interlocutor, and that acceptance carries with it a vague obligation to come up with a counter-gift at some unspecified later stage. A tie is being formed, where the one who is able to offer a gift and have it accepted gains recognition and the potential position of power that comes with being the party who can afford to part with something. At the moment the Hirogen accept the gift, then, their way of life as hunters who have no dealings with their prey other than to hunt it down comes to an end. By the same token, the Federation has succeeded in building a foundation for diplomatic relations, and the Hirogen cease to be diplomatic liminars. Instructively, after this incident, they disappear from the show, and when they reappear in its seventh and final season, they partake of what must be called regular diplomatic contacts with the Federation representatives.

The major diplomatic liminar in *Star Trek*, however, are clearly the Klingons. In the *TNG* episode "Loud as a Whisper," chief of security Lieutenant Worf, himself a Klingon, reports about the man who is presented as the best negotiator available in the galaxy, that "Before him, there was no Klingon word for peacemaker." From this, we learn two things. First, peacemaking, in distinction to the unconditional surrender that follows a total defeat in war, is a diplomat function for which the Klingons recently had no concept. Second, it was a Federation diplomat who led them to incorporate that concept into Klingon.

The entire relationship between the Federation and the Klingon empire as it evolves through the first three series—from the initial clashes on faraway planets and space stations, through the first exchange of officers between their fleets and the uneasy formation of an alliance, to the long testing of that alliance in a war against the Founders—can be read as a bringing of Klingon war-like ways into the ambit of the Federation's diplomatic but intermittantly warfighting embrace of the universe.[4] Captain Picard, a key Federation diplomat in this story, comes across as the tamer of the Klingons, and that taming takes the unequivocal form of an ever more firm embedding of Klingon war-like ways in an ever more differentiated and institutionalized Klingon diplomacy. The saga of the Klingons turning away from waging war at the drop of a *bat'leth* is also the saga of the Klingons turning toward diplomacy as a mode of alternative interaction.

To sum up, liminars of diplomacy in *Star Trek* are marked by their corporeality. As we learn more about them, they are invariably brought more firmly into steady diplomatic contacts with the Federation. This must be seen as a celebration of diplomacy as a mode of interaction—but also as an acknowledgement that diplomacy involves a certain customizing of cultural ways. Again, there is a striking parallel between the evolution of what may perhaps be referred to respectively as mundane diplomacy and of galactic diplomacy.

Like other social practices, fully fledged diplomacy must have a certain permanence to be worthy of the name. It is, in Der Derian's definition, "the formal means by which the self-identity of the sovereign state is constituted and articulated through external relations with other states." "Formal" has sometimes been taken to mean "written" (Nicolson, 1939), but this may be overly strict. Be that as it may, the Federation is seen to have treaty-regulated relations with three types of political entities. First, there are the numerous worlds portrayed as clamoring to join the Federation. Second, there are a number of worlds—invariably described as somehow small—that follow a policy of neutrality vis-à-vis the Federation. Third, there are the other great powers of the alpha quadrant of the galaxy. In addition to the Klingons, these include the Romulans and the Cardassians.

There are sound reasons why institutionalized diplomacy is paid little heed in *Star Trek*. First, the subject matter itself: the negotiation game surrounding the drawing up of treaties, the exchange of information, and the other minutia of diplomatic life is hardly of major interest to anyone other than International Relationists and similarly professionally challenged viewers. Second, dramatic requirements: standard operational procedures, and particularly smooth-running ones, are duller than the unexpected. Harmony is duller than conflict. Even in institutes that seemingly specialize in peace research, interest fastens on unruly entities at war and in conflict, not on societies at peace and in harmony. The key reason for this may be a human proclivity for variation. As Tolstoy observes at the outset of

*Anna Karenina,* all happy families have the same story to tell, but every un-happy family's story is unique. A third reason, which may be even more basic, is to do with how becoming is privileged over being in Western culture generally. Business as usual is only seen as interesting if it leads to something that is somehow "new" (but not too new—then, as *Star Trek* points out repeatedly, it cannot be grasped at all).

## PROGRESS, A KEY ISSUE

This privileging of becoming over being may be traced in two different kinds of narrative of progress that are at the center of *Star Trek's* two different representations of diplomacy. One presents diplomacy as dissembling and progress as quantitative, the other presents diplomacy as a universalizing practice and progress as qualitative.

The first narrative of progress is to do with quantitative expansion. In political terms, it takes the form of imperial expansion. The key here is that there is no tension between the specific and the universal. As noted above, the Borg is the perfect image of this process—so perfect that it is almost beyond any perceived need to engage in diplomacy at all. The Cardassians and the Founders make for better examples. Interestingly, the Cardassians are presented as having no diplomats—their diplomatic functions are invariably carried out by the soldiers who run the entire planet.[5] The Founders do have a diplomatic corps. In fact, the Founders have genetically enhanced an entire race, the Vorta (who, understandably, relate to their makers as gods), for the purpose of acting as their intermediaries in relations with other worlds.[6] These diplomats, we learn little by little, are cloned on demand, and so are the perfect diplomats-to-go. For example, Weyoun, the Vorta who is given the most prolonged and in-depth presentation—goes through eight different gestations before he is retired. The diplomacy of the Cardassian soldiers and the Vorta clones is as inauthentic as they are themselves. The first narrative of progress thus spawns a representation of diplomacy marked by dissimulation, subterfuge, a closeness to war, etc.

The second narrative of progress is to do with qualitative embetterment. This narrative has two foci—the bettering and enlargement of the self (barring the phrases "engage," "make it so," and "good work, number one," "we work to better ourselves" may be Captain Picard's most often repeated line), and the bettering and enlargement of the Federation. It is predicated on there being a basic split between the specific and the universal, between microcosmos and macrocosmos, between individual and

Federation. Progress is presented as a move in the direction of a better fit between the two. The show makes a speciality out of exploring questions of identity, and it does so within a tightly scripted band of variety. First, the focus is almost invariably on the individual, not on society as such: "Historical forces remain largely external to character in *Star Trek*," and "the ultimate nightmare the series considers is the breakdown of the inner stability of the individual. The political balance of power is not nearly so important as the inner balance of power inside the individual" (Richards, 1997: 57, 31).[7] Second, the essential sameness of the individual is invariably stressed. The ex post facto change of identity (if any) is always presented as a matter either of breakdown and reconstruction, or of growth; it is never a change in a less linear or "progressive" sense. This is partly a necessity laid down by the kind of framework studio rules that apply to all television shows and for which acceptable scripts must turn in the characters at the end of the episode roughly in the shape in which they were found. But exactly this fact—that the bandwidth of variation is tightly and formally scripted by the studio—bears out how basic this way of seeing identity is to American individualistic culture in general.

In *Star Trek*, the identity of persons as well as of worlds revolves around the need to fit in with an already established social order epitomized by the United Federation of Planets, its Starfleet, and its ships. It is only a question of time before every individual and every world gets there. One of the great throwaway lines of the show is from a eulogy for a recently departed scientist seemingly delivered by Data, but in fact concocted by the dead man himself, who upon decorporation took possession of Data in order to perpetuate his existence. This man celebrates himself by giving a twist to a standard epitaph, insisting that "To know him was to love him. Not to know him was to love him from afar." The basic representation of diplomacy in the show makes the same supposition where worlds are concerned: the Federation should be loved when known, and it is just a question of time before everybody knows it.

The throwaway line from the eulogy is heavy with self irony; *Star Trek* also manages to be ironic about its most dearly held representations. The difference between the two major representations of diplomacy in *Star Trek* turns on two tightly intertwined factors: voluntariness, and the preservation of specificity under potentially universal conditions. Quite literally, a world of difference separates the two. This makes for an obvious question: what if the difference is thinner and more permeable than the Federation makes it out to be? To its great credit, *Star Trek* poses this question a number of times, perhaps most explicitly and incisively through the

character of *DS9*'s Lt. Commander Eddington. Despite his Starfleet uniform, Eddington's principal sympathy does not lie with Starfleet and the
Federation, but with the Macquis, a group of homesteaders cum resistance
fighters on the Cardassian-Federation border. Former guerrillas turned regular soldiers are quite numerous in the show—they even make up one half
of the *Voyager* crew—but the development of these characters is usually
scripted as a pilgrim's progress from a warfare-first approach to the diplo-
macy-first approach that ostensibly characterizes the Federation. Eddington, on the other hand, consciously leaves behind the Federation.
Crucially, Eddington gives as his reason for turning away from the Federation that he finds its relationship to the non-Federation world, that is, its
diplomacy, to be imperial. "You are worse than the Borg," he tells his
Starfleet captain—worse, because where the Borg sets out to assimilate the
rest of the world quite openly, the Federation sets out to assimilate worlds
under false pretenses, and at the cost of making it impossible for other
ways of life, like that of the Macquis, to flourish. In a word, to Eddington,
the difference between the show's two major representations of diplomacy
is not really a difference that makes a difference. To him, when the Federation sets out to find new worlds, it is not to stage a fully fledged dialogue,
but rather to impose itself and its way of life. Inasmuch as this is not acknowledged openly, as it is by the Borg, the diplomacy of the Federation
is dissembling.

The case of Eddington plays itself out during a war. In the *Voyager*
episode "Living Witness," the same theme is handled with a different
twist. It opens with a black-gloved Kathryn Janeway pronouncing that
"When diplomacy fails, there's only one other option—violence." She
then goes on to perpetrate what she acknowledges as genocide on a people
called the Kyrians. It soon transpires, however, that what we are seeing is
not a representation, but a representation of a representation, a simulation
of events, made by Kyrians and placed in a commemorative museum 700
years after the simulated events allegedly took place. The holographic doctor, the "Living Witness" of the episode's title, is retrieved from a museum
exhibit and proceeds to set the record straight. The episode's major interest is in its reflection on revisionist history, and, for our purposes, the relationship between the representations of diplomacy on *Voyager* generally,
and the representation of diplomacy in the post hoc Kyrian simulation of
life on *Voyager*. What is an ever-present possibility in the former, is brought
out and made painfully explicit in the latter. The reading that seems to be
invited is that things *are* like this, that *all* diplomacy may sooner or later
be replaced by the use of physical violence, but that there are counter-

forces in the life of the *Voyager* crew that generally prevents the possibility from being actualized in its most naked form. A similar reading seems to be invited in "One," an episode that turns on the unintended consequences of Captain Janeway's forging an alliance with the Borg. Arturus, the vengeful lonely survivor of a Borg assimilation campaign and the "one" lending the episode its name, appears and informs Janeway that "Your diplomacy destroyed my world." The alliance with *Voyager* had given the Borg the marginal increase in their strength that was needed to assimilate his homeworld. The accusation is a valid one, and Janeway's answer, "We did not know," acknowledges this. Great power diplomacy, or for that matter diplomacy of any kind, may have unintended and morally indefensible consequences. The major interest here is once again that this insight undermines the major representation of diplomacy in *Star Trek* as benevolently universalistic, highlighting instead the possible specificity-erasing consequences of diplomacy, which are usually associated with the more negative representation of diplomacy (as it is practiced by, among others, Cardassians and Founders).

## CONCLUSION

I hope to have demonstrated that the two major American representations of diplomacy are reproduced in *Star Trek*. One key prerequisite for the circulation of representations of diplomacy between *Star Trek* and its viewers, namely isomorphism, has been demonstrated to exist. Yet this demonstration is only a first step—it situates the analysis "at the level of reflection: images of the monarchy, the lower classes, the legal profession, the church, [diplomacy] and so forth. Such studies are essential, but they rarely engage questions of dynamic exchange. They tend instead to posit two separate, autonomous systems and then try to gauge how accurately or effectively the one represents the other" (Greenblatt, 1988: 11).

The analysis of the above does not yet approach the question of distribution between U.S. diplomacy and *Star Trek* diplomacy. As Stephen Greenblatt states at the outset (and not at the end) of an investigation of European representations of the new world, "We can be certain only that European representations of the New World tell us something about the European practices of representation" (Greenblatt, 1992: 7). That *Star Trek* representations of diplomacy, which are American representations, tell us something about American practices of representation, is a truism. It is, however, interesting that *Star Trek* manages to acknowledge the existence of both major representations, to juxtapose them, and with increasing frequency to demonstrate that they do overlap. This compares favorably with a number of U.S. policy debates, in which carriers of one representation frequently do not even acknowledge the relevance, or even the existence, of this tension for U.S. policy. *Star Trek* arguably suggests a more fruitful way of inciting discourse about diplomacy than does the run-of-the-mill American foreign policy debate.

A BBC documentary called *Louis Theroux's Weird Weekend* followed a group of UFOlogists out into the desert and interviewed them about why they were doing what they were doing. A major theme that emerged was the need to organize an extraterrestrial "people's diplomacy" that could play the role of welcoming committee. One participant stated that "We think it is time to launch a diplomatic effort," another that it was all an attempt at "hands across the universe. We think it is high time racism ended—God forbid we should take it off the planet." This was needed, a third UFOlogist insisted, not least since it was the military that was in charge of these things on the state's side, and they were not necessarily the kind of people with the right skills to communicate with off-worlders: "we don't think they are the best representatives of humankind." A key topic in IR research, namely the relationship between the practices of war and diplomacy, crops up here in a fairly far-out setting. Whether *Star Trek* viewing may account for this particular incident or similar ones cannot concern us here (but one notes that the woman who wanted to reach across the universe described *Close Encounters of the Third Kind* as "my favourite movie of all time"). To a student of world politics, the major question of interest may perhaps not be the representations of diplomacy that exist within these marginal groups, but the extent to which these fringe phenomena also represent more widely distributed representations of diplomacy.

A second conclusion concerns how representations of diplomacy look when compared not only to American representations, but to our historical reservoir of knowledge about diplomacy in general. *Star Trek* presents first contact as a contact that is always mediated through expectations, and it presents the most relevant expectations as religious. Myth, it was noted above, tends to lend an initial grammar to interworld contact. Myths are good to think. In his genealogy of diplomacy, Der Derian (1987) stresses how the first diplomacy is mythical and turns on mediation between men and gods. This echoes the historical record: Columbus noted that the people on the new world had to be residents of paradise, thus echoing a Christian myth. The Spaniards were represented as gods by the Aztecs, as was Captain Cook by the Hawaiians.

Dipomacy and war shade into one another. In the Middle Ages, envoys followed the troops, and initiated their talks only when the weapons had fallen silent. The dialogue between diplomats and soldiers—the "pol-mil" of NATO jargon—is an ongoing one, and it concerns the same events.

Where the establishment of full diplomatic contact is concerned, the striking thing is the narrow band within which *Star Trek* lodges its possibility. Again, this echoes the historical record. In took until 1856 for the modern European diplomatic system formally to acknowledge Turkey as a political entity with rights on a par with the system's core members and, informally, it may at least be argued that there are still some problems pending in this regard (Neumann and Welsh, 1991). Historically, the present diplomatic system grew out of, and may in some respects be said still to be lodged in, Christianity. This is to say that a number of similar cultural traits facilitated the establishment of diplomacy. The same can be said for *all* other diplomatic systems known to have existed. The process of regularization and institutionalization of diplomacy was predicated on the existence of common cultural traits. The Amarna system was embedded in a Babylonian-speaking world of already existing trade relations. The diplomatic system of the Greek city-states was embedded in a tightly defined linguistic and religious setting.

It has been argued that "Explorers do not reveal otherness. They comment upon 'anthropology,' that is, the distance separating savagery and civilization on the diachronic line of progress" (Mudimbe, 1988: 15). In the history of the modern diplomatic system, at least, the major theme of the ninetheenth century in this regard was the definition of and the extent to which different political entities met a "standard of civilisation" (Gong, 1984). It is easy to write off the invocation of a standard of civilisation in *Star Trek* as utter prejudice. It is less easy to think how, in a setting where the issue is the forging of dialogue leading perhaps to diplomacy, one could act on other precepts. If there is an interest in institutionalizing relations—that is, if there is a diplomatic intent—then recognition of otherness *has to* be paired with a certain minimum requirement in terms of communication, predictability, and reciprocity. Critiques of how quickly and in what manner those criteria are invoked, are important and indeed necessary. It is also important to highlight the cost of entering into and maintaining diplomatic relations because it necessarily involves effects on the other parties involved. Such critiques must, however, acknowledge the enormity of the dilemmas involved. Perhaps the most interesting, and depressing, thing about *Star Trek* is that these dilemmas are captured and circulated to viewers in ways that do not jar with what we know from the historical record about diplomacy and the prerequisites of diplomacy. It is not only that *Star Trek* props up widely held representations of diplomacy. It is also that it highlights a tension between them that is deeply embedded both historically and sociologically, and from which there is no easy escape.

## NOTES

1. A previous version of this chapter was read at the annual International Studies Association conference, Chicago, February 20–24, 2001. I thank the participants at that occasion as well as the other contributors to this volume, Barry Buzan, Halvard Leira, and Roberta E. Pearson for comments.
2. In the former case, humanity is limned off from pure organic matter (nature); in the latter, from technology (culture). According to episode writers, the reanthropomorphization of Seven is also inspired by a Tarzan-like epic about a wolf boy called "Wolves at the Door" (see Gross 1999: 95).
3. "In 1651 the Dutch republic forbade its diplomats to accept gifts from foreign governments; and in 1692 regulations were issued in Sweden which for the first time specified the value of those to be given to foreign representatives on their departure. In England P. I. Potemkin was the last Russian ambassador, in 1681, to arrive in London bearing gifts to be presented in semi-oriental style to the king; he was also the last to receive a present in the traditional manner when he left" (Anderson 1993: 51; orientalism noted).
4. On the uneasy status of the Federation's Starfleet as an exploratory and diplomatic vs. a warfighting force, see Weldes (1999).
5. "Cardassians. People. Technologically advanced humanoid civilization. In the past, the Cardassians were a peaceful and spiritual people. But because their planet was resource-poor, starvation and disease were rampant, and people died by the millions. With the rise of the military to power, new territories and technology were acquired by violence, at the cost of millions of lives sacrificed to the war effort" (www.kroesen.demon.nl/startrek/rkalien03.html).
6. The official Paramount Internet site notes that the Vorta " . . . served the Founders as the administrators of the Dominion, field supervisors of the Jem'Hadar armies, and envoys for client races such as the Karemma" (www.startrek.com/library/xeno).
7. "The premise of a time travel episode in *Star Trek* is always that the modification of a single life can change history" (Richards, 1997: 68).

## BIBLIOGRAPHY

Anderson, Matthew Smith. 1993. *The Rise of Modern Diplomacy 1450–1919*, London: Longman.

Bundy, McGeorge. 1964. "The Battlefields of Power and the Searchlights of the Academy," in E. A. J. Johnson, ed., *The Dimensions of Diplomacy*, Baltimore, MD: Johns Hopkins University Press, pp. 1–15.

Coward, Rosalind. 2000. "Dennis Potter and the Question of the Television Author," in Robert Stam and Toby Miller, eds., *Film and Theory: An Anthology*, Oxford: Blackwell, pp. 7–15.

Cronin, Bruce. 2001. "The Paradox of Hegemony: America's Ambiguous Relationship with the United Nations," *European Journal of International Relations*, 7(1): 103–130.

Der Derian, James. 1993. "Diplomacy," in *The Oxford Companion to Politics of the World*, Oxford: Oxford University Press, pp. 244–266.

Der Derian, James. 1987. *On Diplomacy. A Genealogy of Western Estrangement*, Oxford: Blackwell.

Fuller, Brian. 2000. "Interview," *The Official Star Trek Newsletter*, December. http://www.startrek.com/production/voyager7/articles/120100.html.

Gong, Gerrit W. 1984. *The Standard of 'Civilization' in International Society*, Oxford: Oxford University Press.

Greenblatt, Stephen. 1988. *Shakespearean Negotiations. The Circulation of Social Energy in Renaissance England*, Oxford: Clarendon.

Greenblatt, Stephen. 1992. *Marvelous Possessions. The Wonder of the New World*, Oxford: Clarendon.

Greenwald, Jeff. 1996. "Write for *Star Trek*," *Wired Archive* 4.01, January, pp. 1–7. http://www.wired.com/wired/archive/4.01/trek.script.

Gross, Edward. 1999. "May the Borg Be With You," *Retrovision*, 2: 92–96.

Hanley, Richard. 1997. *Is Data Human? The Metaphysics of Star Trek*, London: Boxtree.

Helms, Jesse. 2000/2001. "American Sovereignty and the UN," *The National Interest*, 62: 31–34.

Ilchman, W. F. 1961. *Professional Diplomacy in the United States, 1779–1939*, Chicago: University of Chicago Press.

Killian, Jr., James R. 1964. "Science and Foreign Policy," in E. A. J. Johnson, ed., *The Dimensions of Diplomacy*, Baltimore, MD: Johns Hopkins University Press, pp. 57–87.

Mauss, Marcel. 1990. *The Gift: The Form and Reason for Exchange in Archaic Societies*, London: Routledge.

Mudimbe, V. Y. 1988. *The Invention of Africa. Gnosis, Philosophy, and the Order of Knowledge*, Bloomington: Indiana University Press.

Neumann, Iver B., and Jennifer M. Welsh. 1991. "The Other in European Self-Definition: A Critical Addendum to the Literature on International Society," *Review of International Studies*, 17(4): 327–48.

Nicolson, Sir Harold. 1960. "Foreword," in Charles W. Thayer, *Diplomat*, NY: Harper, pp. ix–xii.

Nicolson, Sir Harold. 1939. *Diplomacy*, London: Butterworth.

Norton, Anne. 1988. *Reflections on Political Identity,* Baltimore, MD: Johns Hopkins University Press.

Penley, Constance. 1997. *NASA/Trek: Popular Science and Sex in America,* London: Verso.

Richards, Thomas. 1997. *Star Trek in Myth and Legend,* London: Millennium.

Ruggie, John Gerard. 1994. "Third Try at World Order? America and Multilateralism after the Cold War," *Political Science Quarterly,* 109(4): 553–570.

Silj, Alessandro, et al. 1988. *East of Dallas: The European Challenge to American Television,* London: British Film Institute.

Thayer, Charles W. 1960. *Diplomat,* NY: Harper.

Weldes, Jutta. 1999. "Going Cultural: *Star Trek,* State Action, and Popular Culture," *Millennium,* 28(1): 117–134.

Wight, Martin. 1977. *Systems of States,* Leicester: Leicester University Press.

# Chapter 3

## BUMPY SPACE

Imperialism and Resistance in
*Star Trek: The Next Generation*[1]

*Naeem Inayatullah*

### THE HOOK

Prior to the economic exploitation of third world labor and prior to
the third word's substantive absence in international institutions, international inequality can be seen to emerge from hidden assumptions about cultural encounter. Such assumptions—present in both social
theory and popular culture—create a hierarchically based estrangement
between and within peoples. For example, sixteenth-century Spaniards assumed that the Indians either did not possess language or that it was utterly transparent. In the same way, most if not all science fiction
movies/TV dramas—and *Star Trek* in particular—assume either that aliens
do not use language or that a "universal translator" can easily transform
alien languages into standard North American/British English. The loss of
moorings, the anxiety of miscommunication, and the tortuous process of
trial and error experience are thereby smoothed out. With that smoothing,
the excitement and trepidation of encounter become flattened into epistemologically violent teaching projects where encounters with others serve
missionary purposes. Nevertheless, the urgency of teaching others belies an
anxiety about the teacher's own capacity to change and learn. Alongside
the missionary project is another in which deeper and perhaps healthier
motives leave their traces.

## UNCOVERING AN APOLOGY

Astounding as it may seem, we can hear calls for a return to the colonial mission (Jackson, 1990; Johnson, 1993; Wolf, 2001; Mallaby, 2002). Such avowals surface, in part, from Western frustration with the pace of economic and political development in the third world. When coupled with a shadowy sense of Kipling's "white man's burden," and with what the sixteenth-century Spanish theorist Francisco de Vitoria crystallized as a type of pedagogical imperative, we can discern in this contemporary impatience the irresistibility of the colonial drive. The need to reclaim and reorder the lives of others, however, comes not just from missionary zeal nor only from a sense of responsibility toward others. Ultimately, the demand to revive colonialism comes from divining that the consequences of this legacy were, on the whole, not so bad—an assessment made possible by the extensive and unending debate over the costs and benefits of colonialism. And who could demur when colonial "encounter" is said to bring technological development, democracy, modernity, and civilization itself?

If we are willing, we can peek behind both this complacent apologia and the combative incredulity it provokes as its twin response. Tzvetan Todorov (1984) proposes to move beyond cost-benefit calculations of colonialism by focusing on the *form* of communication. While still holding the belief that some societies may be more technologically advanced, and therefore not altogether severing himself from theories of progress, modernization, and development, Todorov offers a simple test: was colonialism proposed or imposed?

To pose the question in this form is to have answered it. Thus, Todorov claims, "Christianization, like the export of any ideology or technology, can be condemned as soon as it is imposed, by arms or otherwise." Some civilizations can have features that we might say are superior or inferior to others, but, "this does not justify," says Todorov, "their being imposed on others." Indeed, it is this very imposition that suggests a lower level of civilization in that "to impose one's will on others implies that one does not concede to that other the same humanity one grants oneself. . . ." And then with flourish, Todorov gets to the heart of the matter, "No one asked the Indians if they wanted the wheel, or looms, or forges; they were obliged to accept them. Here is where the violence resides, and it does not depend on the possible utility of these objects" (179). The distinction between proposition and imposition enables a shift in the terms of a five-hundred-year dispute. Todorov looks behind the debate over colonial impact and finds imposition. It seems difficult to deny that the Europeans simply did not consider the Indians' needs except as a projection of their own desires.

Seen in this light, *Star Trek: The Next Generation*'s (henceforth, *TNG*) finest moment comes in the episode "First Contact." *TNG* responds to Todorov's shift by having the United Federation of Planets (henceforth, the Federation) take a *propositional* posture toward the Malcorians. Due to their imminent development of warp drive—the ability to travel faster than the speed of light—the Malcorians are about to cross the threshold into interstellar space. Having secretly monitored their advance, the Federation offers to guide Malcor into this new world. When, after much deliberation, the Malcorians reject the offer, the Federation surprisingly honors the rejection. Of course, the reasons Malcor's Chancellor Durken gives for rejecting this offer do not challenge the Federation's temporal occupation of Malcor's future; they do not challenge, that is, the Federation's assumption of a universal development of civilizations based on technological achievement (see the discussion of the Richter Scale in Whitehall, this volume). Instead, Durken points to the internal tension on his planet—the rift between the most tradition-bound elements and those who would eagerly enter the Federation's new world. Nevertheless, the episode's propositional treatment of encounter comes as close to an apology for the meta-violence wrought upon "Indians" as I have seen.

Before we get into the details of this apology and this model for first contact, let us ask a question suggested by Todorov's shift. We can see the question in the following dialogue from "First Contact":

> Chancellor Durken: You speak the language of diplomacy very well, Captain. It's a language I've come to appreciate and understand. But I have learned not always to trust it.
> Picard: Trust takes time and experience.
> Durken: My world's history has recorded that conquerors often arrive with the words, "We are your friends."
> Picard: We are not your conquerors, Chancellor.
> Durken: What *do* you want?
> Picard: A beginning . . .

Durken poses an excellent question: What brings you here? What is your motive? What is your interest in portraying yourself as guides to our future? Picard's answer obfuscates the critical issue: the hidden desires that lie beneath the apparently benevolent intentions of the Federation.

In a later dialogue between the wounded first officer of the Enterprise, Riker, who is laying in a Malcorian hospital, and the Malcorian Minister of Security, Krola, the issue of Federation interests gets a sharper replay:

> Riker: We are on a mission of peace.
> Krola: Such noble creatures. Why [firing Riker's captured phaser] do peaceful people develop such lethal weapons?
> Riker: It is only for defense.
> Krola: Perhaps like so many conquerors you believe your goals to be benevolent. I cannot. For however you would describe your intentions you represent the end of my way of life . . . .

Notice how, like Picard above, Riker provides a rather weak response. In part this is because the show is premised on the Federation's good intentions. But they also deliver weak lines because, in Western life, not much thought has gone into the desires and intentions of missionaries. In contrast to our heroes, Durken and especially Krola make rich sense. It is as if the show is saying: "You know, the Malcorians have a point. What *are* the motivations of the Federation?" Picard tries to turn to political realism:

> Picard: There is no starship mission more dangerous than first contact. We never know what we will face when we open the door on a new world. How will we be greeted? What exactly the dangers will be. Centuries ago, disastrous contact with the Klingon Empire led to decades of war. And it was decided then that we would do surveillance before making first contact. It was a controversial decision. I believe it prevented more problems than it created.

If first contact missions are so dangerous, why engage in them? Picard speaks to the risks but not to the motives of contact.

To begin to get at the motive, we can turn to the episode "11001001." First the plot line: The *Enterprise* comes into a space station for a computer upgrade to be performed by two sets of Bynars, a species who come in pairs and who are a synthesis of organic and silicon life (prefiguring the Borg). The Bynars have created a symbiotic relationship between their people and the main computer on their planet. Their problem is that a nearby star is about to go supernova, creating a storm that will temporarily disable their computer, thereby destroying their planet. The Bynars plan to hijack the *Enterprise,* upload the data from their computer to the ship's, and then download after the storm. The plan goes awry. The Bynars begin to die, but are rescued after Picard and Riker learn of the Bynar's desperation. We turn, for the moment, to a dialogue at the end of the show:

> Picard to the Bynars: Why did you not ask for help?
> Bynars [conferring]: You might have said no.
> Picard: But there is a very good chance we would have said yes.
> Bynars: Our need was too great to risk rejection.
> Picard: So you stole it [the ship and its computer].
> Riker: Their reasoning was part of their binary thinking. For them there are only two choices, one or zero, yes or no.

To make my point about the Federation's deeper motives in its staging of first contacts, I need a license to invert the relationship between the Federation and the Bynars in this dialogue. That is, I want to suggest that Riker's coda serves as a projection. I base this reversal on the not so implausible assumption that our constructions of alien others, whatever else they may be, are also images of inner Others (see Hozic, this volume). Thus, coming to know and understand alien others can also be a manner of coming to know various, often neglected, parts of ourselves. If I am allowed this move, then I wish to suggest further that it is the Federation, representing Western society, that uses binary thinking and, more important, it is the Federation and Western society whose need in encounter is too great to risk rejection. How might this be so? What need of the Federation's is too great to risk rejection?

The opening of each show, as well as the plots of various episodes, makes the seeking after others the result of simple curiosity, a natural drive. But this tells us nothing. Why risk travel and war when the dangers are so great? When the motivating assumption of the show is so consistently ignored, the critic may be allowed to speculate that perhaps it is the Federation's need to communicate with inner and outer selves, to make those selves less alien and more integral, and thereby to learn from them, that serves as the real motive. "To boldly go where no one has gone before" is to extend outwards in space and simultaneously to search inward into our own being. *This* need—the need to learn—is too great to risk rejection. So, when in the last episode of *TNG,* "All Good Things . . . ," the omnipotent Q says, "That is the exploration that awaits you. Not mapping stars and studying nebulae, but charting the unknown possibilities of existence," he gets some of it right. More dialectically, he might have said: "Through mapping stars and studying nebulae, you can also chart the knowable possibilities of inner existence. That is the exploration that awaits you."

There is a reason why *TNG* never makes the need to learn explicit. To do so would suggest the presence of *a lack* within the Federation. Like the United States and Great Britain before it, the Federation does not see itself as develop*ing;* rather, it is already develop*ed.* It understands its mission as filling the lack of others, not searching for, exposing, and filling its own lack. Like all hegemons, it is convinced that it must teach others, not learn from them—even as it pretends otherwise. As the character of Eddington points out (in an episode of another *Star Trek*-based show, *Deep Space 9*), such pretension makes the Federation a far more dangerous imperialist than the Borg, who, at least, remain direct about their assimilationist intentions (see Neumann, this volume). (To combine themes from chapters by Lipshutz and Jackson and Nexon, we might say that the Borg reflect the Federation without idealist trappings: "I have seen the Borg and they are us.") The dominance of the teaching drive over the need to learn sustains the usual props for benevolent imperialism. *TNG* allows itself to pose the question of the Federation's motives but makes Picard and Riker mute lest they reveal the imperialism of the Federation or enable a critical self-consciousness in its audience. The need to learn, the Lacanian real of travel, cannot be the explicit motive for travel because it fits poorly with the imagery of heroic captains and marvelous voyages originating in modern societies.

And yet, the recessive theme that lingers just below the surface is potent. The search for outer Others can catalyze an uncovering of our inner Others if we learn to treat difference as a resource. Such a need places our lack back at the center of our travel, as can be seen in "Tin Man." Plotline: an organic life form resembling a starship is found to be circling a star that is about to go supernova. The *Enterprise* must transport a specialist in first contact, the telepath Tam Elron, and proceed to engage "Tin Man"—the name given to the alien.

Unknown to the *Enterprise* crew, Tam is already telepathically in contact with Tin Man. He explains that long ago Tin Man cared for a crew living inside it who, in turn, gave it a sense of value and belonging. But its crew/comrades have long since died, and Tin Man has been alone, and lonely, for centuries. By orbiting the soon to be exploding star, Tin Man intends to end its loneliness. Tam, in turn, hopes he can replace Tin Man's crew and thereby save the creature.

By naming companionship as its lack, Tam makes Tin Man's need explicit. Nevertheless, Tam's needs are no less clear. He does not fit in with the *Enterprise,* nor with any community he has encountered. He is impatient with the *Enterprise* crew's slow, non-telepathic communication. Nor can he find a way to shut off his extraordinary telepathic powers—powers that force him to listen to the thoughts of all the crew, creating intolerable noise for his psyche. What Tam needs is quiet, coupled with the instantaneous speed of telepathic communication. Of course, this is exactly what Tin Man offers; one's lack fits the other's need. As Tam admits to Data: " . . . he [Tin Man] is going to save me as well." This lesson extends beyond Tam and Tin Man, as is shown by the closing dialogue of the episode:

> Troi: What did happen?
> Data: Individually they [Tam and Tin Man] were so . . .
> Troi: . . . wounded, isolated.
> Data: Yes, but no longer. Through joining they have been healed. Grief has been transmuted to joy; loneliness to belonging.
> Troi: Data, you *do* understand.
> Data: Yes . . . when I returned to the *Enterprise,* I realized this is where I belonged.

The android Data now replaces Tin Man as our representative for the universal search for belonging and meaning. Tin Man and Tam, Data and the *Enterprise;* each travels to the other and through the other both become more whole, healed and joyful.

Here, I believe, *TNG* finally gives an answer to the question it evades: Why travel? The answer: to engage in a process through which we learn how encountering others' differences can catalyze an awareness of our own hidden otherness, thereby making it possible to heal and become whole. *TNG's* evasion of the motivation for travel is pervasive but also partial; in my viewing, almost every show centered on how encountering others presents ways to think and act upon the differences we see within ourselves.

We can now return to "First Contact," the episode with which we started. The Federation performs two years of surveillance in preparation for official contact, *proposes* to help guide others into a new world, refuses to be defensive while the Malcorians pose strong questions about the motivations of contact, accepts their rejection, and then gets the hell out of there. Is this portrayal of first contact not better than what we usually consider? One would have to be in a Bynar-enhanced holodeck to see words and actions like these emerge from recent presidents, secretaries of state, popes, or most leading scholars of International Relations. Giving it a generous reading, I see this episode as an apology to the Indians and other third worlders. "This," I hear *TNG* saying, "is how Columbus, Cortez,

Pizarro, Da Gama, the Christian missionaries, the soldiers, and the intellectuals should have done it. This is how we need to make contact in the future." If part the purpose of fiction and art is to construct worlds that find and mark the wrongs of the past as well as to unearth ideals to strive for, then I remain unabashed in offering *TNG* as meaningful art—which must be one reason why I act like a fan.

## QUANTUM LEAPS CONSERVE THE HEGEMONIC ORDER

A fan's satisfaction aside, it must be said that appreciating *TNG* is a relative proposition. My enjoyment is based on overlooking that, as a commercial operation, it stays within narrow limits and that its ideas serve to sustain the hegemony of an imperial culture. It's time to take a more critical tone.

We can decry impositions upon Indians and still stay locked within the structures that enable the very acts we regret. *TNG* offers an apology and yet continues to perpetuate a kind of linguistic violence upon Otherness. To see this I need to go back to the episode "11001001." Recall that Riker claimed that the Bynar's thinking process was, well, binary. As I said, I see Riker as projecting. If we examine the problem of translating the meanings of aliens in *TNG,* it seems that two modes of approaching meanings are explicitly employed: either communication with alien entities is not possible, let us designate this by 0; or it is perfectly transparent, designated by 1. What is almost never ventured (with the episode "Darmok" as an important exception addressed below) is the possibility of imperfect communication, miscommunication, and poor communication. Stephen Greenblatt (1976) refers to this as "opacity," which we might think of as nether 0 nor 1, but the continuum in between. The space between 0 and 1, between none and perfect communication is what, borrowing and adapting Mary Louise Pratt's term, I want to call the "contact zone." Because this term will play the role of an important shorthand, let me linger on it here.

Pratt defines the contact zone as " . . . the space of colonial encounters, the space in which peoples geographically and historically separated come into contact with each other and establish ongoing relations, usually involving conditions of coercion, radical inequality, and intractable conflict" (1992: 6). For Pratt, the "contact zone is an attempt to invoke the spatial and temporal copresence of subjects previously separated by geographic and historical disjunctures, and whose trajectories now intersect" (7). She highlights the "interactive, improvisational dimensions of colonial encounters so easily suppressed by diffusionist accounts of conquest and domination." As such:

> A "contact" perspective emphasizes how subjects are constituted in and by their relations to each other. It treats the relations among colonizers and colonized, or travelers and "travelees," not in terms of separateness or apartheid, but in terms of copresence, interaction, interlocking understandings and practices, often within radically asymmetrical relations of power. (7)

For my purposes the crucial element of the contact zone, especially in first contact, is its uncertainty, its ambiguity, its deep risk and potentially powerful reward. Slightly shifting the emphasis, I want to highlight two aspects of the contact zone. First, as I mentioned above, the contact zone is filled with the possibility of missed communications. It is a process and a space defined by an opacity of understanding. Second, I want to stress Pratt's claim that the contact zone calls not only for improvisatory actions by all parties (as in jazz ensemble soloing, e.g., *Sun Ra and his Arkestra, Art Ensemble of Chicago,* or the Cuban big band *Irekere*), but also for learning through trial and error; actors plod along, stumbling, and recovering, never quite knowing if what they heard is what was meant, or if what they said was what was understood. In short, the contact zone is much like everyday life outside of scripted routines.

We can anticipate the problem faced by *TNG* writers: How to convey a sense of the perils and possibilities of the contact zone while using a medium that is necessarily scripted. Their solution is to resort to what I call "discrete dynamics"—taking events that are partial and static and pasting them together so that they appear dynamic and whole. The distinguishing marks of discrete dynamics are the obvious truncations in process, revealing the vacuums between points. Such a process can be effective in some media; for example, movies combine vast numbers of still photos, and the digital sound of compact disks is similar. But when such a technique is used in a narrative, it shows vacuums left as marks where the process should be.

The tactic of discrete dynamics is foundational in modern social theory, making *TNG* part of a long and venerated legacy. Hobbes' analysis of the formation of society out of the state of nature and Adam Smith's narrative of the evolution of the division of labor are cases in point. The reference to Hobbes and Smith is illustrative because the problem faced by *TNG* writers is not so much technical as it is social.

As can be seen, for example, in Stanley Kubrick's *2001: A Space Odyssey* (1968), and especially in the Mexican-produced film *Cabeza de Vaca*

(1993), plausible depictions of communication in the contact zone *are* possible without recourse to a universal translator or telepathy. Without these two types of devices, however, *TNG* would have to make almost every show a variation on "Darmok;" all episodes would be about the opacity or difficulty of communication. We might refer to this as the Darmok Problem: either every show is about the difficulty of communication in the contact zone, or that difficulty has to be ignored so that the writers can draw a moral by the end of the show.

Hobbes faces a similar issue in his *Leviathan:* he wants to argue that humans need the Leviathan to live in society. Without the power of the Leviathan, human self-interest would return them to the state of nature—a contact zone in which common language and common interest tend to be minimal. Hobbes has to be careful, though; if he stresses human self-interest, and the inability to cooperate and communicate (translucency), he cannot easily explain how humans can come together and agree to leave the state of nature. If, on the other hand, he allows them a robust ability to cooperate and communicate (transparency), then they have no need to get out of the contact zone, and no need for the Leviathan.

Hobbes' employment of discrete dynamics assumes that there is just enough chaos to create the need to get out of the state of nature. The problem of the contact zone, namely difference, is thereby established. Then, he creates just enough overlap between differences to create some kind of order out of the chaos. An adequate amount of difference is converted into sameness (seen as the ability to cooperate and communicate) to create a solution to the problem.

So also with encounter in the contact zone of space. At first, the writer's efforts are focused on establishing that the difference of the alien being makes communication impossible. The utter difference of the alien must be established. Thus, in "Home Soil," the entity "micro brain" is a non-organic silicon being with which there is, initially, no communication; Nagilum is an utter and endless void in "Where Silence Has Lease;" Gumtoo is at first an unintelligible organic spaceship in "Tin Man;" the Ferengi are mute in the first few parts of the show in "Last Outpost;" the Tamarians are utterly incomprehensible in "Darmok;" and Armus is a living oil slick that remains mute for the first part of "The Skin of Evil." Using a binary base, we can call this move 0—difference produces zero communication. Or, in terms of linear logic, we can think of this as the moment of difference between two categories separated by a vacuum—the excluded middle. This sets up the problem and tension for the audience: What are we to make of this difference? How should we respond to it? The security officers (first Yar and then Worf) always recommend a realist posture—shields up, weapons ready; Troi and Data council a more open and exploratory stance. In the opening segments of these shows the crew's various assumptions and biases about alien entities are a means to evoke the audience's own notions.

Once the crew/audience is drawn in, the next step is to gather more information about the aliens. Three tools are available: (1) the universal translator, of course, is ubiquitous. However, often the translator does not provide sufficient information about the intent of the aliens. And, sometimes, as with "Tin Man" and "Darmok," the translator is inadequate or inoperative. (2) Another tool is the telepathic skill of ship's councilor Deanna Troi. Troi is the most important character for establishing deeper understandings of alien intent/motivations. Her immense empathic powers are downplayed for exactly the same reason that the universal translator's abilities have to be limited. If she were allowed to read every communication perfectly, there would be no obstacle. To get a sense of Troi's potential power, we have merely to imagine how her telepathic powers can be used malevolently, as exemplified by Tarmin's psychic rapes in "Violations." (3) Science is also often used to ascertain context as a means of learning about aliens. Thus in "Last Outpost" and "Darmok," the computer retrieves information about the "Portal" and the meaning of the word "Darmok." The android Data often acts as a computer on legs.

These three tools produce the second move, which in binary is 1. The central result of this segment is that information/communication is perfectly transparent; the universal translator, Troi, Data, and the Computer *never get it wrong;* they do not make mistakes, do not misunderstand, and do not understand poorly. The 0 of no information or communication turns to the 1 of perfect grasping. In linear logic, this is the moment of identity; a quantum leap is made over the vacuum of the excluded middle. Utter difference becomes perfectly overlapping sameness. Now, in the realm of psychic consciousness, we might allow this instantaneous simultaneity. For, if the outer alien represents an inner other, then, indeed, we can access that otherness instantly in a flash of awareness. Of course, such inner awareness begs the question of why we need external aliens or even travel. In the contact zone, however, the alien and its otherness really *are* there and its presence cannot be so easily finessed.

Each of the episodes concerning first contact follows this pattern of 0s and 1s. The purpose of these instantaneous movements from 0 to 1 and from 1 to 0, is twofold. First, as mentioned above, they generate a pattern of tension and partial resolve needed to drive the plot. Second and more important is a hidden social purpose. The movement from utter difference to perfect overlap serves to evade the ambiguity, uncertainty, the improvisatory necessity, and the consequences of trial-and-error learning within the contact zone.

In the contact zone there is always some overlap between 0 and 1, between difference and sameness, and between chaos and order. Instead of either chaos or order, this overlap suggests a kind of anarchy-in-process that is more than chaos because sentient beings are trying to create relations, and less than order because these relations are elusive and precarious. The hidden social purpose of binary logic, I think, is to devalue the centrality of this anarchy-in-process so crucial to the contact zone. To valorize this anarchy-in-process is to begin to make the improvisatory processes of the contact zone relevant to our daily lives. The meta-narrative, in this case, the editorial sequencing of 0s and 1s, instead favors the order already established by the Federation. As such, it emphasizes teaching that order to aliens over the Federation's learning from engaging others. Others must change, while the Federation can continue to clutch the present. Indeed, the Federation can deny the very lack within that might call forth such a change. In short, sedating the danger, immediacy, and radicalism of the contact zone highlights teaching over learning. In this way *TNG*, while it offers apologies for the impositional postures of past exchanges in European history, also continues the deepest legacy of colonialism.

But before we get to some of the examples that would substantiate these claims, I want to note a third theme beyond (or is it within?) the binary logic of 0s and 1s. It is a theme that, while it rarely makes plain what, if anything, the crew of the *Enterprise* has learned in their engagement with aliens, nevertheless points to the necessity of improvising and co-constructing trial-and-error processes with aliens. Here, the pedagogical hierarchy—who is taught by whom, who learns from whom—is (mostly) suspended in favor of co-learners/teachers striving to solve problems. So, while *TNG* is caught, perhaps inevitably, in sustaining the deepest legacies of colonialism, it also struggles to free itself by hinting that we embrace the contact zone as a model for first and all contact.

## EPISODICALLY ENCIRCLING THE REAL

Before I examine a few of these episodes in detail, two notes are perhaps in order. First, of the 178 episodes of *TNG*, I narrowed my focus to themes of first contact by selecting 27 such episodes for re-viewing and closer analysis. In preparing this chapter, I transcribed 15 of these from video.

For reasons of space, however, I will only use 3 episodes from *TNG* and 2 from the original *Star Trek* to support my claims. Second, in what follows below I will interject (0) to mean no communication and (1) to mean perfect communication.

In the *TNG* episode "Loud as a Whisper," the *Enterprise* transports a famed negotiator, Riva, to a planet where rival factions have been fighting for centuries. They have agreed to make peace by asking Riva to help them negotiate. The *Enterprise* crew soon learns that he is a deaf mute and a master communicator. He is an empath who can send his thoughts to his chorus of three vocalizing mediums who translate them perfectly (1), read lips—even when the crew speaks English (1), and use gestures and sign language (which is initially unknown to any of the crew.) When Riva and his chorus are beamed to the planet, a member of one of the factions fires upon the landing party, killing Riva's chorus. Riva is beamed back on board, now without a means of communication (0). The warring factions apologize for the death of Riva's chorus and plead that he return to resume negotiations. Riva is badly shaken and reluctant. Troi and Data must find a way to encourage Riva to return to the planet.

At the beginning of the episode, Riva invites Troi to dinner. Seeking privacy with Troi, he discharges the last of his chorus of translators, leaving Troi to ask:

Troi: How do we communicate? [Since he can read her lips, Troi means how will he *speak*.]

Riva/Troi: [using gestures that Troi vocalizes for both for them] Words are on top; what's underneath them, their meaning is what's important.

Troi: That's true.

Riva/Troi: We both know how to express important words like: dream; being with you.

Telepathy, gestures, and lip-reading are used to convert Riva's differences into a sameness both he and Troi understand. Communication is transparent (1), but becomes a problem again when Riva's chorus is killed and he no longer has the patience to mime out his thoughts. We have gone from 1 to 0; we can now anticipate a shift that allows us to go from 0 to 1 again. With the computer's help, Data perfectly masters all known sign languages (1), through which communication with Riva is restored (1).

While Troi and Data are able to convince Riva to beam down to the planet to assume his duty, the obvious question is, How will he proceed without his chorus? A re-energized Riva states that he will teach them sign language. The key to his negotiating success, he recounts, is taking some small commonality between the parties and using it to bridge their differences. In this case, they have three things in common: they are responsible for the death of his chorus; they therefore have no known method of communicating with Riva; and they will have to learn his sign language in order to communicate. While teaching them sign language, Riva has to drop his usual methods and learn how to improvise in this new situation.

At the end of the show, Picard acknowledges Troi's success in revitalizing Riva: "You read me well enough to sense how I feel about you and what you do on this ship. But I just wanted to say the words: 'Thank you. Well done.'" Here the writers indicate the importance of the spoken word—words that reverberate in space/time. More important, the discrete dynamics of 0s and 1s are countered by the bumpiness of the contact zone: the failure to communicate, the loss of one's medium of communication, frustration over the inability to converse at the pace and with the intent of one's meanings, the long tedious processes of misunderstanding that serve as the background of most (if not all) understanding, and the failures and errors that create miscommunication. Such problems get their most explicit treatment in "Darmok."

The episode makes its usual first move—establishing the utter difference of the alien. We are informed that there have been seven instances of contact with these aliens—the Tamarians—in the last 100 years, but in each case communication was not possible because they were found to be incomprehensible (0). Of course, this claim presents a prior problem: having specified a meeting place—the El'A'Drel star system—the Tamarians must have made themselves comprehensible enough to request formal contact with the Federation (1). In any case, the opening attempt to converse with the Tamarians takes place, as almost always, in English (1). Nevertheless, each crew finds the other incomprehensible (0). The camera pans on Troi's face, who looks completely befuddled (0). But after a few minutes she offers this: "I sense nothing but good intentions from them, captain." She cannot understand a word they say and yet she can read their deepest intentions (1).

A tense conversation between the captain and an officer of the alien ship ends with the alien captain, Dathon, saying with finality: "Darmok and Gilad at Tenagra." The first officer accepts the decision with resignation. The Tamarians then beam both captains down to the ubiquitous class M planet. The *Enterprise* crew try to recover their captain but are blocked by the alien ship.

On the planet, Dathon throws one of his two knives on the ground in front of Picard, saying: "Darmok and Gilad at Tenagra." Picard interprets this as the beginning of a challenge. He refuses, throwing back the knife. Dathon, as we learn later, is offering Picard the knife as protection against the Beast that will soon prey on them both. So, importantly, Picard gets it wrong; and Dathon cannot make himself understood (0). Picard does not know what is happening and neither does the audience. Opacity at last.

At night each captain makes a fire. Dathon throws him a brand and says, "Timba, his arms wide open." Picard interprets this as a reference to generosity and says, "Thank-you." Dathon smiles as if to understand (0/1). By (0/1), I wish to indicate that it seems that they are beginning to communicate, but they do not really know if they are. And neither do we. This is a rare display of ambiguity. Note also that whereas their words do not make sense to each other, the meanings of their gestures seem to be universal. Thus, a smile represents good will and the frustration of incomprehension is expressed identically for humans and Tamarians (1).

Meanwhile back on the ship Data and Troi try to solve the riddle of the Tamarian language. Just before the computer provides them a break in their investigation, Data and Troi express frustration at the risky and trepidatious nature of the contact zone.

> Data: . . . as with the other terms used by the Tamarians, this appears to be a proper noun. The name clearly carries a meaning for them.
> Troi: Computer search for the term Darmok in all linguistic databases in this sector . . .
> Troi: All our technology and experience, our universal translator, our years in space, contact with more alien creatures than I can even remember . . .
> Data: I've encountered 1,754 non-human races in my tenure in Starfleet
> Troi: . . . and we can't even say hello to these people.
> Data: Correct.
> Troi: A single word can lead to tragedy. One word misspoken or misunderstood and that can happen here Data if we fail.
> The computer interjects: Darmok is the name of mytho-historical hunter on Chantil 3.
> Troi: I think we've got something here.

On the planet, Dathon keeps trying to give Picard the knife, always saying, "Darmok and Gelad at Tenagra." It is only when the Beast threatens that Picard finally accepts the knife. In a flash, Picard realizes that the Tamarians communicate by citing metaphorical examples from their culture. But this understanding does not help Picard with Tamarian meanings (0/1).

The Beast attacks Dathon. Picard is unable to help because he is stuck in a heightened transporter beam that his crew has just activated to rescue him. Wounded and lying on the ground, Dathon says: "Shaka . . ." a phrase that Picard, having heard it many times since their arrival on the planet, finishes: "when the walls fell." The audience, by this time, gleans that both captains now understand this as Dathon's way of saying "we have failed." I could place a (1) at the end of the previous sentence. But while Dathon, Picard, and the audience understand the failure, there is more at play here: [Back on the ship]

> Data: The Tamarian ego structure does not seem to allow what we refer to as self-identity. Their ability to abstract is highly unusual. They seem to communicate through narrative imagery. They refer to names and places which appear in their mytho-historical accounts.
>
> Troi: It's as if I were to say to you, "Juliet on the balcony."
>
> Crusher: An image of romance.
>
> Troi: Exactly, imagery is everything . . . it embodies their emotional states, their very thought processes. It's how they communicate and think.
>
> Riker: If we know how they think, shouldn't we be able to get something across to them?
>
> Data: No sir, the situation is analogous to understanding the grammar of the language but none of the vocabulary.
>
> Crusher: If I did not know who Juliet was or what she was doing on that balcony, the image alone wouldn't have any meaning.
>
> Troi: That's correct. For instance we know that Darmok was a great hero, a hunter, and that Tenagra was an island and that is it. Without the details there is no understanding.
>
> Data: It is necessary for us to learn the narrative from which the Tamarians draw their imagery. Given our current relations, that does not seem likely.

But Data's conclusion underestimates the Tamarian insight on how to develop a context for joint meanings. The Tamarians understand that common experiences provide the context essential to shared meanings. This is why Picard was able to finish Dathon's "Shaka," with his own, "when the walls fell."

Dathon dies, but not before establishing the mythology behind Darmok and Gilad at Tenagra, and not before getting Picard to tell him the story of Gilgamesh and Enkidu. The engagement fails, but only partly so. Picard and his crew misunderstand the purpose of the Tamarian captain and they miscalculate the risk that Dathon is willing to take. And the Tamarians were unable to convey their intent as fully as they needed. Had they been able to do so, Picard would have been free to help Dathon resist the Beast. The two parties failed to communicate adequately. And yet, they jointly understood that failure as a failure.

In the end, the Tamarian officer seems to accept Picard's explanation of what happened on the planet. A new mythos is thus created: "Dathon and Picard at El'A'Drel" means neither the success implied by "Darmok and Gilad at Tanagra," nor the utter failure of "Shaka, when the walls fell." "Dathon and Picard at El'A'Drel" means something in between—perhaps the opacity in the contact zone. The episode ends on a note of necessary ambiguity when Riker asks: "New friends, captain?" Picard replies, "Can't say, Number One, but at least they are not enemies." The emphasis on the difficulty of communication forces categories outside the binary "friend/enemy."

Part of the brilliance of "Darmok" comes from its stark contrast to most of the other episodes in which the problems of communication are obviated by the universal translator. The origins of the universal translator can be traced back to "Arena" and "Metamorphosis"—episodes from the original *Star Trek*. In "Arena," much like in the plot for *TNG*'s "Last Outpost," the *Enterprise* is giving chase to an alien ship that has destroyed a Federation colony. As the two ships move through the star system of an advanced species, the Metrons, both ships are stopped. The Metrons announce—in English—their intent to settle this issue by transporting both captains to a nearby planet for a challenge to the death—winner takes all. While we are not told how it is that the Metrons can make themselves understood in English, their ability does become apparent when they declare: " . . . you [the two captains] will be provided with a recording translating device in hopes that a product of this contest will serve to dissuade others of your kind from entering our system." Kirk, of course, wins the battle by creating a gun from the minerals on the planet's surface. But he refuses to kill the Gorn captain. The surprised Metrons come to believe that perhaps, after all, humans have some chance of developing into a civilized species.

Even though there is no indication that the Metrons allow Kirk to keep the translator, it re-appears in "Metamorphosis." Kirk, Spock, McCoy, and a Federation Commissioner, Nancy Hedford, encounter a cloud-like entity that forces them to land on a planet. Initially, as always, the cloud entity cannot be understood (0). On the planet they meet a very young Zephram Cochrane—the inventor of warp drive. The cloud envelops Cochrane and communicates only with him, doing so perfectly (1). Kirk decides they need to converse with the entity directly and produces the device provided by the Metrons. Cochrane asks how the translator works:

> Kirk: There are certain universal ideas and concepts common to all intelligent life. This device instantaneously compares the frequency of brain

wave patterns, selects those ideas and concepts it recognizes, and then provides the necessary grammar.
Spock: Then it simply translates its findings into English.

At one level, these assertions hardly seem to need comment. Without a device of this type the show is reduced to recycling the themes in "Darmok." On the other hand, Kirk's explanation contains a theory of universals that could only be supported at the end of his travels—if then. It also contains assumptions about the relationship between brains, minds, and language over which theorists have been fighting for some time. Some linguist/philosopher is no doubt hard at work using the *Star Trek* series as a popular motivation for just these debates. While it may seem necessary, I for one do not wish to entangle myself in these issues. I want to leave this area by begging the reader's indulgence on two claims. First, as difficult as communication is, we know that it has happened—at least within different cultures of the human species. Second, no translation could be as quick, smooth, and easy as those provided by the universal translator. Allowed these two assumptions, we can defer this entanglement and proceed instead to what the presence of the translator highlights and hides for us.

In "Where Silence Has Lease," the *Enterprise* encounters a void in space that envelopes them and disables all communication outside the ship (0). As is often the case, the writers have strategically to deploy Deanna Troi's empathic skills. When, within the void, the *Enterprise* first encounters an empty Romulan ship and then an empty Federation ship, Troi picks up nothing (0). Everything continues to be utterly mysterious. Finally, of course, she senses intelligence:

Troi: I do sense something unusual.
Picard: Perhaps a different level of consciousness.
Troi: Yes, perhaps an intelligence so vast it eluded me. [The writers explain feebly why she sensed nothing before.]

At long last the mystery is resolved when the entity decides to communicate. Calling itself Nagilum, it presents a humanoid face on the view screen and speaks perfect English (1). The conversation reveals that Nagilum is curious about human mortality:

Nagilum: Is it true that you have only a limited existence?
[Nagilum kills a crew member—the ever-present visiting actor slated for death.]
Nagilum: How interesting.

Wanting to learn more about death, Nagilum declares its intention of conducting an experiment that will kill half the crew. Picard responds by putting the ship on auto-self-destruct. Unable to stop the auto-self-destruct sequence, Nagilum lets go of the ship and crew, allowing them to return to space. At the end of the episode and back in normal space, Nagilum's face appears in Picard's ready room:

> Nagilum: I have learned all I needed to know. [Nagilum lists human frailties] . . . as a species we have no common ground [assertion of the excluded middle, of radical difference and of superiority.] . . . as a species you are too aggressive, too hostile, too militant. [Nagilum projecting; but also the writers projecting human traits for Nagilum to project on to humans.]
>
> Picard: You too have been evaluated. It would seem we have at least one thing in common. [As always the one with the lesser power wants to deny the vacuum, and the inferiority, by highlighting—in this case—the overlapping middle, the commonality, and thus a certain equality between the two.]
>
> Nagilum: Oh?
>
> Picard: Curiosity.
>
> Nagilum: The point is well taken, captain. Perhaps it is a trait we share. [Nagilum allows for the overlap.]
>
> Picard: Then perhaps we shall meet again, but next time it will be out here among the stars. [Out here in the contact zone, and not in the vacuum that is your terrain.]

Note in this last conversation how easily and thoroughly Picard and Nagilum understand each other (1). And yet, there is a decided lack of critical self-consciousness. Where, we can ask, is the ambiguity in their engagement? Where is the possibility of each of them learning? Having just seen how destructive curiosity armed with power can be, why is Picard unable to reflect on the possible destructive power of his own curiosity? At crucial moments the show fails to pursue critical themes so near its reach. This tendency is not accidental.

## SOCIAL SINGULARITY

*Star Trek: The Next Generation* keeps posing the problem of how to communicate with, understand, and assess alien forms of life. And it keeps failing to grasp the deeper difficulties of this problem. The reason for this failure can be traced back to aspects of fifteenth- and sixteenth-century European cosmology. In his "Learning to Curse: Aspects of Linguistic Colonialism in the Sixteenth Century," Stephen Greenblatt (1976) gives the example of Gregorio Garcia's study of the origins of the Indians (published 1607), which allowed him to conclude that there was "something diabolical about the difficulty and variety of languages in the New World: Satan had helped the Indians to invent new tongues, thus impeding the labors of Christian missionaries" (563). Despite the fact that there were traders, adventurers, soldiers, and missionaries who worked with the Indians and who had a functional grasp of Indians languages, there was a pervasive view that the Indians spoke nonsense. Indeed, according to Greenblatt, "the view that Indian speech was close to gibberish remained current in intellectual as well as popular circles at least into the seventeenth century" (564).

The very same people who were bartering with the Indians, could, in a different venue, recount their experiences so that the overlap of shared meanings was ignored. As Greenblatt points out, "The captain or lieutenants whose accounts we read had stood on the same beach, but when they sat down to record their experiences, powerful cultural presuppositions asserted themselves almost irresistibly" (565). Greenblatt's concern echoes Johannes Fabian's observation that, in their professional writings, contemporary ethnographers place others in a different developmental time from themselves even while their field notes are based on sharing time with those same others. Fabian's emphasis on this "denial of coevality" (1983), and Greenblatt's concern that Indian languages were seen as gibberish, cannot be addressed without recognizing the long history of these issues.

Part of that history is not just the belief in the unintelligibility of Indian languages but also the manner in which that indecipherability becomes—in a sudden quantum jump—perfect clarity. Greenblatt explains that "Arrogant, blindly obstinate, and destructive as was the belief that the Indians had no language at all, the opposite conviction—that there was no significant language barrier between European and savages—has had consequences as bad or worse" (1976: 571). Todorov, after making much of how Columbus does not understand the Indians, makes the same point as Greenblatt:

This [the incomprehensibility between the Indians and Columbus] is not shocking, after all, nor even surprising; what is, on the other hand, is that Columbus regularly claims to understand what is said to him, while giving, at the same time, every proof of incomprehension. For instance on October 24, 1492, he writes: "From what the Indians told me, [the island of Cuba] is of vast extent, great commerce, richly provided with gold and spices, visited by great ships and merchants." But two lines farther, on the same day, he adds: "I do not understand their language." (Todorov, 1984: 31)

A binary response to the other's language is the product of an ontology that denies difference. In regard to Indian languages, the Europeans either "acknowledge it as a language but refuse to believe it is different [which we have represented with a 1]; or . . . acknowledge its difference but refuse to admit it is a language" [represented with a 0] (30).

Of course, the narrative convention in contemporary film, that the Indians have to speak English so that we, their English-speaking audience, can understand them, may be seen as a technical convenience. The convention and convenience, nevertheless, hides a deeper commitment. Greenblatt suggests that " . . . it was immensely difficult in the sixteenth-century narratives to represent a language barrier . . . because embedded in the narrative convention of the period was a powerful, unspoken belief in the isomorphic relationship between language and reality" (1976: 572). Or, in Todorov's words, it was thought that "words are only the image of things." And "since language is natural . . . linguistic diversity does not exist" (1984: 29).

For Biblically based cultures, diversity, and especially linguistic diversity, is a degeneration of God's original perfection. Needing to puncture hubris, God destroys the Tower of Babel and scatters humans into hundreds of tribes whose linguistic differences impede communication. Instead of potential opportunity, linguistic diversity is meted out as punishment. The problem for sixteenth- and seventeenth-century scholars was how to account for the discovery of cultural and linguistic diversity well beyond what the Bible narrated. It is important to note that the basis of this problematic is the valorization of sameness over difference— differences become a problem only when sameness is the ideal (Inayatullah and Blaney, chapter 2, forthcoming).

From such assumptions, it is a small stretch to the conclusion that linguistic diversity was merely illusory, and that creating a universal language was only a matter of effort. In *Star Trek,* that effort (inevitably?) produces the universal translator. With Todorov and Greenblatt's help we can see that the universal translator is produced within a framework: "Behind this project, and behind the narrative convention that foreshadowed it, lay the conviction that reality was one and universal, constituted identically for all men at all times and in all places. The ultimate grounds for this faith were theological. . . . There is a single faith, a single text, a single reality" (Greenblatt, 1976: 572). Emerging from a single faith, Christianity, a single text, the Bible, what James Tully (1995) calls "the empire of uniformity" attempts to create a single order. The translator and *TNG* are embedded in a cultural legacy whose dominant mode is to assert sameness and deny difference.

## REACHING CRITICAL MASS IN BUMPY SPACE

I have embedded *TNG* in the deeper and longer histories offered by Greenblatt and Todorov. So placed, how does *TNG* fare? That depends. If one expects, as I did, that popular culture would more or less faithfully reproduce the hegemonic order, then one can be surprised. Here and there, our heroes do seem to learn. Misread as imperialists, their largesse rejected in "First Contact," they learn that, in the contact zone, shouldering pedagogical responsibility can have unintended consequences. By losing Tasha Yar in "The Skin of Evil" they expose themselves to the zone's stark risks. In not understanding Dathon's intent in "Darmok" and from the death of Riva's choir in "Loud as a Whisper," they begin to sense the opacity of communication and the necessity of shared experiences as a basis for understanding. Nagilum's destructive drive in "Where Silence Has Lease" allows them to question the violence within curiosity. The Bynars suggest that when something as important as one's planet is at stake, one might not risk asking a question whose answer might be "no." So, in "11001001" our heroes can ponder which kinds of issues they can risk opening up to the contact zone and which they cannot. In these ways *TNG* questions the empire of uniformity and pushes us to participate in the frightening and thrilling opacity of the contact zone.

Still, *TNG* never makes its critique explicit. More important, it remains unaware of its overwhelming reliance on the unquestioned and conservative assumptions behind the universal translator. By continuously assuming that language merely mirrors a given universal reality, it absorbs and assimilates—in a manner more efficient than the Borg ever could—the very marrow of diversity. Even as it seems to suggest that, as in "Tin Man," the Other's difference is a difference for us, and is therefore a potential resource, it waves that message on top of an edifice that assumes with Columbus, Cortez, Las Casas, and Francisco de Vitoria that differences are a form of degeneration that must be converted back to a single order.

All in all, *TNG* perfectly mirrors "Western" themes of exploration, encounter, and travel. On the one hand, it supports the basis of a meta-exploitation of the third world by endorsing the idea that alien differences are degenerate forms of a singular unity that must be reconverted to their original either through the pedagogy of force or the force of pedagogy. For those opposed to colonialisms of all kinds, this makes being an unequivocal fan of *TNG* impossible. On the other hand, and admittedly this is the weaker hand, *TNG*'s attempted conversion of aliens also creates an inner resistance within the imperial project. Asking deadly questions about the deeper motivations of travel and exploration exposes the soft underbelly of the beast of power. Such questions suggest that the powerful, despite themselves, imagine others as being necessary for their own inner uncovering, and that they seek contact as a means to recovering their health and wholeness. It is this aspect of the show that intrigues those who, like myself, wish to ally themselves to a hegemonic culture's potential to generate a mass of critical self-consciousness.

## NOTES

1. I wish to thank Joel Dinerstein, Zillah Eisenstein, Iver Neumann, Diana Saco, Showkat Toorawa, and Jutta Weldes for their helpful and generous comments, Michael Ilasi for research assistance, Kamal and Shahid Naeem for enthusiastic viewing, all the authors of this volume and especially Aida Hosic for furnishing a sense of serious fun, and Sorayya Khan for her tolerance, encouragement, and support.

## BIBLIOGRAPHY

Fabian, Johannes. 1983. *Time and the Other: How Anthropology Makes its Object,* New York: Columbia University Press.

Greenblatt, Stephen. 1976. "Learning to Curse," in Fredi Chiapelli, ed., *First Images of America,* 2 vol., Berkeley: University of California Press, pp. 561–80.

Inayatullah, Naeem, and David Blaney. 2002. *International Relations and the Problem of Difference,* manuscript, Ithaca College.

Jackson, Robert H. 1990. *Quasi-States: Sovereignty, International Relations, and the Third World,* New York: Cambridge University Press.

Johnson, Paul. 1993. "The Return of Colonialism," *The New York Times,* April 18, Section 6, p. 22.

Mallaby, Sebastian. 2002. "The Reluctant Imperialist: Terrorism, Failed States, and the Case for American Empire," *Foreign Affairs,* 81(2): 2–7.

Pratt, Mary Louise. 1992. *Imperial Eyes: Travel Writing and Transculturation,* New York: Routledge.

Todorov, Tzvetan. 1984. *The Conquest of America: The Question of the Other,* New York: Harper.

Tully, James. 1995. *Strange Multiplicity: Constitutionalism in the Age of Diversity,* New York: Cambridge University Press.

Wolf, Martin. 2001. "The Need For a New Imperialism," *Financial Times,* October 9. http://news.ft.com/ft/gx.cgi/ftc? [June 5, 2002].

# Part II

*Aliens Among Us*

# Chapter 4

## ALIENS, ALIEN NATIONS, AND ALIENATION IN AMERICAN POLITICAL ECONOMY AND POPULAR CULTURE

*Ronnie D. Lipschutz*

*Cypher: If he had told us the truth. . . .*
*Trinity: That is not true, Cypher. He set us free.*
*Cypher: You call this free?*

—*The Matrix*

*Things are seldom what they seem, skim milk masquerades as cream.*

—*H.M.S. Pinafore*

### THE SKY ABOVE THE PORT WAS THE COLOR OF TELEVISION, TUNED TO A DEAD CHANNEL

For at least a century, Outer Space has been a source of both promise for and threat to the Westphalian state. On the one hand, the Moon, the planets, and the stars offered a vista of limitless *lebensraum*, into which societies of a specific cultural type—usually American, as seen in the more halcyon moments of Ray Bradbury's *Martian Chronicles* (1950) or the less halcyon ones of Robert Heinlein's *Starship Troopers* (1959)—could expand and forever reproduce, meeting, fighting, and vanquishing Others encountered along the final frontier. On the other hand, the cosmos' endless depths threatened unimaginable horrors, as alien Others fell upon Earth, to conquer, occupy, and kill its inhabitants. From *The War of the Worlds* to *The Clash of Civilizations,* the alien has been an omnipresent figure in American politics and popular culture, one whose liminality both beckons and threatens.

In this chapter, I take to heart Jutta Weldes's analysis and admonition, found elsewhere in this book, that, "To the extent that popular culture reproduces extant power relations, we can examine it for insights into the character and functioning of world politics." Applied to aliens, and their representations in popular culture, it begins to appear that they are not only "out there," but also "in here," among us. Perhaps Aliens 'R Us! If popular culture reproduces power relations, as Weldes suggests, it is far from unreasonable to make a connection between aliens in film and aliens in political life. Both demarcate borders that must not be crossed.

It is helpful to recall that aliens are found not only in Outer Space. As both dictionary and discourse remind us, the term has three common uses. The first is, of course, the creature, whether extraterrestrial or of this earth, who confounds "normalcy." The second applies to those individuals who are not native to the country in which they reside, a conception that connotes, as well, a sense of unbridgeable cultural difference. The third means "out of place," a definition that encompasses as well "alienation," a notion that generally refers to those who feel that they do not belong to the society of which they are members (for the moment, I skip over labor's alienation from the products of its work). Aliens are regarded as a threatening presence, possessed of a drive or force that, if not stopped, will absorb, consume, or subvert and transform the body politic. Consequently, much of American popular culture invites and even incites violence and war against aliens.

But perhaps the alien "threat" is better understood in terms of the internal cohesion of the body politic, evidenced in the repeated and destabilizing efforts of the alienated to escape from the containment established around them by dominant social norms and traditions as well as the vigilance of the state, and to subvert the body. The state has long propagated fear of the world outside its borders as a means of internal discipline, and the invocation of aliens can be understood as one tool among many to this end. For Hobbesians, internal discipline has always been both a reason for and function of Leviathan. Yet, the extension of the state of nature among men alienated from one another into relations among states proved essential to Leviathan's survival. Without it, the condition of relative peace and tranquility within the state, and among societies different from one another, might lull both men and women into thinking Leviathan excessive or even unnecessary (a belief that the reassertion of state power after the September 11 attacks on New York and Washington, D.C., was intended to dispel). In other words, the continued power and authority of the state came to depend upon the alienation inherent in a state of nature that must be maintained in order to legitimate the state. What better means to this end than making space, out there between Leviathans, a realm of alienation occupied by alien Others?

At times, as during the 1990s, such claims of danger outside have become difficult to mount and sustain. It is not that states are not armed against each other (so there must be a threat!), or that they have not gone to war and killed millions in the process. Rather, it is that, over the past century, the progressive expansion of economic exchange among societies has repeatedly disrupted the cultural, social, and moral borders established and policed by the state (Polanyi, 2001). During the 1980s and 1990s, social containment was undermined by the growth of deregulated capitalism and the individual self-interest it reified. One result was a gradual escalation of threats, from relatively mundane anarchists, such as Saccho and Vanzetti, to transplanetary terrorists such as Al Qaeda. In both cases, an outcome has been social destabilization and destruction, alienation and the identification of aliens.

Or, is it the other way around?

Indeed, it seems more plausible that it is *domestic social destabilization*—and the specter of domestic illegitimacy haunting political and economic elites—that is responsible for generating the fabulous panoply of dangers said to threaten the United States (and that successive American governments have tried to urge upon allies). Most, if not all, of the hijackers who took over planes on September 11, 2001, were educated, middle-class men, much of whose anger seems to have derived from disgust with *their* Leviathans and whose hope was to bring *them* down. The sources of destabilization are always internal, but to acknowledge this truth would be to destabilize the belief system that legitimates the social system overseen by Leviathan (Altman, 2001). Hence, I argue, the invocation of alien threats so common in popular culture.

In this chapter, I reflect on these arguments and claims. I examine three films, released between 1980 and 1999, that address the theme of aliens, alien nations, and alienation: *Blade Runner, Falling Down,* and *The Matrix.* I argue that each of these films poses the alienation of individuals as a problem for the body politic and a threat to a destabilized polity. In these films, each produced courtesy of the American political economy for the edification of American consumers, the genesis of aliens, alienation, and alien spaces is capitalism. Each film offers a different means of dealing with the internal and social contradictions resulting from life under post-modern capitalism. And each film puts its audience in a curious and paradoxical position, problematizing good, evil, and everyday life even as it alienates viewers from what happens on the screen.

The first and third films are clearly science fiction, while the second appears more as a macho fantasy (which it is not). *Blade Runner* (1982), based upon Philip K. Dick's 1968 novel *Do Androids Dream of Electric Sheep?*, addresses the "manufacture" of human beings in and by post-modern capitalism, and forces us to ask how we can distinguish the "artificial" from the "real," when the real might be the more alien. This is an especially apposite question today, when the self-production of highly artificialized bodies is so integral to capitalism's success. In *Falling Down* (1993), a survivor of the cold war, alienated from his crusade to protect the country, embarks on a pilgrimage across the territories of "alien nations" that appear to be occupying spaces in his homeland, Los Angeles. In so doing, he finds himself turned into an alien (a cyborg, of sorts). Finally, *The Matrix* (1999) introduces us to a dystopic future in which the fruits of post-modern capitalism are a burned-out world in which humans are cultivated for their wattage by the robotic products of human ingenuity. Dreaming of life and love in a capitalist virtual reality engineered by a computerized Leviathan, the humans are alienated from the external devastation even as some seek to return "home" to it. I begin this chapter, however, with a brief discussion of aliens in U.S. history and political economy.

## ALIENS ARE HERE! NOW!

While the Martian fighting machines of H. G. Wells' *War of the Worlds* (1898) are considered by many to be the classic popular depiction of evil extraterrestrial invaders (consider how often their tentacled likenesses, whether organic or mechanic, appear in film), even as Wells was writing, aliens from unknown spaces were also found on Earth (as they continue to be, today). The imminent end of the nineteenth century, a period of growing economic exchange among the Great Powers, was also accompanied by a considerable amount of social and economic turmoil as well as the first frictions between Britain and Germany. These conditions led a number of authors to write speculative, sometimes utopian, and often violent, visions of the future. One of the best known of these works is Edward Bellamy's *Looking Backward* (1888), in which the benevolent hegemony of white Europeans and Americans is extended to all parts of the world.

Even as white dominion and domination was expanding, events in Asia at the turn of the century led American eyes to look to the Far East. What concerned Americans the most, at that time and in subsequent decades, was the imagined rise of Japanese power (in a potentially conspiratorial alliance with Britain after their treaties of 1902 and 1905) and the burgeoning population of Asia, in search of living room and a place in the (rising) sun. These racialist and racist tendencies were evident not only in law but also in literature. Among the many books warning of the alien threat from Asia were Arthur Dudley Vinton's *Looking Further Backward* (1890) and Floyd Gibbons' *The Red Napoleon* (1929). Both depicted conquest of the United States, the first by the Chinese, the second by a Mongol leader of the Soviet Union. Space operas of the 1930s, such as *Buck Rogers* and *Flash Gordon*, also cast Asians as villains. Even as late as 1951, Robert Heinlein's *The Day After Tomorrow* (originally published in serial form as *Sixth Column*, just six months before the Japanese attack on Pearl Harbor) posited occupation of America by the military forces of a pan-Asian coalition.

That such narratives were not simply the product of imaginative minds or public fantasies is clear from the history of imperialism. The earlier works listed above were informed by the Social Darwinism of the nineteenth century, which, somewhat along the lines of Samuel Huntington's *Clash of Civilizations* (1996) and more recent discourses about Islam, pictured world politics in racialist terms, with whites "bound to lead" and dominate the rest. But Americans and Europeans were never confident of their hegemony and always felt beleaguered. Even as the Great Powers extended their imperial tentacles into Africa, Asia, and the Pacific (and corporations such as Standard Oil extended theirs), thereby demonstrating the supposed superiority of the white race, growing concerns were expressed about decadence, decline, and the sheer weight of numbers of non-white peoples (not unlike contemporary population discourses).

But even in 1890, the "alien threat" to America was hardly a new one, as Michael Hunt (1987) has shown. Until the so-called closing of the American frontier, announced by Frederick Jackson Turner in 1893, it was the "savage Indian" who lay in wait, across the line, for the proper moment to invade and pillage American towns and settlements and kill their inhabitants (Campbell, 1992: 122–29; Drinnon, 1990). Never mind that it was the European settlers who were the true aliens, the invaders who de-stroyed Native American society with guns, germs, and steel, as they pushed westward. The source of threat lay in the dark forests, in the dark spaces outside of the light of "civilization." In a similar fashion, Asian invaders were always depicted as less civilized than those they conquered: inconsiderate of life, disrespectful of American ways, and ignorant of the United States' worldly mission. We see here mirror imaging for, even as Americans imagined invaders from Asia, they were busy invading Asia, via commerce and conquest.

It is not surprising, then, that the idea of alien visitors took hold of the popular imagination and, during the first decades of the twentieth century, was rather quickly integrated into film (Dean, 1998). Periods of political and social uncertainty lead people to generate abnormal explanations for conditions and events, attributing to sinister conspiracies (are there any other kind?) consequences that might more easily be explained by coinci-dence or complexity. The "Communists" exposed by Richard Nixon, Whittaker Chambers, Joseph McCarthy, the House Un-American Activi-ties Committee, the media, and others were, for the most part, not of for-eign origin, but there was no denying that they were "alien" to American society. Behind this fifth column, moreover, there were countless, unseen manipulators doing the bidding of Moscow and Peking, as well as the fel-low travelers who were their unconscious dupes—a conceit nicely satirized in Richard Condon's *The Manchurian Candidate* (1960).

The appearance of aliens, whether of this Earth or not, inevitably draws out the military power of the state (usually the U.S. armed forces). Local authorities are never smart or strong enough to take on an alien challenge and, who knows, they might be aliens, too! In *The Day the Earth Stood Still* (1951), Klaatu's spaceship is immediately surrounded by military units; the scientist of *Red Planet Mars* (1952) finds his project brought under military control; the pods of *Invasion of the Bodysnatchers* (1956) can only be defeated by the FBI; the mutated ants of *Them!* (1954) are only de-feated through military "know-how" (but only after atomic know-how creates them). Throughout these films, the audience is reassured that they are in good hands with the all-powerful state. (It comes as something of a shock, then, to realize that Klaatu and his robot, Gort, are emissaries from a still larger "state" that threatens to turn Earth into a "burnt-out cinder" if its inhabitants disturb interplanetary order.)

With respect to state power, the alien films of the 1950s differ from those of the 1980s and 1990s. During the Eisenhower years, the state was still the ultimate repository and defender of values held dear by Americans, and patriotism went unquestioned as *the* core value of all citizens. There might be Communists in the State Department, but the armed forces remained loyal. By the 1990s, the seat of American government was not only infested by aliens and under their control, it had itself become something of an alien space. *The X-Files* articulated not only skepticism about the good intentions of the U.S. federal government, but also suggested that no good could come of trusting its agents (aside from Muldar and Scully, of course).

As with many other things, I would suggest, the end of the cold war is central to the alien revival of the 1990s. The loss of the United States' primary enemy created a considerable amount of disarray in U.S. foreign policy and a never-ending search for new threats (Lipschutz, 1999). In popular culture, aliens became one stand-in for the enemy yet-to-be found (others included comets, asteroids, terrorists, and a resurgent Russia). But this connection is far from complete. Fears of aliens, whether terrestrial or not, appear to peak during times of social uncertainty, when the erosion of previously existing hierarchies, class relations, and structures of authority raise troubling questions of security, identity, and stability (Altman, 2001).

While we ordinarily associate xenophobia with economic recession, it also flowers during times of prosperity, when social mobility is increasing and the need for cheap labor peaks. Established status hierarchies can change; cultures diversify; hegemonic groups and classes feel threatened by those less fortunate (Lipschutz, 1998). Often, it is the poor, marginalized, new arrival, and not the newly bourgeoisified, who come to stand for the new threat. Being poor, they are thought to be dissatisfied with their lot and therefore the likeliest source of resistance and prone to invade wealthier precincts. (This fear should be understood as paranoia on the part of the better-off, although it might well be that the disappointed middle classes pose greater problems for the state and social stability). The 1980s and 1990s were a period of relative security and prosperity, but also decades of high levels of immigration, multi-culturalism, and conservative backlash. No surprise, then, that aliens loomed so large on the radar screens of both popular culture and political economy.

## WHO ARE WE? WHAT ARE WE DOING HERE?

Fears of social disarray and aliens were already evident in films that appeared in the 1980s, such as Ridley Scott's *Blade Runner*. Scott taps into three themes, salient in 1982 but equally important today: Who belongs in a particular political community? How can its "real" members be identified? Who ensures that outsiders (aliens) don't get in, especially when they are indistinguishable from insiders? In *Blade Runner,* as is often the case, the job of maintaining the boundaries of identity falls to the state, in this case, the police. Rick Deckard, the film's apparent protagonist, is a blade runner, a killer. It is his job to make sure that "outsiders"—in this case, artificial humans, or "replicants"—don't get in.

*Blade Runner* depicts Los Angeles in 2019, a city perpetually shrouded in clouds and smog and drenched by constant rain (quite unlike the sunny LA we know from film and television). The city is inhabited by a polyglot mixture of Hispanics, Asians, Middle Easterners, and others, who continually perambulate through a city full of crumbling, abandoned structures and crowded, torn-up streets. High above, those few remaining Anglos who haven't migrated off-planet get around in flying cars, live in opulent, elaborate, and highly secured buildings, enjoy the latest in electronic gadgetry, and avoid the poor. Enormous wealth exists side-by-side with grinding poverty; quite literally, the rich are on top and the poor are on the bottom. All that keeps LA together is the Thin Blue Line, the cops, who protect and serve. As Rick Deckard's supervisor, Sergeant Bryant, puts it, "If you're not cop, you're little people." The cops fly over the little people and make sure they remain small and in order. There is a strong suggestion, moreover, that the "little people" are alien to LA; the cops do not do much to maintain order "on the ground." They are there to protect the few big people who remain and to keep the two orders apart.

It is too costly and troublesome to ship little people off-planet to do heavy labor and service jobs in the off-planet colonies, so replicants (androids) have been created. Replicants are "more human than human," says Emmett Tyrell, the founder of the company that makes them. Judging from four who appear in the film, moreover, all replicants are white (which makes the little people even more alien). Indeed, the only difference between a "real" human being and the Nexus–9, the latest model of replicant, is the latter's four-year life span. And, until the appearance of this model, the only way to tell the difference between human and replicant is to test retinal response to emotional stimuli, via an interrogation having to do with the killing of animals. As in Dick's novel, virtually all animals are extinct, and a real human's empathic response to animal abuse is much stronger than that of a replicant, who does not possess a complete range of emotion and has not been fully socialized where animals are concerned. This shortcoming has been greatly reduced in the Nexus–9.

Replicants, it seems, pose a threat to the social order. They have been banned from Earth because, in the past, they had banded together to kill their human masters. The blade runner is trained in detecting replicants and eliminating them (according to the law, he must first test a suspected replicant in order to determine whether he has arrested a real human or an artificial; this requirement poses some evident problems for both replicant and blade runner). The blade runner maintains the "proper order of things" by seeing that replicants remain outside of human society. But the blade runner is also an outsider in his own way; he also lacks certain attributes possessed by other humans. Individuals' empathy extends to other humans, all of whom cannot kill either replicants or humans, for the same reason they cannot imagine killing animals. The blade runner, who tests others for such empathy, seems to feel no such empathy himself (some have proposed that Deckard himself is a replicant; I think he is merely an emotionally damaged human being).

Can the social order be maintained? Not if capitalism is involved.

When Deckard goes to interview Emmett Tyrell about the Nexus–9, he is introduced to Rachael, Tyrell's niece. Tyrell asks Deckard to test Rachael, which he does. Deckard discovers that she is not his relative but, rather, a replicant, with the implanted memories of his niece. Memories make replicants more accepting of their short lives, says Tyrell, by making them recall the long ones they imagine having lived. Memories also enhance both emotion and empathy, an improvement that makes it all the more difficult to tell replicants from humans. Rachael's nature is detected only after Deckard tests her at great length; otherwise, she is indistinguishable from humans and is therefore, for all practical purposes, a human being. Rachael and Deckard fall in love—another disruption of order—and violate the taboo of emotional bonding between replicant and human. As Deckard later discovers, this destroys his capabilities as a blade runner.

Deckard's love for Rachael, the replicant, stands in stark contrast to his assignment, which is to hunt down and kill four others—Roy, Leon, Zhora, Pris—who are loose in LA. Roy is a soldier, Leon a worker, Zhora an entertainer, and Pris a "pleasure unit." None would be easily mistaken for a member of the white upper class, but their mixing with the lower classes is easily as threatening to the social order as their infiltration of white society would be. Under Roy's leadership, the four have hijacked a spaceship and arrived on Earth, where they seek to have Tyrell extend their lifespans. This would make them even more like humans (except that they have killed humans in order to get to Earth). Tyrell informs Roy that this cannot be done because the necessary cloning creates fatal mutations. By the end of the film, all four are dead, but not all by Deckard. The blade runner has been "turned" by Rachael and has only managed to kill one of the four by himself. Deckard's profession requires that he be alienated from humanity; having acquired empathy, by the end of the film he is alienated from both his work and human society.

I want to leave post-modern exegeses of this film to others (see, e.g., Bruno, 1990) and focus, instead, on *Blade Runner* as a reflection of transformations already taking place in the political economy of the United States. Scott's film suggests a bifurcation of humanity into served and servants, big and little, those who are human and those whose humanity is in question (the replicants are, after all, servants to humans), those who are high and those who are low. The rich cannot survive without the poor, but the rich want to remain as far from the poor as possible. In order to emphasize this status distinction, Scott has imagined his city along vertical lines, more akin to Hong Kong than the sprawling Los Angeles with which we are so familiar, although, even today, the rich live in the hills and the poor in the flats. Still, in contemporary LA, rich and poor, white and people of color, "natives" and "immigrants" move across horizontal, rather than vertical, space, and continuously come into contact. In Scott's city, such exposure is limited: vertical access is easier to control than horizontal (see Davis, 1990).

Replicants force us to ask, What makes someone human? The four replicants whom Deckard pursues so laboriously have been manufactured to labor but not, as free humans, to *sell* their labor. They are mentally and physically superior to humans, but they are slaves all the same. They are commodities, service mechanisms, for sale. And, the replicants are alien, if not for their off-world origin, then for their hopes and dreams, their dreams of a life past (c.f. Leon's photographs, and Deckard's, as well), their hopes for longer life in order to experience the future. Somehow, the replicant Roy Baty's life, for all its brevity, has been richer and more meaningful than Deckard's or the lives of any of the other big people. He, unlike Deckard, is not alienated but more human than human. Having fallen in love with Rachael, Deckard has become more human than human, too.

The arrival of *Blade Runner*'s alien workers reminds us of the "alien invasions" threatened during the early 1980s, triggered by the Reagan administration's wars in Central America and Ronald Reagan's warnings about the northward march of "feet people" (Reagan, 1983; a charming image if applied to extraterrestrials). While many Central Americans fled northward to escape U.S.-sponsored violence, others came, as they had done for centuries, in large numbers and in search of employment. The decimation of the American industrial base, a casualty of the Reagan recession of 1982–83, was accompanied by the rise of the service economy and its need for low-cost labor. The Reagan administration linked the

"Communist threat" to this infusion of immigrants, thereby enabling the American state to marshal its defenses against alien invaders and mobilize public support for both foreign and domestic policy initiatives. We see much the same dynamics in the current hysteria over immigrants and terrorism. As is the case with most dystopias, *Blade Runner* had little to do with the future.

## OVER THE HILL?

One of the more provocative "alien" films of the 1990s was *Falling Down.* Michael Douglas plays the role of Bill Foster (DEFENS, according to his personalized license plate). Foster is an engineer, recently laid off from his job at a defense corporation where, as we, and the LAPD, are later informed by his mother, he "protected us from the Communists." Little does she imagine that her son will become a new alien threat, a "normal" white male transformed by his economic woes into an alien cyborg, bristling with weapons, searching for a past he imagines he once knew. Alas! You can't go home again, especially if you've been alienated from it.

The film opens on one of those blisteringly hot days so familiar to Angelenos. Foster is stuck in a traffic jam. It is a place and situation as familiar and banal as one could imagine, a moment frozen in time for all time. But while his fellow travelers wait, like sheep, for the highway flagman to let them go with the flow, Foster rebels. He breaks ranks and breaks away. "Hey! Where are you going?" asks an irate driver, angered by Foster's escape. "Home. I'm going home," he replies.

Foster abandons his car, climbs the freeway embankment, and goes AWOL, over the hill into the 'hood on the other side. There he expects to find familiar space through which he can gain free passage to his home. Instead, he finds himself in alien territory—or, rather, *he* is the alien. Foster neither understands nor realizes that the cold war, and the 1960s, are over (a can of Coke costs a dollar!). He does not speak any of the languages of Los Angeles (Korean, Spanish, or even English); he cannot read the writing; he doesn't understand local customs or practices. Marked as an outsider by his haircut, tie, white shirt, and Samsonite briefcase, Foster has become an alien being. Foster has not only crossed the physical barrier by going over the hill, but also traveled through time, from his remembered past to an unrecognizable future.

His westward trek across Los Angeles toward Venice and the Pacific Ocean recalls that of the United States, its aliens moving through alien territory, toward their Manifest Destiny, a march that ultimately collapsed on the shores of Asia. Foster, akin to an (anti)hero in a picaresque novel, marches through a series of increasingly hostile terrains and adventures (12 or 14, depending on how you count them). There are no friendly people in LA; even those who appear friendly are hostile underneath. A normal guy turned into a monster as a result of betrayal by his government, Foster ultimately comes to the attention of the LAPD (another avatar of the "state").

In a recapitulation of the establishment of the sovereign state, Foster becomes increasingly militarized, militaristic, and machine-like. He acquires a gym bag full of guns, a camouflage outfit, and a bad attitude. By the time he reaches the Pacific shore, where his ex-wife and daughter live ("Home," where he is an unwanted alien, too), Foster has become fully alienated from his surroundings. But Foster is hardly aware of his transmogrification; he seems puzzled when people suggest that he has become irrational and violent and when they shy away from him in fear. After all, his intentions are good. To Foster, DEFENS is the only response to the dangerous and alien world *he* has encountered, which stands between him and the past to which he so longs to return. By the end of the film, Foster might as well be one of H. G. Wells' tentacled aliens, loose in the sewers beneath the City of Angels. The policemen of Planet Los Angeles hunt him down and kill him. Foster dies for our sins.

My intent is not to make Foster a sympathetic character, although I do think that those who saw him as an "angry white male" acting out his revenge on both minorities and the politically correct are far off the mark. Foster more closely resembles the commuters from Santa Monica who were forced to go to ground after the Northridge earthquake, thereby finding themselves in unfamiliar (alien) territory. Having left the protective cocoon of his automobile, he is exposed to the natural environment of the urban "jungle," something the off-track Santa Monicans were able to avoid. But Foster is so thoroughly alienated from that environment and its recent history, that, like the innumerable organisms exposed to atomic radiation in the films of the 1950s, he is transformed into something unrecognizable and dangerous, a simulacrum of the American state. Inasmuch as he is the quintessential "American," Foster's growing alienation amid a multi-cultural, confusing, and apparently hostile city does suggest something about changes in the country itself.

On its release, *Falling Down* angered almost everyone. Liberal reviewers took it to task for legitimating the false anger of white males and, somehow, making the literal bashing of minorities acceptable (Giunti, 1993; Raferty, 1993). One conservative reviewer described it as a liberal "fascist fantasy" that implied that only Bill Clinton could save the country from such nuts (Bowman, 1993). And *Newsweek,* always quick to spot a market opportunity, published an issue with a cover story linked to the film, entitled "White Male Paranoia" (Gates, 1993). It took a British reviewer, Lizzie Francke (1993), to suggest that all of these commentators might have it wrong. She wrote: "In the new world order, with no discernible outside enemy for America to define itself against, it's not just D-Fens who is cracking up, but his country. It is the status of the States that's under question here."

As I have suggested elsewhere (Lipschutz, 1998, 2000), this "cracking up" is attributable to the very success of the United States in the cold war, especially the globalization fostered (no pun intended) by its economic and strategic policies (Rupert, 1995). That victory, so loudly proclaimed in 1989 and 1991, is also the cause of Foster's dilemma. He made us safe from the Communists and now, not only is his work alienating, but he is alienated from it and those meanings that gave his life some purpose. The creative destruction of post-modern capitalism has destroyed the material base of Foster's imagined past. He is no longer "economically viable," as another character in the film puts it; there are no openings for his skills and knowledge, and there is no one to explain this world of the future to him.

If Foster is a representation of "the United States"—at least, as many imagine it once was—then his Pilgrim's Progress across Los Angeles, the quintessentially American city that has always been ethnically mixed but also controlled by a small group of Anglo power brokers, is something akin to the American trek from the certainties of World War II and the early cold war to the confusion of the present. In 1945, the United States was "in control" and "in charge." Americans went out into the world to establish order, but things got sticky. Eventually, even familiar things became strange and had to be confronted in the only well-known and seemingly reliable way: with guns (see, e.g., the "War on Drugs" and the "War on Terrorism"). Now, we don't know what to do, except use guns and sell them, at home and abroad.

Although *Falling Down* is hardly cast in the mold of a classic science fiction film, it incorporates elements of both fantasy and science fiction. Bill Foster, a transformed cold warrior transported into an alien environment, might as well be a visitor from another time or planet. But the film would resonate much less strongly were Foster to have been equipped with the conventional appurtenances of the alien or time traveler, or even with a narrator to explain what is going on.

The audience becomes both narrator and subject, and those who are curious enough about the epistemology behind the methodology, so to speak, must explain Foster's travels to themselves. They must imagine their own trek through those once-familiar spaces that have now become alien ones, and from which they have been alienated. It is only when the conventions of "normality" are overturned in a comprehensible way that we begin to discern just how out-of-place and -time we might really be. This is a trick further amplified in *The Matrix*.

## JACKING INTO THE MARKET

With *The Matrix,* we approach the end of our journey through fin de siècle capitalism. Although this film is hardly a great work of art, it has achieved cult status and generated a plethora of learned journal articles on its structure and symbolism (see, e.g., Žižek, 2001: Ch. 6.2). That such a film should be such a hit, especially with the academic literati, is somewhat puzzling. For one thing, it is an extraordinarily violent work (much more so than *Falling Down*), and not in the post-modern, self-referential fashion that we see, for example, in *Pulp Fiction*. The director attempts to aestheticize the violence through, for instance, the liberal use of slow-motion choreography, as the main characters engage in virtual gun battles with their opponents.[1] At the end of the day, however, all the antagonists are really doing is emptying imaginary assault weapons at each other. Moreover, there is nothing particularly insightful, innovative, or even provocative about the film's basic plot device: the search for the "true" reality. As the film reminds us with its sly reference to Baudrillard, these days everyone who is anyone writes about simulation and reality (as I do here). So what's the fuss about?

I suggest the fuss is about the film's commentary on contemporary capitalism, playing, perhaps, with concepts of false consciousness writ large. *The Matrix* can be understood as an inverted allegory of globalization, about the consumer's alienation from physical reality promoted by commodity fetishism, the broadly advertised opportunities they are offered to purchase escapes into fantasy worlds, and a general inability on their part to perceive how the capitalist system operates. The everyday "reality" encountered by the participants in the simulacrum of contemporary life depicted in *The Matrix*—whose location is never specified (although filmed in Vancouver) but might as well be Los Angeles—is not only a fully bourgeoisified one that the moviegoer comes to view with a certain degree of repulsion. It is also a mirror of the very world in which the audience lives.

As in the 1988 John Carpenter film *They Live!,* however, the underlying conceit is that there are Others ("alien forces") who are in control. These Others, who materialize as "Men in Black" (MIB), are the avatars of the totalitarian market utopia in which billions of humans believe they are living. Those who discover the "truth"—that in this virtual world, they are alienated from a much more sordid reality that some imagine is nevertheless "free"—are marginalized or vaporized. So it is in our contemporary globalized market utopia (Lipschutz, 2001), with the exception that *our* alienated seek succor in electronic fantasy-worlds, some of which are rather desolate and grim but promise a certain form of "freedom" to the player and capital to the producer.

Dualism, the notion that the physical world we perceive and in which we live is not the "true" reality, is as old as (if not older than) organized religion, and as recent as certain versions of post-modernism. We find it in Plato, the Old and New Testaments, Hinduism, both Christian and Jewish Kabbalah, in romanticism, and even, as Wendy Brown (2001) points out, in Marx. In more recent times, the works of C. S. Lewis, best known for *The Chronicles of Narnia,* are also largely based on a neo-Platonic division between the "shadowlands" and the real world. And even Baudrillard's simulacra suggest that there might be a reality from which we have been distracted. These parallel-world dualisms all bemoan human ignorance, error, and folly. We pursue what is bright, glittery, and immaterial, and ignore what is true, concrete, and critical. It is not that we lack wisdom; rather, our baser appetites dominate our ability to reason and see what is true. Why this is so, and who makes it so, is more problematic: does the source of error lie within, or is there someone or something Out There, pulling our strings?

*The Matrix* draws on these and numerous other works of both fiction and non-fiction. The film therefore treads well-worn ground in positing evil beings manipulating the truth, controlling the destiny of the world's inhabitants, and limiting the possibilities of doing and being good. But, as I suggested above, there is another theme here that is not, for the most part, prefigured in these dualist literatures: paraphrasing Max Weber, *The Matrix* might also be understood as an allegory about the "iron cage" of globalized market capitalism and its totalitarian qualities.

In explaining the origins and organization of the virtual world, Morpheus, the leader of the cyber-terrorist freedom fighters, tells Neo that the Matrix is everywhere. It is control and every human being is a prisoner within it. "As long as the Matrix exists," intones Morpheus gravely, "the human race will never be free." He does not appear to recognize the irony of this claim—or if he does, he doesn't let on. In what might be yet another case of false consciousness, Morpheus ignores the material basis of the Matrix, and its origins in the human search for artificial intelligence. Nor does he stop to consider whether the illusion of freedom in a virtual, albeit totalitarian, utopia might be more attractive than the terror of freedom in a devastated and hostile dystopic reality (Cypher, by contrast, tries to be free to choose but, having left the Garden, can never return).

Those (things) who manage the Matrix are also its Leviathan: they manage the comforting illusion in which humans "live"; they discipline those who reject the fantasy. As the creations of human beings, these tentacled artificial intelligences and their virtual avatars are the materialization of humanity's quest for a Utopian Order. Behave. You won't be bothered and you can live a life of illusory freedom in the market utopia of 1999. We can begin to see here how the iron cage of capitalism figures in *The Matrix*. Although not an explicit part of Morpheus's History as told to Neo, we can presume that artificial intelligence was a commercial venture designed to generate profits, and only secondarily oriented toward the perfection of human capabilities. The search for human perfection, in the face of what is commonly accepted as fallible human nature, is another well-known mythological and literary trope. As those stories warn, such hubris is often a cause for divine displeasure. But self-perfection is also part of the teleology of liberalism. While perfection is unachievable, it is often said that unfettered markets will improve the human condition until the world is a happy place and every human being's wants are being met.

So far, the reality appears quite the opposite; as Karl Polanyi (2001: 3) wrote in *The Great Transformation:* "Our thesis is that the idea of a self-adjusting market implied a stark utopia. Such an institution could not exist for any length of time without annihilating the human and natural substance of society; it would have physically destroyed man and transformed his surroundings into a wilderness." *The Matrix* is a story of such a stark utopia. It is also our story. We are all born into the matrix of capitalism, as it were, and escape is impossible. We have come (or have been made) to believe, moreover, that there are no alternatives except those too awful to contemplate, such as are readily visible in places like Africa or the old Socialist Bloc.

In *The Matrix,* the contrast between the cornucopia of the virtual capitalist world and the poverty of the real world appears most clearly in the comparison of foods, and their tastes and textures (see also clothing: rags in the real world; designer leather in the virtual one). After nine years in the resistance, Cypher offers to betray Morpheus and his crew. At dinner with the head MIB on the case (who does not eat and, in fact, finds such practices disgusting), Cypher savors the steak he imagines he is eating and the wine he imagines he is drinking. As the price of his betrayal, Cypher asks for wealth and fame. He requests, moreover, that all memories of the interlude in the real world be erased from his mind. For his betrayal, he is eliminated.

This scene in the upscale but virtual restaurant is followed immediately by one of the Nebuchadnezzer's crew of freedom fighters at breakfast, eating "real" food. It is a mush that looks like tapioca and oatmeal in milk and has neither texture nor taste but is, nonetheless, nutritionally complete. Who would exchange the pleasures of the virtual dream world for the tribulations and impoverishment of the real one? Who would willingly eschew the fleshpots of market utopia for the empty pots of deprivation? What, exactly, is freedom worth?

This is an especially telling question in the aftermath of the attacks on New York and Washington. In the United States, at any rate, we are told that some freedoms may have to be sacrificed in the pursuit of security, that panoptic surveillance will be necessary in order to distinguish good people from bad ones, that the latter move through a subterranean world of which most of us are only dimly aware but that will control us if we do not control ourselves. Meanwhile, shop 'til you drop. After all, isn't that what freedom is all about: the freedom to choose in the market, to make and remake yourself and your identity, to consume the fruits of the Matrix—excuse me, the Market?

Perhaps the greatest irony offered by *The Matrix,* and one that bears careful reflection, is that we, the movie-going audience, are led to think that we are seeing a possible future, in which alien and omniscient Others control our lives and destinies through their control of civilization's electronic brains and our organic ones. Those Others could be very human, or they could be corporations, or governments or . . . who knows? In any event, we *are* buying the product, although, even as we watch, we are prisoners in a Matrix, one of our own making. As consumers of a slyly self-knowing exposé of our collective condition, and observers of a film full of special effects that not only sell the product but also incite us to break out of the iron cage, we are being inducted into a kind of false consciousness that tells us to pay no attention to our alienated condition. This, I propose, may be the greatest special effect of all those offered by *The Matrix.*

## SOME CONCLUDING REFLECTIONS

I have argued in this chapter that such critiques of American capitalism can be seen in three particular science fiction films (out of many) produced during the period we associate with the rise of globalization, from 1980 to 2000. As dystopias, these films focus on the alienation of three men—Rick Deckard, Bill Foster, Neo Anderson—from the societies in which they (seem to) live, all rooted in the capitalist system of the late twentieth century. Amid the illusion of freedom, all three men are trapped in prisons from which there is no escape. As are we.

It is not surprising that we find the sub-structures of capitalism and its material aspects embedded in Hollywood's economic products. I suspect that the films' critiques are rooted in the political economy of Hollywood, which has always both mirrored and molded hegemony. Such films reflect, therefore, a kind of dialectical love-hate relationship that filmmakers have with the system that permits them to make their films. On the one hand, film-makers (in the very broad and collective sense of the term) have a fairly clear idea of what kind of intellectual product they want to produce, and how to go about it; on the other hand, producers, financiers, and studios have a fairly clear notion of what will sell and make a profit. That the two are often out of synch, as evidenced by the many films that fail at the box office, is not so surprising. Public tastes tend to be fickle, and the growing segmentation of markets makes it ever-more difficult to feed everyone.

Any film that posits outright, in a direct narrative fashion, that things are out of whack or under conspiratorial control (one thinks here of Oliver Stone's films, in particular), is likely to be attacked by cultural critics and the guardians of hegemony alike as inaccurate and ideological. So if there is a message, it has to be hidden behind a curtain, like the Wizard of Oz and the bankers against whom that critique was aimed. The curtain is only a metaphor, after all, for our inability to see what is patently obvious. Science fiction fills a similar role. It provides an ideal vehicle through which to offer both critique and warning, and it is never really about the future or strange, new worlds where "no one has gone before." It is about us and the world in which we live. We should peek behind the curtain more often.

## NOTE

1. I should note that *The Matrix,* which combines virtual utopia with "real" dystopia, can also be seen as a satire, along the lines of Orwell's *1984.* Perhaps what follows should therefore be read with a certain degree of irony. Pay particular attention to the peals of thunder during the sequence of scenes in which Neo finds out about the "real world."

## BIBLIOGRAPHY

Altman, Dennis. 2001. *Global Sex,* Chicago: University of Chicago Press.

Bellamy, Edward. 1888. *Looking Backward, 2000–1887,* Boston: Ticknor and Co.

Bowman, James. 1993. "Friends of Bill," *The American Spectator* (May): 58–59.

Bradbury, Ray. 1950. *The Martian Chronicles,* New York: Doubleday.

Brown, Wendy. 2001. *Politics Out of History,* Princeton, NJ: Princeton University Press.

Bruno, Giuliana. 1990. "Ramble City: Postmodernism and *Blade Runner,*" in Annette Kuhn, ed., *Alien Zone,* London: Verso, pp. 183–95.

Campbell, David. 1992. *Writing Security: United States Foreign Policy and the Politics of Identity,* Minneapolis: University of Minnesota Press.

Condon, Richard. 1960. *The Manchurian Candidate,* New York: New American Library.

Davis, Mike. 1990. *City of Quartz: Excavating the Future in Los Angeles,* London: Verso.

Dean, Jodi. 1998. *Aliens in America: Conspiracy Cultures from Outerspace to Cyberspace,* Ithaca, NY: Cornell University Press.

Dick, Philip K. 1968. *Do Androids Dream of Electric Sheep?* New York: Doubleday.

Drinnon, Robert. 1990. *Facing West: The Metaphysics of Indian Hating and Empire Building,* New York: Schocken Books.

Francke, Lizzie. 1993. "Deadbeat White Male," *New Statesman & Society,* May 29, pp. 31–32.

Gates, David. 1993. "White Male Paranoia," *Newsweek,* March 29, pp. 48–53.

Gibbons, Floyd. 1929. *The Red Napoleon,* New York: J. Cape & H. Smith.

Giunti, Matthew. 1993. "Urban Catastrophe," *Christian Century,* June 2–9, pp. 605–8.

Heinlein, Robert. 1951. *The Day After Tomorrow,* New York: New American Library.

Heinlein, Robert. 1959. *Starship Troopers,* New York: Putnam.

Hunt, Michael H. 1987. *Ideology and U.S. Foreign Policy,* New Haven, CT: Yale University Press.

Huntington, Samuel P. 1996. *The Clash of Civilizations and the Remaking of World Order,* New York: Simon & Schuster.

Lewis, C. S. 1956. *The Last Battle,* New York: MacMillan.

Lipschutz, Ronnie D. 1998. "From 'Culture Wars' to Shooting Wars: Cultural Conflict in the United States," in Beverly Crawford and Ronnie D. Lipschutz, eds., *The Myth of "Ethnic Conflict,"* Berkeley: University of California, Berkeley Institute of Area Studies Press, pp. 394–433.

Lipschutz, Ronnie D. 1999. "Terror in the Suites: Narratives of Fear and the Political Economy of Danger," *Global Society,* 13(4): 411–439.

Lipschutz, Ronnie D. 2000. *After Authority: War, Peace and Global Politics in the 21st Century,* Albany: SUNY Press.

Lipschutz, Ronnie D. 2001. "Who You Callin' 'Hegemonic'? Or, What Kind of Democracy Do You Want With Those Markets?" Hong Kong Convention of the International Studies Association, July 26–28, Hong Kong, SAR, PRC.

Orwell, George. 1949. *1984: A Novel,* New York: Harcourt Brace.

Polanyi, Karl. 2001. *The Great Transformation,* second edition, Boston: Beacon.

Raferty, Terrence. 1993. "Slow Burn," *The New Yorker,* March 8, pp. 98–99.

Reagan, Ronald. 1983. Remarks at a Mississippi Republican Party Fundraising Dinner in Jackson, June 20. http://www.reagan.utexas.edu/resource/speeches/1983/62083b.htm [May 2, 2002].

Rupert, Mark. 1995. *Producing Hegemony,* Cambridge: Cambridge University Press.

Vinton, Arthur Dudley. 1890. *Looking Further Backward: Being a Series of Lectures Delivered to the Freshman Class at Shawmut College, by Professor Won Lung Li (successor of Prof. Julian West),* Albany, NY: Albany Book Company.

Wells, H. G. 1898. *The War of the Worlds,* New York: Harper & Brothers.

Žižek, Slavoj. 2001. "The Matrix, Or, the Two Sides of Perversion," in *Enjoy Your Symptom: Jacques Lacan In Hollywood and Out,* New York: Routledge, pp. 213–33.

# Chapter 5

---

## DEMON DIASPORAS

Confronting the Other and the Other-Worldly
in *Buffy the Vampire Slayer* and *Angel*[1]

*Patricia Molloy*

> *The community's idea of itself in history cannot be disentangled from the
> ways it represents death. At the extreme this can be understood as refer-
> ring to those it chooses to kill.*
>
> —Bronfen and Goodwin, 1993: 15

### INTRODUCTION: WEREWOLVES OF TORONTO

According to a Toronto film critic, the Canadian film *Ginger Snaps* (2001) puts a "post-Buffy spin on an old familiar tale" (Harkness, 2001:99). The tale is of the werewolf, or, as it is referred to more properly, and consistently, throughout the film, lycanthrope; from the Greek *lukanthropia,* meaning *lukos,* wolf, and *anthropos,* man. It is an old tale indeed, dating back at least to Pliny. And while modern werewolf chronicles are not foreign to celluloid, director John Fawcett's *Ginger Snaps* ups the ante with a parallel tale of the horrors of puberty and high school in suburban Toronto. This much (aside from the Toronto part) it does share with *Buffy the Vampire Slayer*. But in Fawcett's film, the lycanthrope is not a "man" transformed into beast, but a teenaged girl, already with a lust for the morose, morphing into beastly form and sexual awakening after being attacked on the day she first begins menstruation—by a creature who's been doing in the neighborhood dogs.

That Ginger is a "kick-ass" high-school chick who embraces rather than fights the forces of evil is decidedly different from both the equally kickass but demon-slaying Buffy and her reluctant werewolf cohort, Oz, to whom I shall return later. Prior to her transformation, however, Ginger and her sister Brigitte were resident outcasts, gothy geeks obsessed with death, and each other. Although it is no doubt the gender-bending characterization of the horror tale, and its high-school-as-hell theme, which puts the post-Buffy spin on *Ginger Snaps*, Ginger's outsider status (which she shares, to a degree, with "I-just-wanna-do-girly-stuff" Buffy) makes her beastly makeover historically logical. By its earliest definition, the werewolf itself was an outcast, a bandit, expelled from both the forest and the city (Agamben, 1993: 105). And as remarked above, the werewolf's tale dates back to antiquity. Indeed, the werewolf is as old as the origins of sovereignty itself. Let me explain.

Giorgio Agamben finds in Rodolphe Jhering's 1886 treatise on Roman law a likening of the liminal werewolf in ancient Germanic texts with the figure of *homo sacer,* sacred man. For Jhering, the bandit and the outlaw, the "sacred wolf," are the brother of *homo sacer,* who within ancient Roman law can be killed yet not sacrificed, murdered without the commission of homicide. The laws of Edward the Confessor (1030–35) also define the bandit as a *wulfesheud,* a wolf's head, consigning him to the status of werewolf: "He bears a wolf's head from the day of his expulsion . . . ." The life of the bandit is not, however, a matter of mere animal nature without any relation to law and the city. "It is, rather, a threshold of indistinction and of passage between animal and man, *physis* and *nomos,* exclusion and inclusion: the life of the bandit is the life of the *loup garou,* the werewolf, who is precisely *neither man nor beast,* and who dwells paradoxically within both while belonging to neither" (1993: 104–105). It is only, Agamben insists, with this understanding that the Hobbesian "state of nature" begins to make sense. The state of nature is not a real epoch in the chronological sense of appearing prior to the foundation of the City, but rather a principle *internal* to the City.

> Accordingly, when Hobbes founds sovereignty by means of a reference to the state in which "man is a wolf to men," *homo hominis lupus,* in the word "wolf" (*lupus*) we ought to hear the echo of the *wargus* and *caput lupinem* of the laws of Edward the Confessor: at issue is not merely *fera bestia* and natural life but rather a zone of indistinction between the human and the

animal, a werewolf, a man who is transformed into a wolf, and a wolf who is transformed into a man—in other words a bandit, a *homo sacer* (106).

Thus it is not so much a matter of a war-of-all-against-all but a condition in which everyone is reduced to "bare" (biological) life and a *homo sacer* for everyone else, a condition in which everyone becomes the werewolf. This simultaneous lupization of man and humanization of the wolf happens in a "state of exception," a suspension of law through the sovereign ban. And "this threshold alone, which is neither simple natural life nor social life but rather bare or sacred life, is the always present and always operative presupposition of sovereignty" (ibid.).

It is precisely these zones of indistinction between man and beast, the worldly and the other-worldly, good and evil, that form the thematic of Twentieth Century Fox's hit television show *Buffy the Vampire Slayer* and its spin-off series *Angel*. While the ambiguities of these couplings have been widely commented on (see Braun, 2000; Byers, 2000), I wish to reveal how these zones of indistinction and their increasing complexity write *Buffy* as a modern tale of sovereignty. Only then can we get at what a "post-Buffy" spin might offer the werewolf in us all.

More specifically, I examine how the radical hybridity of characters such as, for example, a vampire with a soul (and one with a microchip), a reluctant werewolf, and a fallen demon prevents their assignation as *homines sacri*. I also discuss that "demons" are not a homogenous group, but bear their own distinctions of kind—and worth. But while the first years of the series saw a relatively clear demarcation of good from evil, and the goodness of the demon-human hybrid decided on an individual basis, in the fourth season of *Buffy*, the arrival of The Initiative—a military commando outfit prone to confining, torturing, and conducting medical experiments on demons—begins to raise the issue of the ethical treatment of the demon qua demon and his/her place in the (human) world. I then examine how *Buffy*'s spin-off series, *Angel*, further complicates the boundary that separates humans from demons and the spaces in which they both uneasily dwell. Indeed, on *Angel* we encounter more varieties of demon beings and more complex forms of demon-human hybridity, thus more possibilities for community building. But since *Buffy* spins a web of mythology, it is to ancient mythology that I first turn.

## A TALE OF TWO SOVEREIGNTIES

In his analysis of the mythologies of ancient Indo-European languages, Georges Dumezil discovered two orders of sovereignty: the juridical (expressed through the flamines in Rome/brahmans in India) and the magico-religious (Luperci and Ghandarva), represented by the earthly kings Mitra and Varuna (with corresponding gods Numa and Romulus; Jupiter and Fides), which, in operating in opposition to each other, form a complete and unified expression of political sovereignty. The flamines and brahmans are guardians of sacred order, the Luperci and Ghandarva of sacred disorder. One pole is static, regulated, and calm; the other dynamic, violent, and free (Dumezil, 1988: 33–34). As sovereign kings, Mitra is benevolent, just, and priestly, and Varuna terrible and war-like with the automatic blind law of the Jurist in strict opposition to the flexible counter-law of the warrior Magician (72, 110).

Because of its "inherently explosive nature," the magico-religious can remain dominant for only so long, in fact "the time it takes to purify and revivify, to 'recreate' the [flamines and brahmans] in a single tumultuous irruption of energy." Moreover, the Luperci and Ghandarva are recognized as being of the infernal regions of "the other world." The Luperci, says Dumezil, grew apart from human societies. Prone to raids and incursions they were the "brigands of the bush" to the more socially inclined "city dwellers" prior to the founding of Rome. The Luperci and Ghandarva are the bearers of mystery, "mere transients in the world to which brahmans and flamines rightfully belong" (34, 53). Indeed the "good" side of the coupling, the flamines and brahmans, bear no trace of the supernatural. They are instead the "guarantors," the embodiment of rules and social prescriptions that in India are manifest in ritualistic knowledge and philosophy, and in Rome, in the advancement of human law (34). Nonetheless, and however temporary, of the two sovereigns it is the "terrible magician," Varuna, who predominates over the ordered and just Mitra (116, 133–134). In sum, "the couples expressing the Roman and Indo-Iranian conceptions of sovereignty present themselves with a *de facto* hierarchy which does not exclude a *de jure* equality" (116).

Now, this dualist notion of sovereignty does not, Dumezil makes clear, determine the general bipartition of all levels of the universe. In the Indo-European system, sovereignty is but the first of three levels that make up the universe and society (179).[2] And although the other levels are also headed by paired divinities, their formula is markedly different from the antithetical and complementary coupling of Mitra and Varuna. They are, rather, "equivalent and indistinguishable." One should not be tempted, then, to make a direct comparison between the "good" Mitra and the "terrible" Varuna with "certain forms of messianism known in the ancient near East, or with the great Christian dogma of the 'son' as intercessor and saviour juxtaposed to the avenging, punishing father" (179–180). And it doesn't seem, at least to Dumezil, that this has been initiated in any region except Iran, where Plutarch took Mithra as being "a mediator," therein providing a salvation religion ("Mitraism") that almost tipped the scales of Christianity, however briefly. Yet this was a very specific type of mediator, one between the principle of good and the principle of evil (180–181).

As indicated above, it is quite easy to identify Buffy as a mediator between the forces of good and evil, between "this world" and the "other-worldly." In the 1992 feature film and early years of the series (which began as a mid-season replacement in 1997), Buffy, blonde and virginal, represents all that is good and innocent and, in her capacity as "the Chosen One," is the protector and guarantor of a moral order vulnerable at all times to overthrow by all that is evil. We see two orders of sovereign rule in *Buffy:* the just and human mortal dimension, and the terrible and inhuman, the demon dimension, both of which *and equally* (as we shall see) make up earthly life. With representative adversaries as evil as the Master in season one, vampires Spike and Drusilla in season two, the demon-wannabe Mayor and his cohort, the rogue slayer Faith, in the third season, we see the magico-religious order of the explosive other world predominate over the more just and rational order of human sociality. But, as in Indo-European mythology, only for so long. Indeed, Buffy may lose a few battles, but she always manages to win the apocalypse (totaling seven at the end of season five).

It is precisely in "kicking serious demon ass," however, that *Buffy* could be seen to depart from Indo-European mythology. As Dumezil sees it, the antithetical characteristics of the various pairings of the bipartite sovereign system could, in theory, develop in two different directions. As the term "antithetical" means both "opposed" and "complementary," an antithesis could be expressed either by conflict or collaboration. And "there is no trace of conflict, either mythic or ritual, between Mitra and Varuna," but rather, collaboration (1988: 113). In fact, whenever a coupling finds itself engaged in conflict, its adversary is always *external* to its constituent components. Moreover, both components of the Mitra/Varuna, Romulus/Numa coupling are "equally legitimate, equally necessary, equally worthy of imitation, and equally 'good' in the broad sense of the word." Terrible kings, says Dumezil, are not necessarily "bad" kings. And although history may have pronounced the Roman god Romulus as a strictly warrior-type, all four embody something quite distinct from "military leaders" per se. "Varuna and Mitra, Romulus and Numa are all kings in their essence, one pair by virtue of their creative violence, the other by virtue of their organizing wisdom" (114–115).

As earlier mentioned, the arrival of the military unit, the Initiative, in the fourth season of *Buffy* introduces an element that disrupts any easy notions of a "good humans" vs. "evil demons" scenario suggested (for the most part) in the first three seasons, the initial seeds of doubt being planted toward the end of season three. Here, in seasons three and four of *Buffy* and the first season of its spin-off *Angel* (which began in *Buffy's* fourth season), we see the hierarchies of modern sovereignty at work in the hierarchies of killing: with questions of who can legitimately be killed and who cannot, who can legitimately *kill,* and who cannot. Before I address this, however, some elaboration of *Buffy's* own genealogy is necessary.

## DEMON SLAYERS, SLAYER DEMONS, AND OTHER HYBRIDS ALONG FOR THE RIDE

The story is well familiar to any fans of *Buffy the Vampire Slayer.* Into each generation is born a slayer, a young woman, the Chosen One, whose duty is to fight the vampires who roam the earth and threaten the future of humanity. There is only ever one slayer in the world and when one dies another takes her place.[3] In the original feature film (written by Joss Whedon and directed by Fran Rubel Kuzui) we learn that Buffy, a 16-year-old (and rather vapid) high school student, is unaware of her birthright, having been misplaced by the Watchers Council, which presides over, prepares, and trains the slayers. When eventually discovered and approached by her assigned Watcher, she is reluctant to fulfill her birthright as it will cut into her social life, particularly her cheerleading. However, when her Watcher is killed by an especially nasty vampire (Lothos) before her very eyes, Buffy accepts her responsibilities and averts a near apocalypse—at the high school senior dance. The television series picks up with Buffy having been expelled from her Los Angeles high school (for wanton destruction) and relocated with her (now single) mother to the small town of Sunnydale, which unbeknownst to our Slayer is located on a "Hellmouth," a portal between two realities: the earthly and demon dimensions. This does not bode well for Buffy, who, once again, just wants to fit in. But she finds it impossible to shed her birthright, especially when dead students start popping out of school lockers (the school being situated directly atop the Hellmouth).

That Buffy is a reluctant slayer is significant for a number of reasons. First, it indicates that the act of slaying, and saving humanity, is not a choice but a duty, an ethical responsibility that one may accept, or not. Second, and related, it presents Buffy as a "normal" teenaged girl, but one whose normalcy is threatened by her status as the Chosen One. I will expand on the first point later in the chapter. For now, I want to emphasize that Buffy herself is a liminal figure, an outcast. Try as she will, and she certainly does, she cannot lead a normal life. Neither fully a high school student nor fully a slayer, Buffy is a sort of hybrid figure, her radical difference from her peers a source of alienation (but also providing much of the show's humor).

However, Buffy is not alone in her alien/ated existence. She soon attracts a motley crew of other misfits whose fit into the Sunnydale scene approximates her own. Indeed, all of the supporting characters in the show display an Otherness that separates them from the (seeming) homogeneity of the "one-Starbucks" California town in which they (anxiously) dwell. Buffy's new best friend, Willow, is a brainy and shy fledgling witch whose mother still buys her clothes. There is the awkward and decidedly uncool Xander, whose best friends are girls he has little chance of wooing. The wealthy and snobby cheerleader, Cordelia, who inadvertently becomes part of the "Scooby Gang," is set apart by her popularity, which is itself threatened when she begins to date the uncool Xander (Byers, 2000: 217). Oz, who joins the show in the second season, is, on the other hand, cool, intelligent, and pensive, albeit a werewolf. Anya, whom we meet in season three, is a 1,000-year-old demon, who, when stripped of her powers, is suddenly thrust into life as a teenaged girl. The brooding Angel, who becomes Buffy's lover, is a 240-year-old vampire unlike any other, having been cursed with a soul and attendant conscience by a gypsy family some 100 years ago. And the nasty vampire Spike, unable to perform his vampirism following the insertion of a microchip into his brain in the fourth season, reluctantly joins the gang as well.

Rounding out the Slayer's entourage is the figure of Giles, Buffy's Watcher (in the guise of school librarian) who wants to go by the book, so to speak, but whose young charge renders his buttoned-down Englishness virtually impossible. In short, as much as it is a tale of good and evil, *Buffy the Vampire Slayer* is a demonstration, indeed a *performance*, of identities in crisis (see Byers, 2000). Sunnydale, and Sunnydale High in particular, is where modernity's binarisms of masculinity and femininity, the living and the dead, the normal and the pathological, become undone, the fixity of their boundaries unglued. Neither Buffy, nor her friends, nor for that matter a good many of the vampires and demons we encounter, are able to be contained within the spheres that produce them. Any performance of identity, of course, is a political performance, a sovereign expression, and in *Buffy* the constant negotiation and refashioning of identity is a struggle over the moral spaces of political community, a struggle in which sameness ought to win out over difference in order for the community to survive intact and Otherness to be kept at bay.[4] To be sure, with sovereignty founded upon the principles of inclusion and exclusion—the annihilation of difference—a few monsters are needed every now and then to remind us that we are human. The monster, which Derrida defines as a "hybrid of heterogenous organisms," reveals what normality itself is. A future without monsters is no future at all, "it would already be a predictable, calculable, and programmable tomorrow" (Derrida, 1995: 385–387).

Dusting vampires, then, is a way of policing, maintaining, indeed *renewing* the moral boundaries of social space. As Michele Byers argues, hunting vampires in *Buffy the Vampire Slayer* is a means of forming a moral community. Buffy and her friends are on a "righteous crusade in which they represent the good and the moral." But the undead also form a sort of moral community that is itself "constructed by some governing concept of 'truth' which the hunters do not have exclusive rights to. As figures of the Other, the vampires are subsumed to the negative of a binary—the necessary evil without which the moral crusade would be unnecessary" (Byers, 2000: 178). Slayers and vampires (or Mitra and Varuna) are therefore mutually constitutive. The hunter requires the vampire in order to establish him/herself as morally "good" and the vampire requires the hunter in order to accumulate space, power, and strength. Both, Byers adds, are needed to move the story forward. Morever, "Othering the vampire" provides the basis for the very community that needs to be eradicated. Drawing upon Rene Girard, Byers suggests that the destruction of the vampire be read as the production of a "surrogate victim" that thereby ends the "'sacrificial crisis' of the Sunnydale community."

> In this performance the vampiric Other stands in for the threat of violence which exists within the community itself. It is important that the violence against the vampire be normalized as heroic action while the hunt distracts the community from the violence which erupts within it. The vampire helps redefine the boundaries of the moral community its presence breaches. Without the vampire there is no story; without the Other there are no lines to draw, no battles to win and no community to forge (178–179).

Without the monstrous vampire, then, humanity itself is at stake (pun intended). In fact, the monstrous narrative through which our identity is inscribed not only reassures us that we are human, but that as humans, we are only steps away from being monsters ourselves. Monster narratives continue to fascinate because "the monster attracts those who imagine themselves as 'normal' because of the lurking suspicion that they too can be made monstrous" (207).

And this happens repeatedly throughout the series. The condition of Angel's curse is such that in achieving pure happiness, e.g., sexual union with Buffy, the curse will lift and he will revert to being evil (this formed the main narrative arc of the second season). There was always the threat that Oz would break out of his cage (ironically enough the book cage in the school library) on the next full moon and wreak havoc (which indeed has happened). Faith, whom Joss Whedon described as the show's "first human monster," descended into evil upon (accidentally) killing another human. Anya, although up to this point resigned to and even embracing her new mortal form, could presumably be restored to her former demon self; as could Spike if he loses his chip (which he has tried to do). Giles, we learn in the second season, was a "ripper" in his past, and in the finale of the fifth season deliberately took a human life (something Buffy could not bring herself to do). But even Buffy herself has been temporarily transformed as monstrous when in one fourth season episode Faith claimed her body and soul as her own. The threat of sudden irruption into the monstrous is not so much the "trust no one" mantra of *The X-Files,* however, but rather an indication of the fluidity of the boundary that seemingly separates the human from the monster, good from evil, the normal from the pathological. In *Buffy,* the human condition *is* its radical hybridity.

While the hybridity of figures such as Oz, Anya, Spike, and Angel ultimately saves them from the stake of the Slayer (for the most part),[5] in the demon dimension hybridity is not an automatic ticket from destruction into dust. The Otherness of the vampire in particular is not only his/her distinction from the human, but from the "pure" demon as well. Indeed, the Master's plan in season one, as with the Mayor in season three, is to restore the earth to the pure hell it once was before becoming "tainted," not so much by humans, but its hybrid form, the vampire. The earth, we learn from Giles in the very first episode, "Welcome to the Hellmouth," was originally more the domain of demons than of humans. Demons roamed the earth for eons, but they gradually came to "lose their purchase on earthly reality," which, says Giles (albeit without qualification), "in a way was made for mortal animals, for man." All that remains of "the old ones" are vestiges and certain magic and, Buffy adds, vampires. As told in the ancient texts that guide the Watchers and Slayers, the last demon to leave the earthly reality fed off of a human, thereby creating the first of the vampires that now walk the earth "feeding and . . . waiting for the animals to die out, for the old ones to return." And this was almost accomplished when, 60 years ago, a very old and powerful vampire, the Master, made his way to Sunnydale, located on a hellmouth, with the intention of opening it and bringing the demons back. Unfortunately for the Master, an earthquake struck (this is California after all) burying him and half the town below the surface. In a ritual known as the Harvest, the Master was to rise again and open the hellmouth. Buffy, however, averted the plan and in the second season he meets his demise at the hand of the Slayer.

As we learn in the third season, the hellmouth that is Sunnydale did not spontaneously appear as a center of mystical energies (as Giles earlier puts it). Rather, the town was created 100 years before by a mortal demon-wannabe, now the Mayor, to serve precisely as a feeding ground for demons. The former demon Anya, still regarded suspiciously at this point by the demon-savvy slayer's circle, recounts how "all the demons walking the earth are 'tainted'; human-hybrids like vampires." Through "the Ascension," which coincides (not so coincidentally) with the Sunnydale High School Graduation, the equation is to be reversed through a human, the Mayor, becoming "fully demon." (This he briefly does before Buffy, once again, saves the day, and the world.)

Perceived as being on the lowest rung of the demon ladder, being other to humans and pure demons alike, the vampire, therefore, like the werewolf (and the teenager for that matter; see Molloy, 2002), becomes the equivalent of *homo sacer:* suspended in a zone of indistinction between the worldly and the other-worldly, being of both, but belonging to neither. Vampires like Darla and Luke in the first season of *Buffy* are mere minions to the Master and hunted by the Slayer, their lives considered expendable by both.

## THE VAMP AND THE CAMP

As argued in the previous section, sovereign communities are maintained as moral spaces through the eradication of their (desired) undesirable elements, those elements being those who dwell on the fringes, the margins and borders, of the moral order that cannot contain them. Vampires like Angel and Spike, in particular, oscillate between "good" and "evil" with the potential to perform both equally well. The vampire thus performs what could be considered a double border crossing, being doubly inscribed as necessary *and* undesirable, a threat to both proper humans and demons proper. Deciding when, under what circumstances, and by whom a vampire can legitimately be killed is therefore a most tricky business. For example, when the Master kills one of his minions, his ruthlessness is emphasized, whereas if Buffy were to kill the same character, it would not disrupt any moral code. Killing the figure of *homo sacer,* as I have also pointed out, is considered legitimate, a murder that is not homicide because the life taken is politically unqualified. It is important therefore that in *Buffy* the term "slay" is used when speaking of ending the life of a demon. ("I prefer to refer to it as slaying," says Buffy in one episode.) Slaying demons and vampires is legitimate (always depending on who's doing the slaying), whereas killing humans is of a different order altogether.

The hierarchy of killing in *Buffy* is not only linguistically, but also visually coded. Joss Whedon explained in an interview that each vampire story has its own mythology: *Buffy* is no exception. Thus while it is common in many vampire narratives for "older vampires" to crumble into dust when killed, *Buffy*'s vamps all explode into dust even if they're only freshly dead, in order to emphasize that they truly are monsters. As Whedon put it, "I didn't really want to show a high school girl killing *people . . . .*" And when "people" *are* killed the repercussions are serious. This is particularly evident in the third season when the "bad girl" slayer, Faith, accidentally killed a human being (thinking he was a vampire), sending her into a downward spiral of denial, death, and destruction—and into the service of the Mayor. As a "human monster," Faith, in other words, crossed the line not just between good and evil but between the just juridical order of sovereignty and the unjust order of the magico-religious.

It is however with the fourth season of *Buffy* and the first season of *Angel* that the fixity of this boundary becomes most seriously undermined. Buffy has now graduated from high school and, along with Willow and Oz, enters college at U.C. Sunnydale. (Xander and Anya try the working world, Cordelia moves to LA, ostensibly to become an actress, and Angel also moves to LA, having realized that his relationship with Buffy, were it to continue, would literally mean the end of the world.) If Buffy thought high school was hell, college presents a whole other other-world when a wholly different type of adversary and threat to her moral universe is introduced. For whereas her previous adversaries were of the other-worldly ilk, Buffy's new adversary is in human form. Unbeknownst to Buffy (at first), her Psych 100 Professor, Maggie Walsh, and the Teaching Assistant, Riley Sims, with whom Buffy eventually falls in love, are part of a covert U.S. military operation known as the Initiative. The Initiative is as dedicated to ridding the world of evil as the Slayer is, but uses profoundly different means and methods—and moral codes. Armed only with wooden stakes and medieval weaponry and guided by dusty old books, the pert blonde Buffy stands in direct contrast to the hypermasculinized and highly technologized U.S. military. When the Slayer's presence is made known to the Initiative, she is initially considered more a nuisance than a threat to its imperative. However, Professor Walsh discovers quickly enough that Buffy may be a more formidable presence than originally anticipated. In an effort to contain Buffy's strengths and abilities, Walsh invites Buffy to work with the Initiative.

The Initiative has a commando outfit, complete with camouflaged soldiers equipped with night-vision goggles and sophisticated weaponry, that raids more than patrols Sunnydale's cemeteries, streets, and campus, not just killing but also capturing, torturing, and conducting experiments on unsuspecting vampires and demons. One such victim is Spike, who, in being coded by the Initiative simply as Hostile 17, not only has his identity erased, but also has his vampirism neutralized with the insertion of a microchip into his brain. The microchip provides a nasty jolt should he attempt to harm a human. Spike escapes and, in finding himself hunted by the Initiative and unable to function as a vampire, seeks asylum with the Slayer's circle—which they reluctantly and suspiciously grant him.

These events, as I have earlier intimated, present something of a turning point in the series, marking the moment in which the order of Buffy's moral universe unravels as she finds herself fighting humans and saving demons. To be more precise, with the entrance of the Initiative the worldly and other-worldly become virtually indistinguishable and, as I shall elaborate shortly, we come to recognize sovereign power as biopower. As the Chosen One, the sovereign, Buffy had been in a position of operating both within and above the law in what Agamben defines as a state of exception. "We don't need the law," as Faith points out to Buffy in "Bad Girls" (season three), "we *are* the law." As the sovereign, it was Buffy who decided whose life was qualified, that is, who would live and who would die. Now, however, it is the Initiative through which we witness the suspension of law: the point where the violence of law and the law of violence enter a zone of indistinction (see Agamben, 1993: 31–32) or, in Dumezil's terms, where the Jurist becomes the Magician.[6] It is also with the revelation of the sovereign violence assumed by the Initiative that we see, in Levinasian terms, the passivity of the ethical relation with the Other come to the fore. For Buffy cannot ignore the possibility that even demons, when subject to acts of sovereign violence, are worthy of some basic rights, if not compassion. As regards Spike himself (who had been a thorn in the Slayer's side since the second season), now that he is "neutralized," de-vamped if you will, he cannot in good conscience be killed by the Slayer. But what rights can Spike possibly lay claim to? Under whose jurisdiction and in whose community? As a vampire, he's not demon enough. As a neutralized vamp, he's not even vampire enough. But does his new altered state make him not-vamp enough to qualify for full inclusion as a citizen-subject in the human world? Can Spike ever be anything other than bare life? It would be helpful here to return to the distinction Agamben makes between bare and politically qualified life and then move to its implications for "the camp" as the paradigm of modern (bio)political life.

As I have already pointed out, the bare life of *homo sacer* is a life that is expendable, politically unqualified, not worthy of being lived. In sum, it is upon the body of *homo sacer* and in the realm of bare life that state power is organized and exercised. Sovereign violence is "founded not upon a pact but on the exclusive inclusion of bare life in the state" (Agamben, 1993: 107). But it is also in the realm of bare life that *homo sacer* is emancipated, with the birth of democracy and the demand for human rights. For Agamben, "the declarations of rights is the originary figure of the inscription of bare life in the juridico-political order of the nation-state" (127). It is in the form of rights that politically unqualified bare life now fully enters into the structure of the state becoming the very foundation of its legitimacy. Natural bare life as such vanishes into the figure of the citizen in whom rights are preserved. Put differently, rights are available *only* to the citizen, accomplished in the passage from a divinely assigned royal sovereignty of the ancient regime to the form of national sovereignty we associate with the modern state. In the process of the new state order, the subject is transformed into a citizen, thereby severing the distinction between "the principle of nativity" (simple birth, or bare life as such) and "the principle of sovereignty" (the politicization of bare life through biopolitics) that had been separated in the ancient regime (127).[7]

In Agamben's analysis, the most extreme (and logical) consequence of this "hidden difference" between birth and nation in the twentieth century appeared in the form of Nazism and fascism, as "two properly biopolitical movements that made of natural life the exemplary place of the sovereign decision" (128–129).[8] Foucault's own formulation of biopolitics was, therefore, for Agamben, an incomplete project, accounting for the asylum and the prison but stopping short of the concentration camp as the paradigm of sovereignty, the "absolute space of exception," in which bare life and juridical rule enter into a threshold of total indistinction (20, 174). The camp is the very paradigm of political space. "Insofar as its inhabitants were stripped of every political status and wholly reduced to bare life, the camp was also the most absolute biopolitical space ever realised, in which power confronts bare life without any mediation." The camp constitutes the space at which "politics becomes biopolitics and *homo sacer* is virtually confused with the citizen" (171).

The camp, then, becomes the hidden regulator of the inscription of life in the juridical order (175).[9] The state of exception, once a temporary suspension of the juridico-political order, now becomes a new and stable spatial arrangement inhabited by the bare life that can no longer be inscribed within it. The political system no longer orders forms of life in a determinate space, but "contains at its very center a *dislocating* localization that exceeds it and into which every form of life and every rule can be virtually taken" (175). The camp, then, as the paradigmatic structure of modernity, the camp as "dislocating localization," is the "hidden matrix" of the politics in which we are still living and that metamorphasizes into detention zones in our airports and city outskirts (176).

A camp, in other words, can (and will) appear anywhere. No longer confined to a particular place or a definite category, bare life "now dwells in the biological body of every living being" (140). Including, I would add, the tortured and persecuted bodies of the undead. Just as the monster narrative reminds us that we can at any time cross the threshold to the monstrous, the (monstrous) narrative of sovereignty writes us all as potential *homines sacri,* without exception. As Jenny Edkins writes:

> From time to time, the attempt is made to produce a unified political community by exterminating those that occupy the place of *homines sacri,* or bare life, whether they be slaves, Jews, gypsies, people of the Third World, or the underclass. Such attempts inevitably give rise to a new *homo sacer,* in an endless cycle of exclusion, obliteration, and reincarnation. In this way, every society decides who its "sacred men" will be (2000: 20).

To return to Spike: although the escape from the Initiative may have saved his (so-called) life, the sanctity he initially finds with Buffy is deceptive. He may not be able legitimately to be killed by the Slayer, but he is still subject to the laws of the camp: his body still scrutinized, but now cared for, fed, and protected—his biological needs thus regulated—by the Slayer under the guise of humanitarianism (see Agamben, 1993: 133).[10] He is still, in other words, bare life. Lacking the rights of a full citizen-subject, he can't be anything but, to and within any order of governance, however ostensibly altruistic. What hope is there, then, for those who have no permanent home within the nation-state system that is constitutive of "humanity"? What kinds of communities can the radically dispersed, the diasporic nomads such as Spike, Oz, and Angel—or any other "demon"—possibly forge in such an inhospitable world?[11] And, moreover, what is our responsibility to such figures? In the following section, I argue that with *Angel* we see a treatment of the Other that reaches beyond the calculated humanitarian gesture, grounded rather in the incalculable, the ethical relation with the absolutely Other that precedes the constitution of the Self. "Buffy and I," says Angel, "don't belong to ourselves. We belong in the world fighting." As we shall also see, in fighting the good fight Angel comes close to losing his soul. He is nearly broad-sided on the road to redemption, until, that is, he has an epiphany.

## ANGEL/FACE

Now, Angel, be it reminded, departed Sunnydale not in the hope of finding a better place, but in fear of what might happen were he to remain with Buffy (his curse being that he would relinquish his soul upon attaining happiness). Having a soul does not automatically imply, of course, that Angel is "good," but that he has a conscience and thus cannot kill or harm humans with quite the same gusto he once enjoyed. But having a conscience also means that the sins of the past weigh heavily upon it and for 100 or so years a haunted and tortured Angel, bearing the unbearable trace of his former Angelus self within, roamed the earth aimlessly—trying to stay out of harm's way, yes, but not out of any aspiration to do more than that. Until, that is, he met and fell in love with Buffy. And then went to hell and back. Indeed, the path of redemption, for Angel, is a process of becoming and thus never fully attainable.

Shortly upon arriving in LA, a still aimless Angel meets Doyle, who had been sent by "the powers that be" precisely to seek out our cursed vampire. Doyle possesses the power to receive visions of people in distress and enlists Angel's help in finding a young woman who appeared in one such vision. While Angel was unable to save her from the clutches of the vampire, he encounters the now aspiring actress, Cordelia, and saves her from the same vamp (the host of the party). Impressed with the rescue, Cordelia suggests that Angel and Doyle open their own business, hiring her as well of course, and thus is born Angel Investigations, specializing in "helping the helpless," those for whom the traditional bounds of the law offer no protection and have no jurisdiction.

The demon scene that Angel encounters in LA is markedly different from the one he left behind in Sunnydale. Demons live closer to the surface in LA. Whereas Buffy and friends rely on ancient texts, Cordelia finds a demon database on the internet. In fact, "demonology" is an accepted academic field (Doyle's ex-wife is a demonologist). And in season two, Angel encounters a vampire-run motivational seminar (complete with a pyramid scheme) and a demon karaoke bar. As Byers points out, although it's never referred to explicitly as such in *Buffy*, vampires exist within Sunnydale as a sort of community in themselves, "one that lives on the fringes of acceptable society, is seen as dangerous and constantly threatening to overrun the borders of acceptable society." Indeed, the vampires in *Buffy* plan to make the world their own (Byers, 2000: 58, 161), sometimes with a little help from humans, e.g., Faith. In *Angel* we also see humans collaborating with demons, most notably the lawyers of Wolfram and Hart.[12] And whereas we do see many a menacing demon, we also see more fully formed communities of demons who wish simply to live in peace. That is, it becomes possible for demons to be "not human" rather than necessarily *in*human.

Several episodes provide examples of organized resistance to demon oppression, with Angel often protecting harmless demons (something we seldom encounter in *Buffy*) from nasty ones. For example, in "She" (season one), Angel helps a demon princess save the persecuted women of her own dimension from a life of subjugation and sexual slavery. Angel's motivation is not altruistic; rather he wants to prevent a war in another dimension from spilling over onto "his" turf and harming innocent humans. "I'm going to help you whether you want it or not." However, Angel admonishes the princess following the rescue—during which she was prepared to sacrifice the lives of Cordelia and Wesley—proclaiming the necessity to protect "the innocents of *any* dimension." And in the following episode, "I've Got You Under My Skin," Angel responds to the plea of the parents of a young boy believed possessed by a powerful and destructive demon. Upon performing an exorcism, however, he discovers that the boy himself is the murderous monster with the demon within calling out for rescue.

In sum, the categories of human and monster, good and evil, though tested and found faltering on *Buffy*, are even less distinct on *Angel*: the diversity among the demon (as with the human) population is greater in LA than in the more homogenous sunny dales. We learn from the outset that Doyle himself is of both demon and human extraction, a type of hybridity not entertained on *Buffy*. And one that has its price. In "Hero," Doyle has a vision that leads to the discovery of a family of asylum-seeking half-demons stranded when their money and passports are stolen by a man they had entrusted with their safe passage to Equador (where others of their people had found sanctuary on a neighbouring island). The half-demons mistake Angel for The Promised One they believe has been sent to protect them from The Scourge, an army of pure blood demons, complete in SS-type regalia, hell bent on killing all "mixed breeds," or "vermin," who threaten the purity of demonkind. But it turns out to be Doyle who is the hero of the episode's title, as he grapples with his own identity as half demon. Doyle recalls a visit he received from a fellow Bracken demon warning him of the coming Scourge and pleading for his help. As he was raised human, Doyle insisted that this was not his concern. However, he subsequently experienced his first vision (which he mistook for a dream) of a grisly scene of a group of slaughtered Bracken demons, his kin. Doyle thus convinces Angel that the group is in terrible danger and later, when a mystified Cordelia points out that "these are demons" and perhaps they shouldn't be helping them, Doyle's reply is that being demon "doesn't make them bad people," that we have "oppressed demon people here." In reconciling himself to his demon heritage, Doyle not only realizes the degree of persecution people of "mixed blood" face, and share, but also that it's high time to reveal his true yet secret self to Cordelia, the object of his desire. "I want to know if this is a face you could learn to love," he says to her, as his face transforms into demon, before sacrificing his life to save the demon refugees from the Scourge.

Doyle's act of heroism, however sympathetic, is nonetheless based on the fact that these particular demons are only *half* demon, thus worthy of being saved. A hierarchy of life is still in place. In a later episode entitled "The Ring," however, Angel finds himself unable to allow the continued persecution of an enslaved group of pure demons. In this episode, Angel is lured to what appears at first to be an exclusive gambling club but turns out to be a human-run fight club that, like a gladiator ring, pits captured demons against each other for human entertainment and profit. The rules are simple: a record of 21 kills earns a demon his freedom. Thrown into the ring at the threat of his own death, Angel tries at first to throw the fight and allow his opponent to live. But his opponent won't cooperate and Angel ends up killing him. Angel next tries to convince the demons that they can fight their captors, "but only if we stop fighting each other." Unsuccessful in this attempt as well, Angel tries to overthrow his captors, fails, and is brought to the club's office, whereupon he discovers that the club is backed by Wolfram and Hart. When offered his freedom ("keeping you around would be more trouble than it is worth"), Angel refuses to accept the condition that he not reveal the goings-on at the club and join forces with Wolfram and Hart (which he considers "a pact with the devil") and insists that he be returned to the barracks. In what follows, Cordelia and Wesley (who joined Angel Investigations following Doyle's demise)[13] come up with a rescue plan just as Angel is finally successful in convincing the demons to revolt. In the final scene Angel and his cohorts leave the club trailing behind the freed demons:

> Angel: I think we did a good thing here tonight.
> Wesley: Yes. We set the captives free.
> Cordelia: Well, actually, didn't we set—a bunch of—demons free?
> Wesley: Oh. Well. Technically—yes.

In this episode we thus see several levels of collaboration between humans and demons: we have humans consorting with demons; humans helping demons; demons helping humans; demons helping other demons. We also have humans, brothers in fact, fighting each other. The ring is run by the MacNamarra brothers, one of whom kills the other in the course of the episode. Indeed, it is the human dimension that enjoys the ownership of evil in "The Ring." But whereas Angel recognizes that there are moments in which demons deserve protection from the forces of human evil, the possibility that some demons are capable of being and doing good is not fully explored until the second season. In the season opener, aptly titled "Judgment," Angel in fact kills a "good" demon who had been protecting a pregnant woman from "bad" demons. When a shaken Angel relays the incident to the group, Wesley tries to rationalize it: "What, we're supposed to think a creature like that can suddenly change his modus operandi overnight? Turn into a defender of . . . Oh god." That it didn't occur to any of them that a demon could be anything but trouble weighs on Angel's conscience almost as much as the realization that he had killed "an innocent being," moreover, "a soldier like [him]self." The vampire with a soul thus resolves to make the demon's mission his own.

The road to redemption has a number of twists, however. According to an ancient prophetic text that Angel had found in the Wolfram and Hart offices, his destiny is to find his humanity and become mortal again—upon his prevention of an apocalypse. The problem is that for Angel the quest to become human, his desire to be rewarded with mortality, soon becomes an obsession, taking over his will, and ability, simply to do good things. As the second season progresses and the distinctions between hell and earth, good and evil, continue to disintegrate, so too does Angel begin to unravel—in accordance with Wolfram and Hart's master plan. Briefly, in an effort to get to Angel, the firm resurrected his former flame, the vampire Darla, whom Angel had killed in the first season of *Buffy*. Darla begins to infiltrate his mind, occupying his thoughts and dreams, plunging Angel into the solitude and despair of his memories. He fires his staff when they begin to fear that he is reverting back to his evil ways and attempts to take on Wolfram and Hart on his own, and to "save" Darla in the process.[14]

In "Reprise" Angel discovers upon a visit to the psychic demon Host of the karaoke bar that the lawyers from Wolfram and Hart have been hanging out there in deadly fear of an impending visit by the senior partner from "the home office." Angel crashes the meeting/ritual in an effort to get to the home office, which he assumes is hell, and stop the evil at its source. When Angel encounters none other than Holland Manners, who had been (presumably) killed in a bloodbath by Darla and Drusilla, he accepts Manners' offer to escort him to the home office, through the doors of an elevator opening onto the street outside of the Wolfram and Hart office tower. On the descent Manners tells Angel that destroying Wolfram and Hart will solve nothing insofar as they have been and will always be around: from the time the first caveman clubbed his neighbor, through the Inquisition to the Kamir Rouge. "This world doesn't work in spite of evil. It works with us. It works because of us." And when the doors open, Angel is confronted with the identical scene of homeless people, despair, and crime, the reality he thought he had just left. Hell, in other words, is where he already was.

> Manners: Welcome to the Home Office.
> Angel: This isn't . . .
> Manners: Well, you know it is. You know that better than anyone. The things you've seen. The things you've, well, done. You see, if there wasn't evil in every single one of them out there, well, there wouldn't be people. They'd all be angels.

A brooding Angel makes his way through the streets of the hell which is LA and finds Darla waiting for him at home. Given the futility of his efforts to retain his soul, Angel gives in to his desire for Darla and after a night of passion wakes up in terror. In the next episode, entitled "Epiphany," Angel is quite surprised to discover, however, that he has not lost his soul and descended into evil, but has instead "seen the light." Aware that there is nothing he can do to save Darla, he leaves in order to make amends to those he damaged on his "road to redemption." In the final scene he is sitting with his estranged friend, Kate, the police detective whose career he had inadvertently destroyed and who had earlier in the episode attempted suicide (though Angel saved her). For Kate, no longer being on the police force means that nothing she does has any meaning. But for Angel this is exactly the point. Nothing we do matters in the greater scheme of things, he says, because "there's no grand plan and no big win":

> Kate: You seem kind of chipper about that.
> Angel: Well, I guess I kind of worked it out. If there's no great glorious end to all this, if nothing we do matters, then all that matters is what we do. Because that's all there is—what we do now, today. I have fought for so long for redemption, for a reward. Finally just to beat the other guy, but I never got it.
> Kate: And now you do?
> Angel: Not all of it. All I want to do is help. I want to help because I don't think people should suffer. And if they do, it's because there's no bigger meaning. As long as I have the kindness—it's the greatest thing in the world.
> Kate: Sounds like you had an epiphany.
> Angel: That's what I've been trying to tell people!

It may seem a simple moral tale, but in Angel's epiphany rings a distinctly Levinasian moment of clarity: that we are passive before the call of the Other. We have not choice but an obligation to respond to the Other's face, which cries out to us in its nakedness, its destitution and suffering. The ethical relation is a responsibility for the Other that stems not from altruism but from obligation. For no one, says Levinas, is good voluntarily (1981: 11).

What both Buffy and Angel learn is that the response to the Other is a decentering of Self, for the Other precedes the Self, calling its existence into question (Levinas, 1989: 83). As noted above, Angel well recognizes that neither he nor the Slayer belong to themselves; rather, they have a responsibility to the world.[15] Within this supposed televisual fantasy, therefore, we learn not about "facing our own inner demons" (in an individualist sense), nor that "evil lurks everywhere" (in a sovereign sense), but that the face of the demon is our neighbor. And being a good neighbor means welcoming the Other in all its wretchedness and without exception—the poor, the widow, the orphan, and the stranger; all of the *homines sacri* who dwell in this world, the other world, and the not-so-distinct spaces, the camps, in between. This, then, is not an *extension* of sovereignty to those who lack it, but an abandonment of its ban. A "post-

Buffy spin" on the sovereign tale would, then, be one that refuses to ban the outlaw and invent the bandit, and might possibly even give us pause before dusting the vamp or the werewolf next door.

## NOTES

1. This paper would have remained in the realm of fantasy were it not for Mark Clamen, Hilary Davis, Aida Hozic, and Julian Reid.
2. The other levels are that of the warrior and the third estate, victory and prosperity.
3. There are exceptions of course. When Buffy's heart stopped in season two, Kendra was summoned, and upon Kendra's death, Faith became the (other) Chosen One.
4. For more on the threatening presence of the alien Other, and its necessity in maintaining the social cohesion of the body politic, see Lipschutz in this volume.
5. When need be, Buffy has in fact killed Angel.
6. Whereas Dumezil recognizes two antithetical orders of sovereignty, the juridical and the war-like, which in combination form the complete picture of sovereign rule, for Agamben the juridical enters a zone of indistinction with the violent.
7. In other words, the principles of nativity and sovereignty are now united in the body of the "sovereign subject" which becomes the foundation of the new nation-state. "Birth" immediately becomes "nation" such that there is no longer a distinction between the two terms.
8. Agamben argues that Nazism's racism and eugenics are comprehensible only in the context of the birth-nation link that had lost considerable force by the time of the First World War, and has led to the demand for "human rights" (1993:132–133).
9. For Agamben it is not insignificant that the concentration camp appeared alongside new laws on citizenship and the denationalization of citizens. This is true not only of the Third Reich's laws on citizenship at Nuremberg, but also laws on denationalization in almost all European states, including France, between 1915 and 1933.
10. Agamben argues that humanitarian organizations can only grasp human life in the form of bare life and thus "despite themselves, maintain a secret solidarity with the very powers they ought to fight" (1993: 133). For an extension of this argument and its implications for the new humanitarianism of NATO, see Edkins (2000).
11. Oz, I should point out, leaves the show mid-way through the fourth season, when an affair with a girl werewolf, and the destruction it unleashes, makes him question how successfully he can keep his "man" and "wolf" selves separate. He departs Sunnydale in search of the answer.

12. Faith was but one of a replenishing source of adversaries for the Slayer. The presence of Wolfram and Hart, on the other hand, has sustained itself through two seasons of *Angel* and isn't going to go away anytime soon.
13. As with the characters of Angel and Cordelia, Wesley originated on *Buffy*, having been Faith's ineffectual Watcher. Fired from the Watcher's Council, Wesley arrives in LA as a "rogue demon hunter" (prompting Cordy to ask, "What's a rogue demon?").
14. Darla had been brought back by Wolfram and Hart in mortal form. Before she had become a vampire, however, Darla had been a prostitute and was dying of syphilis. When she and Angel discover that she is now dying, Angel tries to restore her health and, failing that, to help Darla reconcile with her past and find her own redemption. This gets thwarted however when Drusilla comes to town and turns Darla back into a vampire.
15. Cordelia (to whom Doyle transferred the ability to receive visions of the helpless) comes to the same realization in season three. Given the choice of giving up the visions, which had been causing severe health problems (the human brain not having the synaptic strength to withstand their intensity), or submitting to becoming part demon in order to continue to receive them, Cordy chooses the latter. That one has to become demon in order to continue to do good, needless to say, further undermines the bad demon/good human distinction.

## BIBLIOGRAPHY

Agamben, Giorgio. 1993. *Homo Sacer: Sovereign Power and Bare Life*, translated by Daniel Heller-Roazen, Stanford, CA: Stanford University Press.
Braun, Beth. 2000. "*The X-Files* and *Buffy the Vampire Slayer:* The Ambiguity of Evil in Supernatural Representations," *Journal of Popular Film and Television,* 28(2): 88–94.
Bronfen, Elisabeth, and Sarah Webster Goodwin, eds. 1993. *Death and Representation,* Baltimore and London: Johns Hopkins University Press.
Byers, Michele. 2000. *Buffy the Vampire Slayer: The Insurgence of Television as a Performance Text,* Toronto: University of Toronto PhD Dissertation.
Derrida, Jacques. 1995. "Passages—from Traumatism to Promise," in Elisabeth Weber, ed., *Points . . . : Interviews, 1974–1994,* Stanford, CA: Stanford University Press, pp. 385–387.
Dumezil, Georges. 1988. *Mitra and Varuna: An Essay on Two Indo-European Representations of Sovereignty,* translated by Derek Coltman, New York: Zone Books.
Edkins, Jenny. 2000. "Sovereign Power, Zones of Indistinction, and the Camp," *Alternatives* 25(1): 3–25.
Harkness, John. 2001. "Witty Werewolves," *NOW Magazine,* 20(36): 99.
Levinas, Emmanuel. 1981. *Otherwise than Being or Beyond Essence,* translated by Alphonso Lingis, Dordrecht: Kluwer Academic.

Levinas, Emmanuel. 1989. "Ethics as First Philosophy," in Sean Hand, ed., *The Levinas Reader,* Oxford: Blackwell, pp. 75–87.

Molloy, Patricia. 2002. "Moral Spaces and Moral Panics: High Schools, War Zones, and Other Dangerous Places," *Culture Machine* (February). http://culturemachine.tees.ac.uk.

# Chapter 6

## FORBIDDEN PLACES, TEMPTING SPACES, AND THE POLITICS OF DESIRE

### On *Stalker* and Beyond

### *Aida A. Hozic*

*What was that? A meteorite that fell to Earth? Or a visitation from outer space? Whatever it was, there appeared in our small land a miracle of miracles: the Zone.*
   *We sent in troops. None returned. Then we surrounded the Zone with police cordons. We did right. Although, I am not sure. Not sure. . . .*

—From an interview with Professor Wallace, Nobel Prize Winner, for RAI press (in *Stalker,* a film by Andrey Tarkovsky, Mosfilms Studios, 1979)

*The Zone is a complex maze of traps. All of them death traps. I don't know what it's like when there is no one here, but as soon as humans appear everything begins to move. Former traps disappear, new ones appear. Safe places become impassable, and the way becomes now easy, now confused beyond words.*
   *Because this is the Zone.*
   *You might think it's capricious but at each moment it's just what we've made it by our state of mind. Some people have had to turn back empty-handed after going half-way. Some perished at the threshold of The Room. Whatever happens here, depends not on the Zone, but on us.*

—Stalker (also in *Stalker)*

A ndrey Tarkovsky's film *Stalker*, produced in the late 1970s in the now defunct and nearly forgotten Soviet Union, is one of those rare cinematic masterpieces that rattle all our preconceptions about the relationships between politics and art, popular culture and the state, science fiction and international relations. Funded by the Soviet government, yet hailed as a dissident work of art in the West, *Stalker* defies easy political categorizations. It is neither a perpetuator of existing power relations nor a predictable counter-narrative of the Soviet regime. Instead, the film subverts the science fiction genre to tell a complex and metaphysical story about law, desire, and sovereignty in which characters' relations toward an extra-juridical space called The Zone form a set of different political subjectivities and different visions of the international system.

In this chapter, I explore the constitution of these alternative political stands by relying on Giorgio Agamben's (1998) analysis of sovereign power and bare life, on the one hand, and on the category of the sublime (particularly the feminine sublime), on the other. The sublime, which, as Jean-Luc Nancy notes (1993: 25), has lately become a fashionable term, allows us not only to connect the aesthetic and ethical aspects of Tarkovsky's work to science fiction as a genre, but also carves a rare opening for subject positions located beyond and above sovereign power. For, ultimately, as we shall see, *Stalker* suggests that it is the seemingly apolitical sublime love of a woman—in this age in which we have "quite forgotten how to love" (Tarkovsky, 1987: 199)—that creates an ethical and political stance with the greatest emancipatory potential and the most unsettling effects on sovereign power as we know it.

## THE STORY

*Stalker*, Andrey Tarkovsky's film based on the science fiction novel *Roadside Picnic* (1977) by the brothers Arkady and Boris Strugatsky, depicts the journey of three men through The Zone—the place where a meteorite had once fallen, or the site of a possible alien visitation (we are never quite sure). The Zone is suspected to have strange and mystical powers and it is, for that reason, cordoned off from the rest of the world. Access to The Zone is forbidden: those who venture into it risk either disappearing within The Zone or being arrested outside of it. The three men in Tarkovsky's film—Writer, Scientist, and their guide, Stalker—travel through The Zone in search of The Room, the place where everyone's deepest desires allegedly come true. According to the Scientist, The Room is indeed the main reason why authorities so jealously guard The Zone.

For, as the Scientist says at one point, "who knows what wishes people might conceive?"

As the men enter into The Zone, they are reminded of the fate of another stalker, Porcupine, who apparently went into The Room to ask that his brother, for whose death Porcupine had felt responsible, be brought back to life. However, when Porcupine returned home from The Zone, he found himself incredibly rich—The Room had exposed his real wish. Ashamed of his own selfish desires, Porcupine eventually hanged himself.

When the men finally approach The Room, the Scientist and the Writer realize that they do not have the courage to enter it. The Writer concludes that it is better to continue to get "quietly and peacefully drunk" than humiliate himself by praying in The Room. Besides, he says—where is the proof that the miracle of The Room really exists? In Porcupine's death? The Scientist, on the other hand, attempts to destroy The Room with a bomb that he has brought with him. The Room, he claims, has obviously not made anyone happy, so why risk having it fall into the wrong hands? Stalker wrestles with the Scientist over the bomb, warning both men that The Room is the only place to come to if one has nothing else to hope for, and that destroying it would mean destroying faith. The Scientist, though hardly convinced, eventually defuses the bomb and the three men are seen in The Zone resting on the wet walls of The Room, their desires left unspoken.

Upon their return from The Zone, the men are aimlessly drinking at a local bar when Stalker's wife comes to take him home. Their daughter, Monkey, cannot walk—she is a genetic mutant, a result of Stalker's frequent visits to The Zone. Stalker carries Monkey home on his shoulders, his wife helps him into bed, and then—in a stunning monologue—explains her relentless and selfless love for him. In the last scene of the film, Monkey recites a poem, written by the nineteenth-century Russian poet Fyodor Tyuchev:

> How I love your eyes, my friend,
> With their radiant play of fire,
> When you lift them fleetingly
> And like lightening in the skies
> Your gaze sweeps swiftly round.
>
> But there is a charm more powerful still
> In eyes downward cast
> For the moment of a passionate kiss,
> When through lowered eyelids glows
> The somber, dull flame of desire.

Then, Monkey gently lowers her head and looks intensely at a few empty glasses on the table. The glasses, apparently guided by her telekinetic powers, start to move. Perhaps—the viewer is left to ponder—miracles can still happen.

## POLITICS

In the late 1970s, at the time of the film's original release, *Stalker* was perceived to be a thinly veiled critique of the Soviet regime. The early interpretations of the film emphasized its alleged allusions to Stalinism. Apparently, the word "zone" was frequently used in colloquial Russian for gulags, Stalker's shaven head evoked the look of Stalin's prisoners in Siberian camps, and one of the first sentences that Stalker utters in the film— "I am imprisoned everywhere"—were taken as proofs that Tarkovsky's real subject in *Stalker* was the enduring legacy of Stalin's terror (Žižek, 1999). The hints at Stalinism, the critique of the scientific state through visualization of its ecological disasters inside and outside The Zone, and the portrayal of the heavily policed border around The Zone, led many observers to conclude that *Stalker* was nothing but a metaphor for the physical and spiritual imprisonment within the Soviet Union and across the Eastern Bloc (Johnson and Petrie, 1994; Goulding, 1994; Le Fanu, 1987).

The fact that the production of *Stalker* was mired in difficulties served as an additional proof that the film was not to the liking of the Soviet authorities. Aside from personnel problems (the firing of the film's first cameraman and set designer), it was also discovered during the location shooting—after nearly half of the film had been shot and two-thirds of the money spent—that the film stock was defective and could not be developed. In order to finish the film, Tarkovsky needed to reshoot it, and that required both additional funding and additional film stock. Goskino—the State Committee for Cinema under the Council of Ministers of the USSR—initially refused to cover the losses but eventually provided additional funds under the pretext that *Stalker* was now becoming a two-part film (which allowed new deadlines and extra funding) and by changing the genre from science fiction to "moral-philosophical parable" (Johnson and Petrie, 1994).

Tarkovsky completed *Stalker* in 1979, two years after the initial shooting began. According to some accounts, the authorities, particularly military leaders, were very concerned about its release: "Where is it taking place? What are these people, whose helmets are they wearing? What is this zone?" (ibid.: 139). Surprisingly, the head of Goskino, Filip Yermash, came to the film's defense and allowed its release. However, as Boris Strugatsky notes in a volume in which a number of Tarkovsky's friends and collaborators commemorate his opus, only 196 copies of the film were distributed in the entire Soviet Union, and only 3 in Moscow (Tarkovskaya, 1990). The film was almost totally neglected in the official Soviet press and it was denied a public screening at the 1979 Moscow Film Festival. Only after the film's successful showing at the 1980 Cannes Festival did positive reviews of *Stalker* appear in the Soviet Union (Johnson and Petrie, 1994: 140).

At the time of *Stalker*'s release in the West, the press frequently referred to Andrey Tarkovsky as a dissident. Serge Schmemann, for instance, writing in the *New York Times* (October 24, 1982) used Tarkovsky as the example of a filmmaker whose works belied the stereotypes of Soviet power. The political label was a necessary tool of aesthetic legitimation if Tarkovsky's artistic genius was to be recognized in the free world. It was reinforced by Tarkovsky's own decision to remain in the West after filming *Nostalghia* in Italy in 1984. The decision was prompted by the refusal of the Soviet government to grant him indefinite permission to stay in the West. But Tarkovsky himself resented the term. "I am not a dissident, I have no conflict with the Soviet government," he said briskly after announcing that he would not be returning home to the USSR (Reuters, December 30, 1986). Similarly, he rejected any overt politicization of his films, including *Stalker*. For him, the mission of art transcended mundane politics. "Art," wrote Tarkovsky, "must carry man's craving for the ideal, must be an expression of his reaching out towards it; must give man hope and faith" (1987: 192). As such, he claimed, it could not, by its very nature, be commercial or plebian or political in a trivial sense. Tarkovsky's vision of art, and of his role as an artist, was always—by Western standards—a romantic one: the artist was a genius whose mission was to aid others to achieve moral and spiritual perfection through an aesthetic experience. Thus, although occasionally criticized for his elitism or self-absorption, Tarkovsky had relatively little trouble co-existing with the Soviet state. The latter's own emphasis on high culture as a way of edifying the population remained wedded to the eighteenth- and nineteenth-century idea of art, and funding for works with such aspirations was abundantly available.

Tarkovsky's interpretation of *Stalker*, then, was very different from the one put forward in the West. For Tarkovsky, *Stalker* was a film about "human dignity; of what that dignity is; and of how a man suffers if he has no self-respect" (1987: 198). Like most of his other films, said Tarkovsky,

*Stalker* too was a film about "people possessed of inner freedom despite being surrounded by others who are inwardly dependent and unfree; whose apparent weakness is born of moral conviction and a moral standpoint and in fact is a sign of strength" (181). Hence, Stalker, the guide, although objectively much weaker and more frightened than the Scientist and the Writer, turns out to be "invincible because of his faith and because of his will to serve others" (ibid.). But ultimately, Tarkovsky said, *Stalker* was a film about love. For the real miracle in the film, he wrote, is the selfless, unthinking love and devotion of Stalker's wife, "the final miracle which can be set against the unbelief, cynicism, moral vacuum poisoning the modern world, of which both the Writer and the Scientist are victims" (198). In *Stalker,* concluded Tarkovsky, "I make some sort of a complete statement: namely that human love alone is—miraculously—proof against the blunt assertion that there is no hope for the world. This is our common and inconvertibly positive possession. Although we no longer quite know how to love . . ." (199).

## THE ZONE

It appears at first that the central concept in *Stalker*—and the key to its political interpretation—is The Zone, a heavily guarded extra-juridical space whose relationship to the film's main characters and to the world outside its boundaries allows for different mappings of sovereignty, the international system, and political subjectivity. As Slavoj Žižek notes (1999), film critics have generally described The Zone as a forbidden place, constituted by prohibition and authority and thus as tempting and alluring. On this view, the dynamic relationship between The Zone and the world outside it is predicated upon the existence of a firm border between them and a transgressive desire to cross it. Not surprisingly, then, during the cold war The Zone could easily be interpreted as a metaphor for the world behind the Iron Curtain. For Tarkovsky, on the other hand, The Zone was nothing but life itself. "People have often asked me," wrote Tarkovsky,

> what The Zone is, and what it symbolizes, and have put forward wild conjectures on the subject. I'm reduced to a state of fury and despair by such questions. The Zone does not symbolize anything, any more than anything else does in my films: the zone is a zone; it's life, and as he makes his way across it a man may break down or he may come through. Whether he comes through or not depends on his own self-respect, and his capacity to distinguish between what matters and what is merely passing. (1987: 200)

Hence, as Žižek claims in an essay about *Stalker:* for Tarkovsky "the mysterious zone is effectively the same as our common reality, and what confers on it the aura of mystery is the limit itself, that is the fact that the zone is designated as inaccessible, prohibited" (1999).

These two interpretations of The Zone—as a fantastic world distinct from the real world, and as an extension of the world or life itself—embody two different visions of sovereignty, the international system, and political subjectivity. The first one closely resembles traditional understandings of world politics, including conventional theories of international relations—the world of tightly controlled borders is also the world that entices us into the quest for power, into territorial hunger, into a desire for conquest, into the fear of and the thirst for the unknown. This is also the view of the international system most often affirmed and reaffirmed in science fiction films: the journey, as the principal narrative vehicle of the genre, is generally an outward journey of exploration, encounter, and subjugation, while space itself becomes nothing more than a different theater for well-known terrestrial power relations and ambitions. Science fiction thus lends itself most easily to parallels with colonial expansion and fantasies about the *Other* (see, for example, the chapters by Inayatullah and Neumann in this volume).

However, The Zone in *Stalker,* particularly in Tarkovsky's interpretation, allows for an alternative reading of the international system, one in which traditional assumptions about the ways in which power operates are called into question. The external journey in *Stalker* is then supplanted with an internal journey of the three main characters, the movement through space is always circuitous ("In the Zone, the straight road is not the shortest," says Stalker), and The Zone quickly folds into itself as a reflection of its visitors' states of mind. Analogous to a world beyond Westphalian sovereignty, which Blaney and Inayatullah describe as the world of heterogeneous power arrangements that blur the boundary between the inside and the outside of states (2000: 56), the world in which The Zone is situated then becomes indistinguishable from The Zone itself. The inward-oriented journey forces characters to discover and confront their enemies within, and to realize that the other, the desired, the fantastic is never located on the other side of any border, but rather among us.

Visually, too, Tarkovsky was careful not to emphasize the fantastic attributes of The Zone. While lusciously green in contrast to the sepia-colored world outside of it, The Zone is nonetheless just as much an ecological wasteland as "the reality," the outside world, to which it is supposed to be contrasted. The film is minimalist: there are no special effects in *Stalker* and, indeed, no visual distractions. The events themselves, as well as the situations with which the characters are confronted, have no elements of fantasy to them. As Tarkovsky emphasized over and over again, "the film was intended to make the audience feel that it was all happening here and now, that The Zone is there besides us" (1987: 200).

On this interpretation, The Zone is no longer a space that has to be eradicated, absorbed, or expanded upon because it is a challenge to sovereign power, but rather a place that needs to be policed, patrolled, and cordoned off because it makes sovereign order possible. Just like a refugee zone in Africa, an export-processing zone in Southeast Asia, a buffer zone in Israel, a *zone sannitaire* in central Europe, a safe zone in Bosnia, or a rebel zone in Colombia, The Zone in *Stalker* is a place where the established (legal) order has been suspended. Neither chaotic nor idyllic, zones—paradoxically—do not abolish or challenge the law but affirm it. As Giorgio Agamben (1998) notes in his analysis of sovereignty, the power of a sovereign ruler is not so much defined by his or her ability to create law and order, but by his ability to suspend them. The state of exception, created through this suspension of juridical order, makes sovereign rule possible. There—in this "zone of indistinction" between order and chaos, law and its suspension—the sovereign confronts her ultimate power: the ability to encounter and, if need be, to extinguish bare life. "The sovereign sphere," writes Agamben, "is the sphere in which it is permitted to kill without committing homicide and without celebrating a sacrifice, and sacred life—that is, life that may be killed but not sacrificed—is the life that has been captured in this sphere" (83). Similarly, anything can happen in The Zone—people can disappear, previously passable roads can turn out to be closed, new traps can emerge where there were none, desires can be articulated and realized. Whatever happens, it is obvious that the rules have been suspended—"Because," as Stalker says, "it is The Zone."

The paradox of sovereignty, its incestuous co-dependence on the "zone of indistinction," represents, according to Agamben, the cause of democracy's "decadence and gradual convergence with totalitarian states in post-democratic spectacular societies" (1998: 10). But the zone—the state of exception—also contains an additional ambiguity: it cannot be localized. "One of the theses of the present inquiry," adds Agamben, "is that in our age, the state of exception comes more and more to the foreground as the fundamental political structure and ultimately begins to become the rule. When our age tried to grant the unlocalizable a permanent and visible localization, the result was the concentration camp" (20). In the camp, the state of exception, originally envisioned as a temporary measure, "is now given a permanent spatial arrangement which as such nevertheless remains outside of normal order" (169). The camp is, therefore, a peculiar juridical and spatial construct, which contains in itself both the state of exception and the law (or the norm) itself, "a hybrid of law and fact in which the two terms have become indistinguishable" (170). Hence, the camp is the "nomos of the modern" (Agamben, 1997). Envisioned as such, as the forcefully localized state of exception that conceals its co-extension with sovereign order thanks to the strictly controlled boundary, *Stalker* and The Zone problematize, rather than affirm, the once important political border between East and West and the still important ideological border between the real and the fantastic. The Zone beside us is the result of the forceful localization of troubles within us.

But what, if any, kind of agency is possible vis-à-vis The Zone? And what kind of subjectivities do these different portrayals of The Zone and the international system produce? As Blaney and Inayatullah note, in traditional depictions of the international system, the other, difference, the fantastic, the desired are always located on the other side of a state boundary. Remaining within state bounds are law-abiding citizens and a "realm of relative 'sameness'—a cultural homogeneity and a uniform constitution . . . —is presumed" (2000: 44). However, although law is installed to control popular passions and desires, prohibition nonetheless creates its own transgression. State borders, intent on controlling the anarchical nature of the international system, only perpetuate its insecurities and foster a desire for territorial expansion as a way of securing those very borders. Hence, in traditional, state-centered visions of world politics, the heavily policed border between The Zone and the "real world" constitutes political actors as desiring, and inherently sinful, subjects. The main characters in *Stalker,* on such a reading, are also subjects who imagine that they can only realize themselves and their innermost desires by trespassing into The Zone. Conversely, the authority (law) patrols the border because The Zone as the locus of desire and its realization may also potentially be the site of absolute power. As the Porcupine story reveals, there is no ethical limit on the nature of the characters' desires: once visitors step into The Zone and enter The Room, their utmost wishes—be they for wealth, control, violence, immortality, or health—will be realized. Hence, the law banishes desire into The Zone, and by doing so purports to create socially conforming subjects in the "real world" while criminalizing or estranging those who dare to evade it.

An alternative understanding of political subjectivity begins to emerge if we assume that law does not constitute desire but rather forbids it. In other words, society may be founded not on desire but on its repression. Such an interpretation of the relationship between law and desire constitutes a different political subject—not a "subject who simply and unequivocably has a desire but one who rejects its desire, wants not to desire it" (Copjec, 1994: 25). The self-defeating nature of the men's journey in *Stalker* springs to mind. Faced with the possibility that their desires will be realized, the Writer and the Scientist cannot bring themselves to enter The Room. Even Stalker needs The Zone only as a possibility, as a space of hope and faith, but not as a space in or through which his own wishes actually come true. Indeed, he claims, "Stalker cannot ever enter The Zone if he has selfish wishes of his own." Stalker's relationship with desire is the sacrifice: in order to guide others toward their desires, Stalker has to renounce his own. The Zone thus becomes a space not that dissimilar from the world without—whether or not desires will be realized now depends on characters themselves, not on mysterious powers of The Zone. The boundary between the two worlds melts away as it becomes clear that subjects are equally unfree and unsettled in both, just as reluctant to accept law as they are to assume the absolute power that could come with its transgression. Hence, in this reading, the political subject is a much more uncertain entity—split from her own desire, which can never be realized (since the very being of the subject depends on the negation of desire), notes Copjec (1994), desire becomes a self-hindering process. The subject emerges as both conflictual and culpable, never assured of her own place and never at peace with herself. The international system, on such a representation, can only be mapped as a space of multiple, overlapping sovereignties, zones and non-zones—the space of perpetual unease but also the space where power relations are never fixed and where the actors' own conscience and fantasies define the character of the system itself. Blaney and Inayatullah (2000) are hopeful that such spaces of heterogenous authority, where subjects willingly confront the other within them, constitute the possibility of a more ethical and tolerant international community. A less optimistic view is also possible. As Stalker's characters suggest, subjects may realize the futility of boundaries but remain paralyzed by their own anguish, unable to learn from their own failures, equally cynical about the world and still, in one way or another, defined by their relation to The Zone.

So is there a world in which The Zone itself is redundant? And are there any political subjects who are detached from the vicious circle of law and desire? For as long as interpretations of *Stalker* and the international system—whether envisioned as a rigid world of states and borders or as a fluid world of overlapping boundaries and mutually constituting desires and anxieties—revolve around The Zone, attendant subject positions are nothing but its derivatives, bare life. Once The Zone fades into the background, however, it is possible to see that the sublime love of Stalker's wife—the ultimate miracle of the film, according to Tarkovsky—opens up a path toward a subjectivity that transcends the entanglements of sovereignty, law, and desire.

## THE SUBLIME (LOVE)

"The sublime," writes Jean-Luc Nancy, "forms a fashion that has persisted uninterruptedly into our own time from the beginnings of modernity, a fashion at once continuous and discontinuous, monotonous and spasmodic" (1993: 25). The sublime has long been viewed as a bridge between aesthetics and ethics, between art and politics: a passageway between desire, reason, and law. Situated on the edge of representation—for the sublime, by definition, is an encounter with an event, occurrence, or artwork so immense that it cannot be represented—the sublime, says Nancy, displays the destiny of modern art qua art. It is where art is measured by something other than art, where art "gives itself as a task [of being] something other than art, something other than the world of the fine arts or than beautiful works of art: something 'sublime'" (27). In the sublime pathos passes beyond into ethos, the beautiful is there not to please us but to move us, and enjoyment touches us as well as commands us. Hence, concludes Nancy, "at the limit of the sublime, there is neither aesthetics nor ethics. There is a thought of offering which defies this distinction" (49). The offering of freedom, since the subject—unbound by interests, passions, or desires—discovers herself as the author of law.

It is well known that for Kant (1987), whose analysis Nancy closely follows, the sublime was a concept that enabled a passage from the antinomies of speculative reason to the moral laws of practical reason. In a sublime encounter with nature (or with works of art), man becomes aware both of his utmost insignificance and of his moral imperative: the violent failure of his perceptive or imaginative capacities makes the capacity for rational comprehension—and moral judgment—all the more vivid (Crowther, 1989: 154). Hence, unlike Burke (1990), Kant does not perceive the sublime as a characteristic of the object; instead, in Kantian analysis, the sublime is always a subjective capacity for complex feelings of exhilaration and fear, imaginative impotence and superior moral reasoning. As an "intersubjective relation stimulated but not caused by the external world" (Freeman, 1995: 70), the Kantian sublime opens up the possibility for development of a different kind of political subjectivity in an equally different relation to and with others. Since experiences of the cognitive sublime make us fully aware of the utter extraordinariness of what it is to be human, "then we might reasonably expect that such experiences will be conducive to our sense of respect for persons" (Crowther, 1989: 173). The feeling of the sublime, awakened by the infinite of the world is, thus, "the feeling of community" (Rogozinski, 1993: 151).

Two aspects of the sublime seem relevant to Tarkovsky's *Stalker*. The first is the link between art and politics that defies simplistic politicization. As noted earlier, Tarkovsky himself had always attempted to create works that would move audiences toward a different ethical stance—in other words, his art aspired to foster experience of the sublime. One of the reasons why his works always engaged an element of the fantastic may be the fact that science fiction as a genre lends itself quite easily to the aesthetics of the sublime. "The precise function of science fiction," writes Scott Bukatman, is in many ways "to create boundless and infinite stuff of sublime experience, and thus to produce a sense of transcendence beyond human finitudes (true to the form of the sublime, most works produce transcendence of, and acknowledgment of, human limits)" (1999: 256). But Tarkovsky tried to go a step further by bridging aesthetic experience with ethics. "Art . . . affects a person's emotions, not his reason," wrote Tarkovsky in *Sculpting in Time*. "Its function is, as it were, to turn and loosen the human soul, making it receptive to good" (1987: 165). The artist's duty, therefore, is "to stimulate reflection on what is essentially human and eternal in each soul, and which all too often a person will pass by, even though his fate lies in his hands. . . . to make whoever sees my films aware of his need to love and to give his love, and aware that beauty is summoning him" (200).

The second important aspect of the sublime is the intimate relationship between the experience of the sublime and the ethics of respect. The latter constitutes (and is itself constituted by) a different political subject—one that stands beyond and above the interplay of sovereignty, law, and desire delineated by The Zone and described in the previous section. The sublime entails a degree of self-abandonment and suffering on the part of the subject that has generally not been a part of the economy of subjectivity in late modernity. The liberal ideal of self-realization denies any kind of legitimacy to sacrifice. As Tarkovsky notes, "we demand freedom for ourselves at the expense of others and don't want to waive anything of our own for the sake of someone else: that would be an encroachment upon our personal rights and liberties" (1987:180). Hence, self-abandonment is rare and appears most clearly in sublime love—the only form of love, writes Renate Salecl, that is not driven by insatiable desire for an unattainable object. "Whereas romantic love strives to enjoy the Whole of the Other, of the partner, the true sublime love renounces . . ." (1996). Instead of idealizing the object of affection, "the subject confronts the horrifying dimension of the object, the object as Das Ding, the traumatic foreign body in the symbolic structure" (ibid.). The feeling thus becomes a non-feeling, affection a suspension of affection: the sublime is "what remains of feeling at the limit, when feeling no longer feels itself, or when there is no longer anything to feel" (Nancy, 1993: 46). The sublime experience is "no longer to feel but to be exposed" (ibid.). The subject position of sublime love is the position of absolute exposure and of selfless giving.

In *Stalker*, this complex—and, as Tarkovsky would say, the only miraculous—position is occupied by Stalker's wife, the only character in the film who has never entered or desired to enter The Zone. Indeed, her own experiences with The Zone have only been negative—The Zone is a place that attracts her husband like a magnet, taking him away from home and bringing him into conflict with the law. In addition, The Zone is also the place responsible for her daughter's genetic mutations and paralysis, a curse placed on her family. Only once in the film does she mention the possibility of going into The Zone and then only as a way of comforting Stalker upon his return from the trip with the Writer and the Scientist. "Why don't I go with you," she says, "Do you think that I have nothing to wish for?" But Stalker, despairing over the Writer's and the Scientist's cynicism and failure to articulate their own desires, refuses his wife's offer with a question: "And what if you also fail?"

Firmly located outside The Zone and absent from most of the film, Stalker's wife presents herself as a different kind of subject—and, I would argue, a very political subject—than the Writer, or the Scientist, or even her husband. Interestingly, just like all other characters in the film, she does not have a name, only a function: in her case, that of Stalker's spouse. And yet, this function should not be read as an erasure of her identity, or in any way a sign that she is nothing but a derivative of Stalker himself. Rather, it is the signal of her identity as the one of being-together, companionship, partnership. Engaged in the here and now, in accord with her own desire, and independent of fantasy, law, or The Zone itself, the Wife appears to us self-sufficient and selfless at the same time. Her monologue, spoken directly into the camera at the end of the film, further separates her from the diegetic universe of the film and gives her character unique immediacy and presence in relation to the audience. Her stance, as revealed in the monologue, is one of acceptance of life without the need for any meta-narrative or meta-space; and yet it is her unassuming, quiet love for Stalker that gives her the courage to sustain such a position.

> . . . Mom used to say, "He's a Stalker, a condemned man, always under arrest, and remember what kind of children Stalkers have . . ." I didn't even argue. I knew all of that—that he was a condemned man, always under arrest, and about the children. . . . But what could I do? I was sure I'd be fine with him—I knew, of course, that there'd be a lot of grief too, but bitter happiness is better than a depressing, grey life—or maybe I just told that to myself afterwards. But he just came up to me and said "Come with me." And off I went. And I've not regretted it once. Not once. I've felt bad, I've felt terror, I've felt shame. But even so, I have never had any regrets, nor envied others—that's just how the fate was, how life was, how we were. Even if our life was without grief, it would not be any better for it. It would be worse. Because it would also be without happiness, and without hope. So.

The simplicity of the Wife's statements, lack of regrets, lack of fantastic crutches, her clear sense of priorities, stand in sharp contrast to the anxious, desire-driven journey of the three men. As we have seen, the men, even Stalker, can only define themselves in relation to The Zone and to desire as something other than themselves. Their subjectivity is defined by this sense of permanent alienation and hinges upon a particular mapping of power for which The Zone itself is an absolute necessity—either as a fantasyland or as the ultimate threat. And while the journey forces the men, particularly the Writer and the Scientist, to confront their own failings and weaknesses, its ultimate function is only to make them acquiesce to the world without. Even for Stalker, for whom the journey is a disappointment—the reminder of the extent to which the world has fallen into materialism, cynicism, and pettiness, threatening the continued existence of The Zone itself—the life outside, the prison, is made bearable only by the promise of yet another trip into The Zone.

Stalker's wife, on the other hand, embraces life with a sublime love for her husband and life itself that allows her to be both open to and accepting of its horrors. Her subjectivity thus seems strangely divorced from the known geographies of power: neither governed by law nor driven by desire to transgress, Stalker's wife cannot be easily located in the world mapped by sovereign claims on bare life. As Alenka Zupancic notes, addressing the Kantian link between ethics and experience of the sublime, the openness to the sublime places the subject both inside and outside the law (1998). According to Kant, the sublime entails an encounter with an event in nature—a thunderstorm, a bunch of moving clouds—that makes us feel simultaneously small and insignificant, powerless vis-à-vis the nature, and aware of our "suprasensible vocation," our internal power, the moral law within us (Kant, 1987). Hence, the subject both is exposed to the law, and is its author: "It is not in so far as he is subject to the law," says Kant, "that he has sublimity, but rather in so far as, in regard to this very same law, he is at the same time its author" (in Zupancic, 1998: 88). However, notes Zupancic, there is one additional condition for the experience of the sublime: "as spectators of some fascinating spectacle of nature we have to be placed somewhere safe, that is, outside the immediate danger" (70). This location, then, "where we are at the same time 'inside' and 'outside,' where we are at the same time the 'insignificant trifle,' the grain of sand that the wild forces play with, and the observer of this spectacle" makes possible a Kantian ethics of respect (ibid.).

In her analysis of the "feminine sublime," Barbara Freeman (1995) also links the sublime to the politics and ethics of respect. The sublime, according to Freeman, always entails an encounter with radical alterity that escapes any representation. Such a notion of alterity "eludes particular ethnicity, sexuality, class, race or geopolitical positioning but implies both a general concept of the unrepresentable as that which exceeds the symbolic order of language and culture, and the particular otherness of actual others, who remain nameless insofar as they are outside its borders" (1995: 11). Hence, the politics of the "feminine sublime" involves "taking up a position of respect in response to incalculable otherness" (ibid.). Or, as Bill Readings put it, a sublime politics does not "attempt to subject politics to the radical indeterminacy of the sublime as a questioning of rules and criteria . . . it is to refuse society as the locus of modeling and authority, to argue for heteronomous community in which there can be no absolutely authoritative instance and no consensus that might legitimate such an authority" (in ibid.: 12–13).

Love thus places Stalker's wife into a safe place that appears beyond the reach of sovereign power and can, for that reason, be regarded as politically subversive. It is difficult to imagine what could possible destruct the Wife's love for her husband and for her daughter. What exercise of power would make her regret her devotion? What threat of punishment would make her question the choices that she had made? Love—and the openness to and acceptance of its horrors—makes her irreducible to bare life and constitutes the base for an entirely different mapping of political power, one where the subject would be the author of the law, where desire would not have to be banished on the other side of the border, where radical difference is treated with respect.

## "ALTHOUGH WE NO LONGER QUITE KNOW HOW TO LOVE . . ."

*What is art? Is it good or evil? From God or from the devil? From man's strength or from his weakness? Could it be a pledge of fellowship, an image of social harmony? Might that be its function? Like a declaration of love: the consciousness of our dependence on each other. A confession. An unconscious act that nonetheless reflects the true meaning of life—love and sacrifice.*

—Andrey Tarkovsky, *Sculpting in Time* (1987: 239)

Tarkovsky's project, as he often stated, was to remind people of their infinite capacity to love. To do so, he chose a path where the aesthetic and the political merge. The function of his art was to invoke an ethics of respect that could only emerge from an encounter with the sublime. And yet the sublime itself could not be represented, only evoked. *Stalker,* therefore, takes an elliptical route: seemingly a film about a journey into a forbidden territory of desire, the film actually circles around the love of the only character that never enters The Zone, Stalker's wife. The Writer, says Tarkovsky, perhaps "sets out for The Zone in order to encounter the Unknown, in order to be astonished and startled by it. In the end, however, it is simply a woman who startles him by her faithfulness and by the strength of her human dignity. Is everything subject to logic, then, and can it all be separated into components and tabulated?" (1987: 199).

The outward-inward journey in *Stalker* is then mirrored in the Tyuchev poem that Monkey, Stalker's daughter, recites at the end of the film. In the first half of the poem, the gaze of the lover surveys the world, leaving an impression that the poet himself is swept away by its power. In the second half of the poem, the lover's eyes are lowered, and the gaze reveals "the somber, dull flame of desire." The panoptic gaze turns inward and finds the blind spot of the Other's desire, the unrepresentable finally at peace with itself.

But can the love of a woman really be a political stance? Can the sublime really cut through the knots of sovereignty, law, and desire? And isn't the position of Stalker's wife simply that of a traditional, faithful Penelope who sits at home and patiently awaits the return of her man? Slavoj Žižek is skeptical about the emancipatory potential of the Kantian sublime. What we encounter in the sublime, says Žižek, "is the basic paradox of Kantian autonomy: I am a free, autonomous subject, delivered from the constraints of my pathological nature precisely and only in so far as my feeling of self esteem is crushed by the humiliating pressure of the moral Law" (1994: 275). Barbara Freeman sees a hidden misogyny in the Kantian sublime and the logic of sacrifice that it entails. "Kant's sublime," she argues, "tells the story of internalized oppression, one of the principal strategies through which patriarchy reproduces itself. In particular, however, it describes a specifically feminine mysogyny, for what it narrates are the conditions under which women learn to do to themselves and other women what society has done to them" (1995: 75). So what is it then that would prevent us from cynically dismissing Tarkovsky's musings about love and sacrifice as yet another attempt of law and patriarchy insidiously to affirm themselves?

Ultimately, nothing, but a warning that we no longer quite know how to love. . . .

## BIBLIOGRAPHY

Agamben, Giorgio. 1997. "The camp as the nomos of the modern," in Hent de Vries and Samuel Weber, eds., *Violence, Identity, and Self-Determination,* Stanford, CA: Stanford University Press, pp. 106–118.

Agamben, Giorgio. 1998. *Homo Sacer: Sovereign Power and Bare Life,* translated by Daniel Heller-Roazen, Stanford, CA: Stanford University Press.

Blaney, Davıd, and Naeem Inayatullah. 2000. "The Westphalian Deferral," *International Studies Review,* 2(2): 29–64.

Bukatman, Scott. 1999. "The Artificial Infinite: On Special Effects and the Sublime," in Annette Kuhn, ed., *Alien Zone II: The Spaces of Science-Fiction Cinema,* London: Verso, pp. 249–276.

Burke, Edmund. 1990. *A Philosophical Enquiry into the Origin of Our Ideas of the Sublime and Beautiful,* edited by Adam Phillips, Oxford: Oxford University Press.

Copjec, Joan. 1994. *Read my Desire: Lacan Against the Historicists,* Boston: MIT Press.

Crowther, Paul. 1989. *The Kantian Sublime: From Morality to Art,* Oxford: Clarendon Press.

Freeman, Barbara. 1995. *The Feminine Sublime: Gender and Excess in Women's Fiction,* Berkeley and Los Angeles: University of California Press.

Goulding, Daniel J., ed. 1994. *Five Filmmakers: Tarkovsky, Forman, Polanski, Szabó, Makavejev,* Bloomington: Indiana University Press.

Johnson, Vida T., and Graham Petrie. 1994. *The Films of Andrei Tarkovsky: A Visual Fugue,* Bloomington: Indiana University Press.

Kant, Immanuel. 1987. *Critique of Judgment,* translated by Werner S. Pluhar, Indianapolis: Hackett.

Le Fanu, Mark. 1987. *The Cinema of Andrei Tarkovsky,* London: BFI.

Nancy, Jean-Luc. 1993. "The Sublime Offering," in Jean-Luc Nancy, ed., *Of the Sublime,* translated by Jeffrey S. Librett, Albany: State University of New York Press, pp. 25–53.

Reuters. 1986. "Obituaries: Andrei Tarkovsky Exiled Soviet Director Made Haunting Films Filled with Symbolism," *The Globe and Mail,* December 30, p. D7.

Rogozinski, Jacob. 1993. "The Gift of the World," in Jean-Luc Nancy, ed., *Of the Sublime,* translated by Jeffrey S. Librett, Albany: State University of New York Press, pp. 133–156.

Salecl, Renata. 1996. "I Can't Love You Unless I Give You Up," in Renata Salecl and Slavoj Žižek, eds., *Gaze and Voice as Love Objects,* Durham, NC: Duke University Press, pp. 179–207.

Schmemann, Serge. 1982. "Some Soviet Films Belie the Old Political Stereotype," *The New York Times,* October 24, Section 2, p.13.

Tarkovsky, Andrey. 1987. *Sculpting in Time: Reflections on the Cinema,* translated by Kitty Hunter-Blair, New York: Alfred A. Knopf.

Tarkovskaya, Marina. 1990. *About Andrei Tarkovsky,* Moscow: Progress Publishers.

Zupancic, Alenka. 1998. "The Subject of the Law," in Slavoj Žižek, ed., *Cogito and the Unconscious,* Durham, NC: Duke University Press, pp. 41–73.

Žižek, Slavoj. 1994. "A Hair of the Dog That Bit You," in Mark Bracher, Marshall Alcorn Jr., Ronald Corthell, and Françoise Massadier-Kenney, eds., *Lacanian Theory of Discourse: Subject, Structure, and Society,* New York: New York University Press, pp. 268–282.

Žižek, Slavoj. 1999. "The Thing From Inner Space," *Artmargins.* Online at http://www.artmargins.com/content/feature/zizek1.html [July 12, 2002].

# Part III

---

*Future Worlds, Alternative Imaginings*

# Chapter 7

## REPRESENTATION IS FUTILE?

### American Anti-Collectivism and the Borg[1]

*Patrick Thaddeus Jackson and Daniel H. Nexon*

The *Star Trek* franchise, which now includes ten films and five television series, has long provided scholars and fans with rich material for the analysis of politics in general, and United States foreign policy in particular. Many argue that specific episodes and/or elements of the *Star Trek* mythology—such as alien races and its historical timeline—endorse, critique, or reflect aspects of U.S. foreign policy. Such interpretations are far from uniform. There may be little doubt that the Klingon Empire in *Star Trek: The Original Series* (1966–1969) [*ST:TOS*][2] and such films as *Star Trek VI: The Undiscovered Country* (1991) corresponds to the Soviet Union and that the United Federation of Planets represents the United States, but is the Cardassian Empire of *Star Trek: The Next Generation* (1987–1994) [*ST:TNG*] and *Star Trek: Deep Space Nine* (1993–1999) [*ST:DS9*] Iraq, Nazi Germany, or does it lack a clear referent? For that matter, what does the Borg, the collectivist enemy par excellence and the most popular antagonist in the *Star Trek* universe, represent? Some suggest the Borg is Japan (Sardar 1999), others Communism (Yates 1997), and cases can be made, for example, for religious fanaticism, Rousseauian democracy, capitalism, forces opposed to multi-culturalism, the fear of being consumed, and globalization.[3]

In this chapter, we explore the evolution of the Borg in *ST:TNG*, *Star Trek: Voyager* (1995–2001) [*ST:VOY*], and the film *Star Trek: First Contact* (1996) [*ST:FC*]. The Borg is a cyborg race—a synthesis of organic material (humanoids) and technology—constituted by a single consciousness. The Borg lacks an obvious referent and has no direct parallels with any human system of government.

In the Borg's first appearance in the *ST:TNG* episode "Q Who?" (5/8/89), it is the radical opposite, or Other, of the explicitly liberal ideals and values of the Federation. As the ultimate collectivist "regime," the Borg lacks any internal distinctions of property, privacy, family, hierarchy, or even individual consciousness. It is so alien that communication with it is impossible. When Captain Picard, commander of the *Enterprise,* asks of Guinan, a character whose species has encountered the Borg before, "How do we reason with them? Let them know that we are not a threat?" she responds, "You don't, at least to my knowledge nobody has so far."[4]

Yet by its final appearance to date in *ST:VOY,* the Borg has altered nearly beyond recognition. The Borg is (are?) now analogous to an insect "hive," complete with "drones" and a "Queen," a tyrannical ruler with a distinctive—and very human—personality. She can be reasoned with, even if she is untrustworthy and malevolent. This transformation suggests that the most interesting question to ask about the Borg in the context of U.S. foreign policy is not what the Borg represents, but how it is *represented.*

Following Jutta Weldes (1999), we argue that artifacts of mass entertainment, such as *Star Trek,* are an important but neglected aspect of the study of world politics. Politicians attempt to sell specific foreign policies to the public, one another, and key constituencies by crafting stories about world politics that imply particular courses of action. What kinds of narratives an audience will accept limits what public policies officials can pursue, and similar constraints also restrict the creators of other products for mass consumption, such as films and television programs. In this way, mass entertainment is an excellent window into mass political culture. It is also an important vector in its production and reproduction. By studying mass entertainment we can gain important insights into the changing parameters—the limits of possibility—of what constitutes legitimate political narratives and also into how such parameters may be reinforced through narrative and story-telling.

In consequence, we should expect to find homologies between dilemmas of representation and story-telling in programs such as *Star Trek* and in U.S. foreign policy. Because *Star Trek* self-consciously engages in political debates—including debates about foreign policy—because it is widely interpreted by its viewers as doing so, because of its status as a "cultural phenomenon" in the United States, and because the Federation is a thinly disguised projection of the United States, *Star Trek* presents itself as an excellent candidate for such an analysis.

We choose to focus on the Borg both because of its status as the most popular enemy in the *Star Trek* universe—an enemy that, as we shall see, was used to enhance the profitability of the *Star Trek* movie franchise and the ratings of *ST:VOY*—and because it began as the ultimate collectivist threat to the liberal-humanist aspirations of the Federation. As such, it focuses our attention on the parametric constraints and opportunities for U.S. foreign policy legitimization created by the fundamental role played by liberal ideology in American identity.

## U.S. FOREIGN POLICY AND
## THE LIBERAL IMAGINATION

*After 200 years, two centuries, she [the United States] still stands strong and true on the granite ridge, and her glow has held steady no matter what storm. And she's still a beacon, still a magnet for all who must have freedom, for all the pilgrims from all the lost places who are hurtling through the darkness, toward home.*

—Ronald Reagan, Farewell Address, 1988

In contemporary American politics, the term "liberal" is commonly used to describe left-of-center Democrats. In contrast, we use it in the political-theoretic sense: a broad understanding of society and politics that stresses (1) the individual, rather than state or society, as the most important unit of political life, (2) freedom of the individual against an arbitrary state, and (3) a theory of history as the progressive emancipation of individuals from tyranny (Hartz, 1955).

For nearly all of its history, the United States has self-identified as history's great experiment in liberty and representative democracy (Foner, 1999). American foreign policy, in turn, is often not simply justified in terms of preserving the security of the United States, but, at the same time, as necessary to safeguard the very existence of freedom and liberal democracy in the world. Indeed, no matter what the specific policy recommended, the notion that the United States has a "manifest destiny" as the embodiment of freedom and liberty is a constant theme in American political discourse. It may justly be termed the "master narrative" of U.S. foreign policy, part of a "whole *matrix,* a manner of interpreting the space and time of 'America'" (Stephanson, 1995: 5). This theme runs through the statements and major speeches of most American presidents and continues to this day. In his 2000 inaugural address, George W. Bush encapsulated the world-historical mission of America: "Through much of the last century, America's faith in freedom and democracy was a rock in a raging sea. Now it is a seed upon the wind, taking root in many nations. Our democratic faith is more than the creed of our country, it is the inborn hope of our humanity, an ideal we carry but do not own, a trust we bear and pass along. And even after nearly 225 years, we have a long way yet to travel."

The suffusion of liberal values and its sense of divine mission tend to make U.S. foreign policy narratives overtly moralistic: cast in terms of grand narratives of "good against evil," "freedom against tyranny," and "civilization against barbarism." George W. Bush's reference in his 2002 State of the Union address to Iran, Iraq, and North Korea as forming an "axis of evil" (Talbot, 2002) is but one manifestation of this Manichean tendency. It should not be surprising, then, that the very existence of collectivist regimes and ideologies constitutes an existential threat to "America." In his "Evil Empire" speech of 1982, Ronald Reagan argued that the "hard evidence of totalitarian rule has caused in mankind an uprising of the intellect and will . . . rejection of the arbitrary power of the state, the refusal to subordinate the rights of the individual to the superstate, the realization that collectivism stifles all the best human impulses. . . ." For most of the twentieth century the threat of collectivism was associated with Communism; many Americans understood themselves as part of an epic struggle pitting freedom and individualism (the United States) against collectivism (the U.S.S.R.).

Nevertheless, liberal values—particularly in the realm of foreign policy—are not without tensions and contradictions. For example, the presumption that liberal values are self-evidently true underscores the possibility that other societies could be more like America in practice if given the proper incentives or tutelage. Hence the familiar spectacle of American presidents making appearances in foreign countries and pressing those countries to enact such liberal social institutions as a free market economy, the separation of church and state, and increased freedom of the press. While many non-Americans resent such actions, in the United States they are usually seen as the simple reaffirmation of things that Americans *know* to be true. America imagines the rest of the world as somehow, at base, just like America—if not for the distortions produced by ideology, corrupt regimes, and the historical effects of culture.

At the same time, U.S. foreign policy has actively supported illiberal and oppressive regimes throughout the world, and even covertly intervened to overthrow democratic regimes (e.g., Rabe, 1988). Such policies are justified domestically and internationally as fights against collectivism and barbarism. Yet it is understandable that many observers find them grossly hypocritical—examples of imperialism by an avowedly anti-imperial power and of deliberate violations of human rights and freedoms by a nation that argues its very existence is about embodying and spreading those values. If such policies were justified on the grounds of simple *realpolitik* rather than liberal morality, the United States might appear significantly less hypocritical. But principles of *realpolitik* are fundamentally illiberal, and thus difficult to justify to the American public (Shimko, 1992).

One general rhetorical strategy used by U.S. officials maintains that a particularly evil individual or group of individuals is responsible for deluding populations into hating the United States. As Kevin Phillips (2001) remarks, "Americans like to personalize war, to give the enemy a human face. It's probably a reflection of American individualism, and it certainly goes way back [in American history]." Hitler and Tojo in World War II, Saddam Hussein in the Gulf War, and Osama bin Laden in the war on terrorism are all examples of how U.S. rhetoric often involves a personal embodiment of evil. To give only one recent example, William Clinton explained his decision to intervene in Kosovo on the grounds that "all the ingredients for a major war are there—ancient grievances, struggling democracies, and *in the center of it all a dictator in Serbia who has done nothing since the Cold War ended but start new wars and pour gasoline on the flames of ethnic and religious division*" (in "The Crisis in Kosovo," 1999, emphasis added).

Not all wars have such singular personifications—neither Korea nor Vietnam did—and they vary in importance, but they also represent one way of resolving the tension between the belief that most people in the world are really just like Americans, and yet many are willing to die in wars fought against the United States. Personalizing an enemy also makes for better drama than fighting against faceless masses. The dramatic aspect of these decisions can be glimpsed perhaps more dramatically in a fictional setting such as *Star Trek,* to which we now turn.

## ECONOMIES OF PRODUCTION AND CONSUMPTION IN STAR TREK AND U.S. FOREIGN POLICY

We draw our inspiration from a number of readings of *Star Trek:* hermeneutic (Conslavo, 1999; Ellington and Critelli, 1983; Helford,

1996), deconstructive (Fulton, 1994; Harrison, 1996), and anthropological (Worland, 1994). But we also propose to analyze *Star Trek* in terms of its formal similarities with U.S. foreign policy consumption and production. The position of the formulators of U.S. foreign policy is not unlike that of the producers and writers of *Star Trek:* they both generate an episodic product for consumption that involves the "emplotting" of various characters and themes in a more or less consistent narrative (Ringmar, 1996). Also like U.S. foreign policy, the success for a season of *Star Trek* is measured through demonstrations of approval, whether passive acquiescence to a novel plot twist or the signaling of active support of (or resistance to) a new initiative via a change in viewer ratings.[5] The primary audience for both U.S. foreign policy and *Star Trek* is the same (the American viewing/voting public); the primary medium through which both creative products—episodes in American foreign policy and episodes of *Star Trek*—are disseminated is the same (television). These relational similarities suggest that the study of one arena may shed some light on the other.

There are certain advantages to studying *Star Trek* in order to generate insight into U.S. foreign policy, as opposed to simply studying U.S. foreign policy directly. In analyzing any episodic product for public consumption, there are at least three sets of factors to consider: those "internal" to the narrative universe that the product participates in, those "external" to it, and those concerned with the "material" production of the product.[6] We refer to these three sets as *narrative* considerations (involving the relationship of a particular episode to earlier episodes and the entire virtual universe that all of the episodes inhabit), *audience* considerations (involving how a particular episode is received by the viewing/voting public, and various ways in which producers and writers attempt to expand the appeal of their product), and *technical* considerations (involving the actual crafting of an episode, and the ways in which produces and writers can reach their audience in the first place). These three sets of considerations interrelate in complex ways, and are often empirically indistinguishable from one another, but can be separated for analytic purposes.

Each distinction is easier to grasp with a product that is understood to be fictional, as the different aspects involved in the production of *ST:TNG* are expressed in rather different language. Viewed with an eye to narrative, *ST:TNG,* the film *ST:FC,* and *ST:VOY,* consist of the adventures of the crews of assorted starships (the *U.S.S. Enterprise* in the former two, the *U.S.S. Voyager* in the latter) in the twenty-fourth century as they encounter alien life forms, pursue goals of scientific discovery, engage in military operations, and enforce Federation law.[7] Viewed with an eye to the audience, *Star Trek*—like all television shows and feature films—is a means of attracting viewers, and thus making money either from box office receipts, sales of commercial advertising slots, or syndication. Viewed with an eye to the technical aspects, *Star Trek* is both limited and made possible by the capabilities of make-up artists, CGI (computer generated images), union contracts specifying working conditions and pay scales, and the like.

These three sets of concerns provide three very different ways of explaining particular events that happen on the show, such as the introduction of a new character or plot twist: as a result of narrative or thematic requirements, as a result of the need for increased ratings, or as a result of technical considerations. These are different sets of concerns, enacted for the most part by different groups of people: for example, writers and actors deal with the narrative while network executives deal with the audience (Poe, 1998: 112–5).

Similar kinds of concerns are also present in the formulation of U.S. foreign policy, but they are harder to distinguish in practice. U.S. foreign policy is justified through narratives, which are sold to audiences in an attempt to appeal to particular constituencies and incorporate their concerns so as to achieve reasonably high approval ratings. There is also a technical aspect, involving the need to express and justify policy in sound bites for distribution on television news, and to do so while looking firmly in control of the situation. These parallels suggest that the study of representational dilemmas in *Star Trek* may shed some light on similar dilemmas within U.S. foreign policy.

## COLLECTIVISM AGAINST INDIVIDUALISM

> BORG: Strength is irrelevant. Resistance is futile. We wish to improve ourselves. We will add your biological and technological distinctiveness to our own. Your culture will adapt to service ours.
> PICARD: Impossible. My culture is based on freedom and self-determination.
> BORG: Freedom is irrelevant. Self-determination is irrelevant. You must comply.
> PICARD: We would rather die.
> BORG: Death is irrelevant.
> —"The Best of Both Worlds (Part 1)" (6/18/90)

"The Best of Both Worlds (Part 1)" explicitly sets the Borg collective against the liberal-humanist values of the Federation, embodied, as always, by Captain Jean-Luc Picard of the Starship *Enterprise*. When the Borg was first introduced in 1989 during *ST: TNG*'s second season—in the episode "Q Who?"—it provided the Federation with "a deadly, remorseless enemy that could not be reasoned with or defeated" (Reeves-Stevens and Reeves-Stevens, 1998: 90). The Borg also provided a way of vindicating the core philosophical premises of *Star Trek*, as the Borg "steal the technology they want" and "fail [sic] to respect the individuality that is so highly prized in the Federation world" (Conslavo, 1999: 142).

Right from the start, the Borg is presented as the extreme limit of what the Federation can handle. The *Enterprise* only encounters the Borg because the god-like alien "Q" wishes to disabuse Picard of his belief that he and his crew are ready to "confront" anything that they encounter. Q counters that "You judge yourselves against the pitiful adversaries you have so far encountered—the Klingons, the Romulans, are nothing compared to what's waiting." To prove his point, he instantaneously moves the *Enterprise* 7,000 light years further on its journey to encounter the Borg.

When it first encounters the Borg, the *Enterprise*'s sensors cannot even detect any life signs aboard the Borg vessel, which Data—an android member of the *Enterprise* bridge crew—speculates may have something to with how the *Enterprise* sensors are calibrated: constituent members of the Borg do not register as separate life forms, because they are merely parts of the whole, "working collectively."[8]

The Otherness of the Borg is initially underlined by Q's observation that the Borg does not fit the male/female dichotomy that is apparently still characteristic of human beings in the twenty-fourth century. When a single Borg drone[9] appears on the *Enterprise* and begins to investigate the ship's computers, Q comments that the drone is "not a he, not a she; not like anything you've ever seen"—which is odd, because the Federation has encountered androgynous species before—and refers to the drone as "it" when warning Captain Picard that the drone might try to take control of the ship.

But almost immediately, this representation proves unsustainable. Q switches to referring to the Borg drone as "he" and the *Enterprise* crew follows suit. Additionally, the crew continues to refer to the Borg remaining on the Borg ship *in the plural,* which implicitly presumes that particular Borg drones *are* individuals—contrary to the notion that the Borg is a collective.[10] In fact, the Borg refers to itself in the plural the only time it communicates with the *Enterprise:* "We have analyzed your defensive capabilities as being unable to withstand us. If you defend yourselves, you will be punished."

Why does this happen? The Borg appear as discrete beings. The individual actors playing the drones are male, and thus the use of a masculine pronoun seems sensible (Conslavo, 1999: 178). These technical and audience considerations surely played a part, and suggest why the Borg appears to be made up of many individuals. The writers themselves choose to have the Borg refer to itself in the plural, perhaps to emphasize that the Borg is not a single individual but a collective (but if it is a group mind, it should be referred to—and should refer to itself—in the singular!). The Otherness of the Borg is difficult to represent even in their first contact with the Federation (and the viewing audience).

These slight tensions are the only presentation elements that deviate from the initial depiction of the Borg as a completely collectivist Other. Q characterizes the Borg as "the ultimate user," interested only in appropriating technology from other species and incorporating it into itself—a consumer of hi-tech products run amok.[11] After beaming aboard the Borg ship, members of the *Enterprise* crew discover a Borg nursery, in which babies appear to be "grown" and are already fitted with mechanical implants.

The Borg adapts to every attempt by the *Enterprise* crew to destroy or disable it; after a phaser blast incapacitates the first Borg drone, a second materializes onboard the *Enterprise* and proves immune to similar attacks.[12] The Borg is the ultimate liberal nightmare: a collective entity that does not suffer from the clumsiness and inefficiencies associated with command economies. Indeed, the *Enterprise* only escapes the Borg vessel when Picard admits to Q that they are out-matched, and Q spirits the ship away to safety. All of these aspects of the episode dramatize the Borg as the limit to the Federation's liberal project: it is not interested in negotiating and has no respect for the diversity of individual lives and species.

At the end of the episode, Guinan tells Picard that Q brought about the Federation's "contact with the Borg much sooner than it should have come," and that now the Borg are aware that the Federation exists and has technology that it can use. "They will be coming," concludes Picard, setting the stage for the Borg's return in a future episode. The Borg thus disturbs the liberal triumphalism implicit in *Star Trek*'s portrayal of a universe in which respect for individual autonomy ultimately solves all problems, and suggests a need for military vigilance even after the "end of history" (Weldes, 1999: 125–6).

But the Borg's status as the mysterious, inhuman Other cannot be sustained. This is not merely because of the nineteenth-century utopian ethos that pervades so much of *Star Trek*, in which everyone has redeeming qualities and can actually be redeemed at some point (Boyd, 1996: 100–2).

The story must also become more "interesting," and the Borg must become more dimensional, in order to hold the audience's attention.[13] Inevitably, this involves personalization. Frederic Jameson observes that the fact that American viewing audiences seem to find personalized dramas more compelling "seems to lie in some generalized ideological incapacity of North Americans to imagine collective processes in the first place, and their tendency, in consequence, to fall back on the emotional securities of individualizing narrative paradigms wherever possible" (Jameson, 1992: 41). Absent the narratological resources to do otherwise and still produce a story appealing to the audience, it is little surprise that the initial representation of the Borg is unsustainable.

Hence the dilemma: representing a collective Other to a liberal audience in a compelling manner would involve breaking down the collective, individuating and personalizing the Borg in a performative contradiction of the assertion that the Borg is a collective. To this we must add the factors of the special-effects budget, the fact that extras cast to portray Borg drones are individual human beings underneath their costumes and makeup, and the way in which a televisual medium accentuates the differences between the individual actors portraying the Borg drones. These tensions among narrative, audience, and technical considerations produce the subsequent Borg episodes in which the collective Otherness of the Borg is gradually called into question through a process of personalization.

## PERSONALIZING THE BORG (I)

> PICARD/BORG: I am Locutus of Borg. Resistance is futile. Your life as it has been is over. From this time forward, you will service . . . us.
> —"The Best of Both Worlds (Part 1)"

The Borg make their dramatic reappearance in the *Star Trek* universe in the final episode of *ST: TNG*'s third season, entitled "The Best of Both Worlds (Part 1)."[14] The Borg's objectives have changed. The Borg communicates with the *Enterprise,* hailing Picard and demanding that he surrender himself to it. This is the first time in the series that the Borg takes cognizance of an individual. It soon becomes apparent, as the Borg explains to Picard, that it is now interested in assimilating the citizens of the Federation, and thus adding their "biological" as well as "technological" distinctiveness to its own.[15]

The Borg captures Captain Picard, transforms him into a Borg drone, and sets him up as a kind of Borg spokesman named "Locutus" who will facilitate the assimilation of humanity: "Your archaic cultures are authority driven. To facilitate our introduction into your societies, it has been decided that a human voice will speak for us in all communications." The episode ends with the chilling sight of Picard, now Locutus, demanding the surrender of the *Enterprise* and uttering many of the Borg catchphrases, including the overtly neo-colonial "Your culture will adapt to service us."

Why this change in the Borg? In the course of the episode—and the subsequent episode, "The Best of Both Worlds (Part 2)" (9/24/90)—the change is explained as a tactical decision: Picard, as Locutus, will simply make the assimilation of humanity easier. No explanation is offered for the larger strategic change in which this decision is located; it is simply offered to us as an unfolding back-story providing some kind of motivation for Borg actions. The Borg asks, through Locutus, "Why do you resist? We only wish to raise . . . quality of life . . . for all species." This, of course, could be the claim of any universalist credo, including liberalism.

Viewed narratively, this episode illustrates and explores two basic *Star Trek* themes. First, alien races, like the Borg, can't be simply evil, but need to have goals and motivations that are at least recognizably human, even if they represent a one-sided exaggeration of some human trait (Poe, 1998: 132–3). In these episodes the Borg suggests a number of themes in human history: imperialism, efficiency taken to an extreme, the submergence of the individual in a larger cause. This is part of the reason why the Borg has been interpreted as representing, for instance, *both* communism and capitalism.

Second, even though the Federation model of organization has drawbacks—demonstrated in the episodes through inter-crew conflict—its celebration of individuality and personal freedom is ultimately vindicated. In Part 2 the Borg's "Achilles heel" is revealed: as an interdependent collective, they cannot leave one of their members behind. There are no individuals who might make sacrifices for the greater good, and by playing on this weakness the Borg can at least temporarily be defeated. After a successful rescue operation that returns Picard/Locutus to the *Enterprise,* Data, the android officer of the *Enterprise* whom Locutus dismisses as "obsolete in the New Order," manages to tap into the link between Picard and the Collective, implanting a command that puts the entire Borg ship to sleep. The strategy is suggested by Picard himself, who has somehow managed to "break through" the control of the Collective and communicate with his crew.

A culture of individuals might have made the decision to sacrifice one individual for the good of the whole (a traditional *Star Trek* theme, perhaps best exemplified by Spock's sacrifice at the end of the 1982 film *Star Trek II: The Wrath of Khan*), but the Borg cannot do this. This kind of rhetorical move is important, in that it simultaneously affirms the capacity for self-sacrifice to the *collective* good while criticizing the collective for its inability to sacrifice the individual. Thus the Federation is shown to be, paradoxically, a collection of individuals capable of sacrificing an individual, but that also values individuals as such. Indeed, it is Riker's decision to retrieve Picard from the Borg ship that sets the *Enterprise's* victory in motion, a decision for which Locutus chastises him: "Incorrect strategy, Number One. To risk your ship and crew to retrieve only one man . . . Picard would never have approved. . . ." Yet Riker's decision is ultimately vindicated, and every episode involving the Borg after "Q Who?" portrays *individual* innovativeness and force of will as the key elements that enable the Federation to defeat the Borg.

From a story-telling point of view, the Borg has to grow as a character: there needs to be a rationale for its actions, even if that rationale is abhorrent to the human characters on the show. Otherwise, the Borg would remain a force of nature, and telling stories about it that would appeal to a mass audience might pose an unsurmountable challenge. It is for this reason that the producers intentionally decided to make the Borg a more "dimensional" villain, exploring its purpose and making it possible to tell more compelling stories about it (Bormanis, 2002). Compelling stories—at least stories that a liberal audience finds compelling—also tend to have villains with faces. Personifying abstract themes and larger causes through a particular individual or group of individuals is often a necessary component of dramatic narratives. It helps audiences build a direct, emotional connection to a particular struggle and also provides them with a physical enemy who can be vanquished—whether in fiction or in foreign policy.

Enter Locutus, the first Borg with a name, and the first individual Borg drone that the audience encounters qua individual. This alteration permits the writers to introduce individual drama into a story about the Borg, without having to confront directly the fact that there are no Borg individuals: Locutus is a special case, particularly since the human whom he once was—Picard—is lionized throughout the episode as exemplary of the best of humanity, a true individual.

Indeed, the two episodes involve at least three levels of complementary struggles: liberal humanism against collectivism, the Federation against the Borg, and Picard against the control of the Collective. In some respects, the last is the central drama of the two episodes. Picard is seized, and outfitted with Borg prosthetic implants, without much trouble, but there is a striking close-up in which we see a tear running down Picard's face as further modifications are performed. Numerous visual and spoken cues suggest that Picard continues to struggle against the Borg—and the Borg is ultimately defeated only because Picard is able to assert his individuality against the Collective and suggest that Data enter a command in their network to put them to sleep.

This partial and temporary individuation of the Borg is a particular resolution to the dramatic difficulty of representing a collective entity to a liberal audience. It is also a resolution of the technical problems of portraying a collective entity on screen: any individual Borg drone that was followed closely with a camera would become, in the eyes of the viewers, a familiar individual. By having the camera follow *Picard* instead, the collective character of the Borg can be preserved. In addition, scenes like those in which Picard/Locutus watches the *Enterprise* on a Borg viewscreen can be staged; the Borg itself would have no need for a viewscreen, as information would simply flow along the pathways of the collective consciousness.

But Locutus, as a kind of Borg/human hybrid, might need such a thing—which is fortunate from a technical standpoint, as a bunch of Borg drones sitting around (they wouldn't need to speak to one another, either) does not make for good television. "I am Locutus of Borg," the phrase with which the assimilated Picard identifies himself, encapsulates the doubleness which makes the episode possible from a technical standpoint: Borg but not Borg, individual but not an individual, Locutus *speaks for* the Borg, and can be filmed as their representative. And since he is portrayed by Patrick Stewart, the actor who portrays Picard, the possibility of his rescue from the Borg is already pre-given in the episode's structure: the camera *shows* him to be Picard, at least at some level, and opens the possibility that he can be retrieved.

## INDIVIDUALITY AGAINST COLLECTIVISM

> PICARD: . . . in the short time before they purge those memories . . . the sense of individuality which he has gained here will be transmitted throughout the Collective. Every one of the Borg will have the opportunity to experience the feeling of . . . singularity. Perhaps that would be the most pernicious program of all . . . the knowledge of self, spread through the Borg Collective in that brief moment, might alter them forever.
>
> —"I, Borg" (5/11/92)

The possibility of rescue from the Borg is further explored in the fifth-season *ST:TNG* episode "I, Borg," in which the *Enterprise* encounters a crashed Borg vessel, one member of the crew of which is still alive, but injured. At the urging of the *Enterprise*'s physician, Dr. Beverly Crusher, the crew reluctantly takes the drone on board.

With the Borg drone onboard, Picard floats a plan to end the Borg threat once and for all: the crew will implant the drone with a computer virus designed to destroy the Borg's neural network and annihilate the Borg. All the officers agree that this act would amount to genocide. Picard defends the plan on the ground that "They have declared war on our way of life. We are to be assimilated," to which Riker adds, "There are no civilians among the Borg." Dr. Crusher responds, "When I look at my patient I don't see a collective consciousness. I don't see a hive. I see a living, breathing boy who has been hurt and who needs our help." She is overruled. Apparently, the rules of *jus in bello* do not apply to a collective. Soon, however, Dr. Crusher's response is vindicated. Separated from the Collective, the drone begins to individuate. By the end of the episode, it—now "he"—has acquired the name "Hugh," has affirmed the individual rights of the crew and rejected the right of the Borg to assimilate them, and has become friends with the ship's engineer, Geordi LaForge.

This episode provides further exploration of the Borg's motivations. Early in the episode, Hugh expresses sorrow at his loneliness: "On a Borg ship we live with the thoughts of the others in our minds. Thousands of voices . . . with us always." As LaForge examines Hugh's prosthetics—seeking to find a way to design and implant a computer virus—Hugh asks him what he is doing. LaForge answers: "Part of what we do is learn about other species," to which Hugh responds: "We assimilate species. Then we know everything about them."[16]

Confronted with Hugh's helplessness and individuality, even Picard discards the idea of dooming the Borg to genocide. Picard pretends still to be Locutus, and commands Hugh to assist with the assimilation of the crew, but Hugh refuses. After their encounter, Picard tells his officers that: "if we used him in this manner, we would be no better than the enemy we seek to destroy" (the rules of *jus in bello* do apply to collectives after all, if those collectives can be decomposed into individuals). It is at this pivotal moment that Picard utters the lines that began this section: individuality "is the most pernicious program of all."

But the drama is not over. Individualism cannot be vindicated until Hugh himself chooses to return to the Collective and thus risk losing his own individuality—a choice necessary to save the *Enterprise* and its crew, who would become targets of the Borg is they were to harbor Hugh. Again, the close connection between liberal ideals and self-sacrifice so common in *Star Trek* appears—the tension between the two resolved here by the imperative that it is the individual who must choose to sacrifice himself or herself.

A combination of technical and audience concerns is also at work in "I, Borg." The camera has already shown Hugh as an individual being—an inevitable consequence of focusing on any actor for a time—and the audience expects individual beings to *be* individuals. The episode shows Hugh's development into just such an individual, culminating in his confrontation with Picard and proof of Hugh's embrace of liberal rights and understandings of the individual: when Picard demands that he help assimilate the *Enterprise,* Hugh replies "I will not."

Picard is shocked at this display of individuality, but the viewers should not be so shocked, because the drone already referred to itself as "I" when asking LaForge "Do I have a name?" Although Hugh refers to himself in the plural ("We are Hugh") from the time of his naming until the scene with Picard, the initial asking of the question reveals the representational paradox: either the drone is *already* an individual, in which case the process of becoming an individual is somewhat secondary, or the drone is *not* an individual, in which case "becoming an individual" is not a very well-defined procedure. The episode, drawing on the audience expectation that individual beings *are* "individuals" underneath their make-up and their culture, seems to opt for the first resolution; this is cemented near the end of the episode when Picard offers Hugh "asylum" should he choose to remain on the *Enterprise.* Over the course of the episode, the Borg have gone from collectivist Other to oppressive social system, a resolution of representational tensions quite different from that which characterized the Borg in earlier episodes.

## AMBIVALENCE

HUGH: Before my experience on the Enterprise, the Borg were a single minded collective. The voices in our heads were smooth and flowing. But after I returned, the voices began to change. They became uneven . . . discordant.

[. . . .]

HUGH: You probably can't imagine what it is like to be so lost and frightened that you will listen to any voice which promises change.

WORF: Even if that voice insists on controlling you?

HUGH: That's what we wanted—someone who could show us a way out of confusion. Lore promised clarity and purpose.

—"Descent (Part 1)" (6/21/93)

RILEY: When we were linked, we had no ethnic conflict. There was no crime, no hunger, no health problems. We lived as one harmonious family.

—"Unity" (2/12/97)

In the two-part episode "Descent" (6/21/93 and 9/20/93) the crew of the *Enterprise* encounter Borg who *are* ruthless, war-like, and clearly individuals—referring to themselves as "I." Picard's hopes in "I, Borg" have backfired: the virus of individuality left Hugh's Borg ship in social and political chaos, vulnerable to the machinations of the android Lore, Data's evil twin. In return for their obedience, Lore promised to make them a "superior" race, fully artificial, but soon demanded "sacrifices" involving horrendous experimentation upon the Borg. Lore aims to make a master race in "his own image," and seduces Data into aiding him. Unsurprisingly, our heroes emerge victorious. Data's "ethical program" is re-booted. Despite his anger at the crew of the *Enterprise*, Hugh aids them in overcoming Lore and his minions. Later, Hugh admits, "Perhaps my encounter with the *Enterprise* effected me more than I realized." The episode ends with Hugh taking up leadership of the remaining individuated Borg, declaring that "Perhaps in time . . . we can learn to function as individuals—and work together as a group."

A similar representation of the potential dangers of de-collectivization occurs in the *ST:VOY* episode "Unity," in which a group of ex-Borg are located living on a planet. Members of the group reveal that when their Borg cube was damaged and the "neuroelectric field" linking them together was disrupted, each of the former drones began to remember her or his individual life from before assimilation, and each also remembered her or his name. What was implicit in the depiction of Hugh now becomes explicit: Borg drones *are* individuals, only restrained and restricted by technology and culture.

However, the episode takes a somewhat surprising turn by emphasizing the *positive* benefits of the Borg link. Narratively, the episode explores the conditions under which individuals would willingly choose collectivity over individuality. The Borg link is shown to have medical applications, as it can be used to regenerate individuals—such as Commander Chakotay, who was critically injured in an early part of the episode. Chakotay's newly found friends, who include a former Starfleet officer, call themselves the "cooperative," which connotes a group of individuals voluntarily joining together for common purposes rather than subordinating their individuality to the group (recall Hugh's aims in "Descent [Part 2]").

The "cooperative" ultimately forces Chakotay to help it re-establish the link in order to bring peace and harmony to the individuated Borg. Another motivation for joining a collective entity is developed during the medical procedure that temporarily joins Chakotay with the members of the cooperative: one former Borg describes the experience of gaining access to the memories and thoughts of a new mind in ecstatic terms. Regardless, the episode ends with a new Borg entity separate from the main Borg collective. (It is of interest technically that we never *see* the people we have come to view as individuals after this occurs; we only *hear* their collective voices wishing *Voyager* well and apologizing for having forced Chakotay to act against his will.) Although this episode seems to invert the conventional *Star Trek* privileging of the individual, in another way it may strengthen it: individuals remain the fundamental reality in the universe, even if they sometimes choose to subordinate that individuality for the sake of some higher purpose—neglecting the fact that the "choice" to re-establish the Collective is made by a select few among the former Borg.

Both episodes tap into American fears in the 1990s about the downside of the collapse of the Soviet bloc. "Unity" rather unsubtly invokes the specter of ethnic conflict that consumed Yugoslavia in the 1990s, while both parts of "Descent" present a Weimar-style scenario, complete with the rise of a fascist leader. But while "Descent" tells the story of the impact of the spread of individuality on a collectivist entity, it is "Unity" that firmly opts to resolve the representational tension involved with the Borg by suggesting that the Borg is constituted by suppressed individuals. When combined with a narrative development introduced in the film *ST:FC*—the introduction of a "Borg Queen"—the representational strategy adopted in "Unity" ultimately leads *Star Trek* to portray the Borg as a totalitarian regime, underneath which fester oppressed individuals struggling to emerge.[17]

## PERSONALIZING THE BORG (II): THE "BORG QUEEN" AND "SEVEN OF NINE"

BORG QUEEN: You imply a disparity where none exists. I am the Collective.
—*Star Trek: First Contact*

SEVEN: When I was first captured by the Borg . . . I was young and frightened. I watched my parents assimilated. Then I was placed in a maturation chamber, and the hive mind began to restructure my synaptic pathways—*purge* my individuality. When I emerged five years later, the turmoil of my forced assimilation had been replaced with order.
—"Collective" (2/16/00)

Viewed in terms of audience responses, the Borg are quite a ratings draw. Their popularity as villains is attested to by the myriad fan web-sites devoted to Borg culture, mythology, and technical details. This popularity is also reflected in two major production decisions involving the shape of the *Star Trek* universe: the decision to give the Borg a starring role in *ST:FC*, and the decision to introduce a new character onto *ST:VOY* in its fourth season: a recovering Borg drone named Seven of Nine.

While both decisions can be explained narratively and technically, the audience dimension cannot be overlooked. The Borg were intentionally written into *ST:FC* in order to "draw in the same audience that found the Borg so entertaining in the television series," an effort to exploit their popularity with fans in order to increase box office revenues (Conslavo, 1999: 133). The strategy was to reach out to core fans of *Star Trek*, who would then talk the movie up and encourage casual fans to see it (Bormanis, 2002). Apparently it worked, as *ST:FC* had a bigger opening weekend and grossed more money in the United States and worldwide than any other *Star Trek* film, including its successor.[18] Although there is no way to be certain how much of this success was due to the Borg's presence in the film, it was clearly a contributing factor.

Similar considerations animated the decision to create the character of Seven: viewer numbers were declining by the third season, and the producers decided to spice things up by creating a new character who would introduce some conflict into the *Voyager* crew by taking on the traditional *Star Trek* role of the outside observer of humanity (Poe, 1998: 348). Eventually they decided that this character should be a human woman who had been assimilated by the Borg as a child, opening the way for the writers to explore her journey back to being human—the ultimate vindication of the Borg-as-oppressors characterization.

While overall ratings do not seem to have changed that much, the character did seem to attract some of that young male audience back to the show, judging from anecdotal comments on web-sites and internet bulletin boards.[19] In addition, Borg-focused episodes of *ST:VOY* generally garnered higher ratings than those episodes immediately surrounding them, suggesting that casual *Star Trek* fans made an effort to watch these episodes even if they were not regularly watching others.[20]

One striking thing about both of these later Borg appearances is the sudden appearance of gender in the formerly genderless Borg, but as a malevolent force. In *ST:FC*, we meet the Borg Queen, who introduces herself to Data by saying "I am the collective" and proceeding to direct the actions of the other drones like an insect queen at the center of a hive.[21] The Queen tries to seduce Data, promising him physical pleasures beyond his android experience if he willingly affiliates with the Borg. The Queen's relationship to the other Borg is never really clarified, although there is some suggestion that she is a gestalt manifestation of the Collective itself.

*Star Trek* writer Andre Bormanis refers to the invention of the Queen as an effort to "create a face at the core of that faceless enemy," and compares her to Stalin, Mao, and "Big Brother": the personality at the heart of the collective Other (Bormanis, 2002). She is the malevolent ruler, able to entice people to give up their individuality (or to take it by force if required), seducing them away from their true (individual) selves. It is in keeping with the general thrust of *Star Trek* that she is killed near the end of the film.

If the Borg Queen is a seductive face of evil, Seven represents the extreme possibility of liberation from the Borg. A human girl assimilated at a young age, she has few memories of her life before the Borg, and initially resists being separated from the Collective and joining *Voyager*'s crew in any capacity. Captain Janeway takes her on as a project, engaging in various techniques to help her recover her individuality; this is a constant theme of *ST:VOY* from the fourth season onward. In various episodes, reference is made to Seven's "liberation" from the Borg Collective, and in an episode entitled "Repentence" (1/31/01), she comes to terms with the things that she did while still part of the Collective by declaring that "I was compelled by the Borg" to do those things, and should not be held personally responsible.

Nevertheless, Seven remains a hybrid, a fact underscored by her vestigial Borg implants, her need to "regenerate" in a Borg alcove every evening, and the occasional crisis in one or another of her cybernetic systems. Eventually she ceases to want to return to the Collective, and accepts her individual status—in the final episode we learn that she will even marry one of the crew members. In effect, Seven is the Borg refugee that Hugh declined to become.

The former drone takes the name "Seven of Nine," her Borg designation, as her human name, even after her "real" human name is discovered by the crew. In subsequent episodes we hear *other* Borg using designations as proper names, sometimes with an additional component designating the "unimatrix" to which that drone is assigned. Seven's full Borg designation was "Seven of Nine, Tertiary Adjunct of Unimatrix 01"; this appears to have functioned like a proper name, as she is portrayed in several episodes having flashbacks to her Borg days *and bearing this same designation.* The change is significant: a designation like "third of five" (Hugh's designation before he is named) seems to be temporary, able to change with the mission, but Borg designations in *ST:VOY* seem more permanent. Once again, individuality lurks just beneath the surface of the Borg, awaiting only the proper procedures to bring it to light.

This theme is explored quite directly in a sixth-season *ST:VOY* episode entitled "Survival Instinct" (9/29/99). In this episode we meet three ex-drones from Seven's unimatrix, who have come looking for her in an effort to determine why they remain linked to one another after their Borg implants have been removed. Through flashbacks, we learn that these drones once crashed on a planet (a situation not unlike that of Hugh) and began to revert to their original personalities when their link was severed.[22] Seven was the most uncomfortable with this and tried to induce the others to return to the Collective. When they resisted, she re-assimilated them herself and *forced* them to do so; this second assimilation produced the additional link.

Here we see more clearly than previously that the suppression of individuality is an artifice, requiring continual maintenance. Ironically, it is only Seven's individual resourcefulness that keeps individuality at bay after the technical failure. Upon remembering this situation (it had been blocked from her memory), Seven feels extremely guilty, eventually helping the doctor to develop a procedure for terminating this second link and administering it even though it will cause the ex-drones to die within a month. "They would choose freedom" over continued life as a linked triumvirate, Seven declares, granting the ex-drones death as individuals rather than life as parts of a whole: freedom at any price, achieved by removing the artificial restraints imposed on individuals.[23]

Perhaps the ultimate extension of this theme, though, is the two-part episode "Unimatrix Zero" (6/24/00 and 8/4/00), which provides the cliffhanger for the sixth season and the first episode of the seventh. In this episode we learn about a rare mutation in some assimilated individuals—including Seven—that allows them to access a virtual environment called "unimatrix zero" during their regeneration cycles. In unimatrix zero, the drones are individuals again; their virtual self-images are bereft of Borg implants, their memories are intact, and they are able to interact autonomously (even forming romantic relationships with others). When they awaken, however, their memories of unimatrix zero are repressed by the Borg technology until their next regeneration cycle, when they find themselves in unimatrix zero once again—with their memories intact. This is a kind of Borg *samizdat* existence, a true private space in which individuality is preserved even though the public face of each drone remains in conformity with the Collective.

We meet the Borg Queen again in this episode,[24] and she acts more like a despot or dictator than any Borg we have previously seen: she is desperately trying to find unimatrix zero in order to eliminate this threat to her "control of the hive mind," and destroys drones mercilessly in an effort to do so. The *Voyager* crew creates a computer virus that will permit those drones with access to unimatrix zero to retain their memories upon awakening (external Western funding of *samizdat* literature?) and thus form a "Borg resistance movement." Although they have to shut down the virtual environment in order to do so, they succeed in enabling some Borg to break away from the Collective and actively resist.

The message is straightforward: individuality lurks at the heart of any collective, both in the form of the evil individual who controls it *and* in the form of the individuality of the members of the Collective that has to be artificially restrained in order for the Collective to exist in the first place. Of course, this means that the Collective wasn't ever *really* a Collective, but only *appeared to be* such before the beneficent intervention of the liberal individualist Self. But such is the representational dilemma of *Star Trek* and American foreign policy alike: representation, at least representation of a genuine collectivity, is futile.[25]

## CONCLUSION

*Star Trek's* resolutions of the representational dilemmas involved in dealing with a collectivist Other parallel the resolutions advanced within the discourse of U.S. foreign policy. Personalization, the interpretation of a collective as made up of oppressed individuals, and the re-coding of groups as mere instrumental conveniences chosen by individuals for instrumental purposes: all of these rhetorical devices make their appearance in official discussions of policy toward communism, ethno-nationalism, radical Islam, and so forth. We have suggested that these devices, and their increasing use over time, arise from tensions between the narrative, audience, and technical aspects of the public representation of a collective entity. Whether the setting is "fictional" or "factual"—itself an unstable and somewhat arbitrary distinction—similar problems and similar solutions reveal themselves. The Other becomes the Self, albeit the Self in an oppressed and twisted form; little wonder that the kind of foreign policy produced by such a stance displays all of the characteristics of a messianic crusade to liberate the Other from itself. In the end, is this all that different from being assimilated into the Borg Collective? Both *Star Trek* and U.S. foreign policy try to maintain that it is, but closer inspection should give us pause.

## NOTES

1. We would like to thank Jennifer Lobasz and Vasu Vaitla for their invaluable assistance in researching this chapter.
2. For the remainder of this chapter we will refer to the first *Star Trek* series as *ST:TOS* and use "*Star Trek*" to refer to the entire "mega-text" of televisions programs, feature films, books, web-sites, fanzines, etc. (Conslavo, 1999: 76).
3. Culled from a Google newsgroup search on April 22, 2002, of the terms "borg" and "represent."
4. All dialog from *ST:TNG* transcribed by "Captain Trekker" online at http://www.angelfire.com/scifi/capttrekker/ [April 25, 2002]. Dialog from *ST:VOY* and *First Contact* transcribed by the authors, except for dialog from "Collective," which was transcribed by Jim Wright. Online at http://www.treknews.com/deltablues/collective.html [April 25, 2002].
5. The production schedule of the *Star Trek* television series is such that there is no time to test-market individual episodes, and consequently the writers and producers rely more on the ratings for a complete season to signal whether they are meeting the expectations of their audience (Bormanis, 2002).
6. This tripartite distinction is based on Conslavo's (1999: 109–11) adaptation of Stuart Hall's work to the analysis of *Star Trek*, although we place less emphasis on what the producers *think* about the audience and more on how the audience *responds* to various episodes.
7. As the Borg did not appear in either *ST:TOS* or *ST:DSN,* we neglect these television series for the purposes of our analysis.
8. Presumably sensors on all Starfleet vessels are recalibrated after this initial encounter, because this problem never seems to recur.
9. Individual Borg are not referred to as "drones" until later in the *Star Trek* timeline, but "individual Borg" raises connotations that are somewhat problematic when discussing the Borg.
10. One should say "the Borg is" rather than "the Borg are," even though the latter is the formulation preferred in *Star Trek*.
11. Borg ships appear in *TNG* as menacing cubes (and in *ST:VOY* and *ST:FC* the predominant Borg ship remains the cube, although a "Borg sphere" is also introduced), perhaps signaling a concern with efficiency over (conventional) aesthetics (Richards, 1997: 45–6).
12. No one refers to this as "adaptation" until a subsequent episode, but eventually the cry of "they've adapted!" becomes a signature part of each battle with the Borg, as some weapon is rendered useless by Borg learning.

13. Andre Bormanis (2002) stressed this explanation of the way that the portrayal of the Borg changed as the series progressed; "interesting" and "dimensional" are his words for the shift.
14. This is the first time that *Star Trek* uses the device of a season-ending cliffhanger, in which the storyline begun in one episode is only to be resolved in the first episode of the next season. Two of the four cliffhangers in *ST:TNG* involve the Borg.
15. The Borg does, however, continue to refer to itself *in the plural:* "*we* will add your biological and technological distinctiveness to *our* own" (emphasis added). If it did not, could it consistently display any interest in individual human beings?
16. Apparently the idea that the Borg merely assimilate technology has been completely dropped by this point.
17. There is something of an irony here, since "Unity" is the only episode of *Star Trek* explicitly to endorse collectivism. However, as Weldes (1999) suggests, all of *Star Trek* contains an implicit endorsement of collectivist themes: from militarism (Starfleet is a military institution) to an economy that bears a strong resemblance to Marxist ideals.
18. Film grosses from the Internet Movie Database, www.imbd.com [February 21, 2002].
19. The producers of *Star Trek* do not release information relating to the demographic breakdown of their audience to the general public. Anecdotally, several of the authors' acquaintances did resume watching *ST:VOY* more regularly once Seven was introduced.
20. Episode ratings data from Arlie's Voyager Page (http://members.aol.com/arlie88/index.htm, [March 11, 2002]). Anecdotally, one of the authors followed this viewing pattern, tuning in for publicized Borg episodes but not for others.
21. An insect queen doesn't actually do this, but it is a common literary device all the same.
22. Interestingly, Hugh only begins to become an individual after the *Enterprise* crew members begin actively to try to socialize him into one. This difference has never been explained within the *Star Trek* mega-text.
23. In the seventh-season episode "Human Error" (3/7/01) we learn that Seven *can't* become a fully human individual since Borg cortical nodes are designed to shut down higher brain functions when a certain level of emotional stimulation is reached. The doctor speculates that this is a Borg fail-safe mechanism for preventing drones from re-discovering their individuality. We have heard hints of this idea before, but this is the first time we really see that Borg technology is explicitly designed to repress individuality *on an individual level.*
24. Actually, we met her once before on *ST:VOY,* in the two-part episode "Dark Frontier" (2/17/99). The precise relationship between this Borg

Queen and the one from FC is never clarified; the issue is made more complex by the fact that they are portrayed by different actresses. The writers try not to be too clear about these details, recognizing that the mystery is sometimes more intriguing to viewers than any definitive explanation would be (Bormanis, 2002).

25. One fan, noting these changes and the trivialization of the Borg threat into "a grudge match between [Captain] Janeway and the Borg Queen," nevertheless defends the trajectory of shifts on, among other things, the notion that the Queen makes the Borg more menacing and dramatic (Wright, n.d.).

## BIBLIOGRAPHY

Bormanis, Andre (senior writer and consultant on several *Star Trek* series). 2002. Telephone interview, February 20.

Boyd, Katrina. 1996. "Cyborgs in Utopia: The Problem of Radical Difference in *Star Trek: The Next Generation,*" in Taylor Harrison et al., eds., *Enterprise Zones,* Boulder, CO: Westview, pp. 95–113.

Bush, George W. 2000. "Complete Text of Bush's Inaugural Speech." Online at http://detnews.com/2001/politics/0101/21/–178375.htm [July 10, 2002].

Conslavo, Mia Lynn. 1999. *The Best of Both Worlds? Examining Bodies, Technologies, Gender and the Borg of Star Trek,* Ph.D. Dissertation, Graduate College, University of Iowa.

"The Crisis in Kosovo." 1999. "The Clinton Years, Nightline Transcripts," March 24. Online at http://www.pbs.org/wgbh/pages/frontline/shows/clinton/etc/03241999.html [July 10, 2002].

Ellington, Jane Elizabeth, and Joseph Critelli. 1983. "Analysis of a Modern Myth: The *Star Trek* Series," *Extrapolation* 24(3): 241–50.

Foner, Eric. 1999. *The Story of American Freedom,* New York: Norton.

Fulton, Valerie. 1994. "An Other Frontier: Voyaging West with Mark Twain and *Star Trek's* Imperial Subject," *Postmodern Culture* 4(3). Online at http://muse.jhu.edu/journals/postmodern_culture/v004/4.3fulton_v.html [February 14, 2002].

Harrison, Taylor. 1996. "Weaving the Cyborg Shroud: Mourning and Deferral in *Star Trek: The Next Generation,*" in Taylor Harrison et al., eds., *Enterprise Zones,* Boulder, CO: Westview, pp. 245–58.

Hartz, Louis. 1955. *The Liberal Tradition in America.* New York: Harcourt Brace.

Helford, Elyce Rae. 1996. "'A Part of Myself No Man Should Ever See': Reading Captain Kirk's Multiple Masculinities," in Taylor Harrison et al., eds., *Enterprise Zones,* Boulder, CO: Westview, pp. 10–32.

Jameson, Frederic. 1992. *The Geopolitical Aesthetic: Cinema and Space in the World System,* Indianapolis: Indiana University Press.

Phillips, Kevin. 2001. "Get bin Laden," *Morning Edition,* (12/11). Online at http://www.npr.org/ramfiles/me/20011211.me.04.ram [April 12, 2001].

Poe, Stephen Edward. 1998. *A Vision of the Future: Star Trek Voyager,* New York: Pocket Books.

Rabe, Stephen. 1998. *Eisenhower and Latin America: the Foreign Policy of Anticommunism,* Chapel Hill: University of North Carolina Press.

Reagan, Ronald. 1982. "Speech to the House of Commons," June 8. Online at http:odur.let.rug.nl/~usa/P/rr40/speeches/empire.htm [July 10, 2002].

Reagan, Ronald. 1988. "Farewell address," at "The Ronald Reagan Home Page: Speeches." Online at http://reagan.webteamone.com/speeches/index.cfm [July 10, 2002].

Reeves-Stevens, Judith, and Garfield Reeves-Stevens. 1998. *Star Trek, the Next Generation: The Continuing Mission,* New York: Pocket Books.

Richards, Thomas. 1997. *The Meaning of Star Trek,* New York: Doubleday.

Ringmar, Erik. 1996. *Identity, Interests, and Action,* Cambridge: Cambridge University Press.

Sardar, Ziauddin. 1999. "Science Friction," *New Statesman,* 12(557): 35–37.

Shimko, Keith. 1992. "Realism, Neorealism, and American Liberalism," *Review of Politics,* 54(Spring): 281–301.

Stephanson, Anders. 1995. *Manifest Destiny,* New York: Hill and Wang.

Talbot, David. 2002. "Axis of Stupidity," February 14, Salon.com. Online at http://www.salon.com/news/feature/2002/02/14/iraq/ [July 10, 2002].

Weldes, Jutta. 1999. "Going Cultural: *Star Trek,* State Action, and Popular Culture," *Millennium,* 28(1): 117–34.

Worland, Rick. 1994. "From the New Frontier to the Final Frontier: *Star Trek* from Kennedy to Gorbachev," *Film and History,* 24(1–2): 19–35.

Wright, Jim. N.D. "Unimatrix Zero, Part II." Online at http://www.treknews.com/deltablues/unizero2.html#Analysis [April 26, 2002].

Yates, Steven. 1997. "*Star Trek* and Collectivism: The Case of the Borg," *The Freeman,* 47(4): 200–2.

# Chapter 8

## THE PROBLEM OF THE "WORLD AND BEYOND"

### Encountering "the Other" in Science Fiction

#### *Geoffrey Whitehall*

This chapter flows from the assertion that the enabling foundational myths of modern world politics have been exceeded, and that an adequate conception of the political, one that is capable of dealing with this profound, yet cliché, condition of indeterminacy, contingency, and change, has yet to be generated. "The problem of the world and beyond" represents an epistemological and ontological crisis whereby contemporary events are exceeding the conventional categories of understanding and action in modern politics. Instead of further denying "the problem of the world and beyond" and offering its eternal reification, simulation, and the violence that follows, this chapter explores alternative ways of dealing with the condition of being (or becoming) *beyond* the limits of modern thought and action. My highest concern is that political responses to "the problem of the world and beyond," contemporary failings of security, are nothing short of fanatic attempts to contain movement, deny change, and ignore anything that is different.

The beyond can be introduced as an affirmation of those aspects of contemporary late-modern, high-capitalist life that exceed modern national forms. Jean Baudrillard's 1988 survey of *America,* for example, presents a radically different account of "the nation" than Tocqueville's conducted in 1831 and Sartre's compiled in 1945. Where Tocqueville and Sartre sought America in tangible institutions, and in attitudes, characteristics, and deep mores, Baudrillard presents *America* as an affirmation of spaces of pure circulation, wrapped in "the exhilaration of obscenity, the obscenity of obviousness, the obviousness of power and the power of simulation" (1988: 27). *America* has overcome the traditional classifications, qualifications, quantifications, and essentializations of national political life. Similarly, a world where meaning can be determined, mapped, and shelved, a world that makes *sense* and can itself be *sensed,* has also been exceeded, overtaken, by (virtual) world(s) of change and movement. Contemporary life is deemed one of speed, not order, where speed "creates pure objects. It is itself a pure object, since it cancels out the ground and territorial reference-points, since it runs ahead of time to annul time itself, since it moves (more) quickly than its own cause and obliterates that cause by outstripping it" (6). A condition of speed generates the problem of exceeding one's condition of possibility. Developing this problem, Jean-Luc Nancy suggests that "there is no longer any world: no longer a *mundus,* a *cosmos,* a composed and complete order (from) within which one might find a place, a dwelling and the elements of an orientation" (1997: 4). Instead, he suggests, "the world of sense is cumulating in the unclear and in nonsense" (9). This non-sense is not an absence of meaning but an excess, what Paul Virilio (1997), referring to the gray matter in the brain, calls gray pollution. This gray pollution, this glut of meaning and information that overwhelms the senses, constitutes "the problem of the world and beyond" and the crisis of the day. *If non-sense, speed, and excess have overwhelmed an ordered world, as the beyond, then how does one make sense of the world?*

This contemporary thesis—that the world of sense has been overtaken by a condition of non-sense and thus created the epistemological and ontological crisis of modern politics—relies on a historically and geographically contingent idea: that for every world there is a simultaneous beyond. Immanuel Kant offers an interesting way to explore this Western framing because of the mutual dependency implied between his system of philosophy and politics. Kant links the modern measures of qualified thinking and acting to his mapping of the "world" (Franke, 2001). The question emerges: How does one begin to think and act when Kant's world has become overwhelmed by this beyond?

In terms of philosophy, the beyond can be said to emerge from Kant's distinction between phenomena and noumena. This distinction implies that there are two aspects of any "thing:" what is knowable (phenomena) and what is not (noumena). Kant calls that aspect of the thing that is knowable an *appearance* and that which is unknowable the *thing in itself.* Together they constitute a matrix of intelligibility: the world is the sum of all appearances. This matrix of intelligibility implies that the noumena, a thing in itself, cannot be understood as being of this world, it exceeds our structures of apprehension.

To every world there is a beyond that cannot be known. The relationship manifests itself in Kant's concept of geography and is enforced through his politics. For Kant, geography is a *propaedeutic* (a preparation) for knowledge. Geography prepares "things," as appearances, making them ready to be experienced or knowable (1972: 67). It prepares a world that is the sum of all appearances and it excludes all that which is unknowable (noumena). Once prepared, this world (of things) can then be known via the *a priori intuitions* of space and time. The world cannot be known *in itself;* instead, it is a presentation of empirical objects and appearances, mapped to serve reason's required unity (Franke, 2001: 163–167). The phenomenal world corresponds to a geographic preparation of phenomenal things.

This relationship between the phenomenal thing and the phenomenal world is concisely summarized in Nancy's statement that "the world is not merely the correlative of sense, it is structured as sense, and reciprocally sense is structured as world" (1997: 6). A tautological relationship emerges: reason affirms for itself that beyond the experienced world there is nothing that can be an object of reason (Franke, 2001: 173). The resulting image of the world is "geographically pictured as an island . . . surrounded by the dark, inhuman and unknowable void of the deep waters" (McGrane, in Shapiro, 1999: 88). Outside Kant's island of reason, the beyond becomes constituted as a realm (the sublime) that is unknowable and excluded from Kant's structure of apprehension and modern matrix of intelligibility (the world). "The problem of the world and beyond" is the idea that *for every world there is always a simultaneous beyond that exceeds human sense and human sensibility.*

It is in this *sense* that the question of how to maintain a coherent, secure, and endurable boundary between world and beyond emerges as a key modern political problem. The modern distinction between the world and the unknowable beyond, which manifests itself in Kant's concept of geography, is enforced through his politics. The question most important for International Relations theory and modern explorations of the political is how the boundary between the world and the beyond, between what is sensible and non-sense, and between what can be known and unknown is to be managed, secured, and disciplined. As contemporary issues concerning global justice, diaspora, migration, finance, trade, tourism, terrorism, entertainment, governance, activism, and urbanism increasingly exceed the explanatory and administrative capacities of disciplines of political studies, the political engagement with "the problem of the world and beyond" becomes more urgent. If this "world" has been exceeded by those noumenal qualities of the beyond, as is suggested, then how does one now make *sense* of world politics? This chapter is an attempt to explore how the concept of the beyond can be used to give world politics, in general, and the political, in particular, specific possibilities. Developing these different uses opens up the political "problem of the world and beyond," makes unfamiliar the reification of this problem as modern state-centric politics, and offers a new possible range of political practice.

## SCIENCE FICTION AS A GENRE OF THE BEYOND

Science fiction can help us think about how the beyond can be used to re-imagine the performances of world politics and the limits of the political. This genre has appeal because the modern political imaginary is so deeply committed to a singular reified world political performance. This performance endlessly secures and manages change, movement, and the beyond within the problematic of sovereignty. It is fair to say that science fiction does not necessarily deal substantively with the complexities of world politics; in fact, its themes are often restricted to sterile liberal constructions (i.e., democracy vs. dictatorship, freedom vs. equality, and exploitation vs. self-determination) that this chapter seeks to displace. This may be a blessing in disguise. Although provocative, we cannot rely on science fiction only as a meditation on contemporary political problems. For the purposes of this chapter, science fiction will be treated as a *genre of the beyond*. On this view, the political appears in the different usages of the beyond and not in the specific details of a story's narrative dilemmas. What is said is less interesting than how the beyond is used.

As a genre of the beyond, science fiction is best introduced, as Carl Freedman (2000: 16) does, through Darko Suvin's distinction between estrangement and cognition (Suvin, 1988). Science fiction is a literary genre that champions the tension between the beyond and the known by offering up imaginative alien worlds to scientific laws and cultural norms and mores (Freedman, 2000: 16). At its most basic level, science fiction cannot assume a world; instead, as Albert Wentland suggests, it must convince the reader to encounter, become, or take part in a created reality (1980: 21). The nature of this created reality of estrangement and cognition can be understood through classifying science fiction, as Wentland does, as either conventional or experimental. Whereas conventional science fiction follows a narrow range of plots and devices that reproduce the basic assumptions specific to the genre, author, or society, experimental science fiction attempts to place the genre, author, or society into a condition of estrangement. In this sense, experimental science fiction is a speculative philosophy that constructs thought experiments in the space between *science* and *fiction*. Experimental science fiction, therefore, is portrayed as a creative and progressive classification of literature that explores the (future) limits of humanity (Wentland, 1980: Chapters 2–3). Science fiction is a genre of the beyond precisely because, as a whole, it seems to value experimental variants of its genre over those that might be considered conventional. International Relations literature, by way of contrast, would celebrate the opposite, offering rarefactions of conventional approaches while isolating dissident and experimental ones (Ashley and Walker, 1990).

While the difference is important, distinguishing between conventional and experimental types of science fiction runs the risk of oversimplifying and reifying the modern resolution of "the problem of the world and the beyond." A modern (Kantian) representational structure is not adequately problematized and treated politically if framed in terms of experimental and conventional worlds. A shift from categorizing types of science fiction, to emphasizing different uses, productions, and practices of language avoids these reifying tendencies. Instead of categorizing genres into different language types (i.e., conventional vs. experimental), I follow Gilles Deleuze and Felix Guattari in exploring the major and minor *uses* of language (Deleuze and Guattari, 1987: 105–106).

The major use of language produces a literature that reifies its own authorization by assuming a constant that serves as a standard measure to evaluate its own authority and domination (Deleuze and Guattari, 1987: 105). It is a literature of sovereignty, capable of resolving tensions between universals and particulars by capturing them in a logic of representation. As a major literature, therefore, it imposes a national language of territory, community, identity, subjectivity, and history onto the unbounded construction of the beyond. It uses a geo-political imaginary to capture the beyond and reify the political and philosophical matrix of intelligibility—the world. For example, when *Star Trek,* a major geo-political literature, represents a planet as a home world with a unified territory, identity, and history, a national language is used to manage the beyond within a prepared geo-political logic of national categories.

Minor uses of language in science fiction encounter the beyond differently. Instead of capturing the beyond in order to secure it, the beyond is mobilized to make major uses of language unfamiliar. A minor literature uses language "as seeds, crystals of becoming whose value is to trigger uncontrollable movements and deterritorializations of the mean or majority" (Deleuze and Guattari, 1987: 106). Breaks, stutters, and openings are mobilized to challenge the ability of major literatures to capture meaning within the limits of its own authorization. For example, in the film *Starship Troopers* (1996), a slaughter of an alien species might re-inflect the dominant images of American foreign policy (i.e., the protectors of peace, justice, and democracy), making these images unfamiliar, contingent, and parochial. The beyond, in this minor use of language, is mobilized to create a critical distance from the dominant stories it seeks to problematize.

In addition, this distinction between major/minor literatures must itself be opened. How to use the beyond, other than as a space of difference to be captured, secured, and mobilized, requires that the beyond *in itself* be affirmed through the political event of encounter. By developing a politics of encounter in advance or excess of these distinctions, the beyond is used differently than in either minor or major literatures. Instead of using language to negate difference by politically securing or mobilizing the beyond, it uses language to encounter difference *in itself* through the Event. *The Martian Chronicles* (1950), for example, affirms different uses of the beyond and collapses the distinction between world and beyond. The political becomes an Event that precedes and exceeds the spatial limits of the world.

## REPLICATING A SYSTEM OF REPRESENTATION: *STAR TREK* MANAGING THE BEYOND

Exploring the galaxy and negotiating with alien cultures makes *Star Trek* interesting and politically rich in itself (see Inayatullah and Newman in this volume). Here, however, *Star Trek* is read as a meta-theoretical project to secure modernity from the conditions under which modernity has itself been exceeded. The possibility of modern existence must be *managed* if the world, as the condition under which both knowing and being human are possible, has been exceeded. *Star Trek* represents the dominant political management of the epistemological and ontological "problem of the world and beyond." It captures the beyond in a modern spatial-temporal matrix of intelligibility (the galaxy). *Star Trek* replicates modern disciplining of modern politics: where the world transcends and grounds all horizons of difference.

As explained above, Kant's politico-philosophical matrix resulted in a division between world and beyond, between phenomena and noumena.

Geography prepares a world of sense that can be understood, reasoned, and grounded. Though he played with the idea of alien life, it exists, allegorically, as a realm of danger that excites speaking non-sense and rouses mere opinion. The voyages of the Starship *Enterprise* have a cartographic mission that, by its very nature, are dedicated to trespassing Kant's epistemological territory of danger: "to boldly go where no one has gone before." *Star Trek* must breach Kant's terrestrial propaedeutic and venture outside the geographic matrix of intelligibility and move into a bewildering expanse of uncertainty and danger.

Although *Star Trek* sheds Kant's terrestrial limit, the *Enterprise* does not senselessly wander in space; on the contrary, the operational imperative of *Star Trek*'s journey preserves Kant's "will to truth" as a galactic "will to map." With long-range sensors and a stellar cartography, its continuing mission is "to explore strange new worlds, to seek out new life and new civilizations." The truth is out there. Immanent to this will to map is the drive to actualize humanity. Humanity, the inner space, is as important a territory to be explored (see Inayatullah, this volume). Kant's securing of reason implies and requires that humanity itself be secured. Beyond the world, the question of humanity's worth, character, and essence is urgent and always on trial. The question is always on the lips of Captain Picard (the Shakespearean–Earl Grey Tea ambassador of humanity), Data (the android who desires to be human), and Q (the omnipotent being with a perverse curiosity about human development). *Star Trek*'s mission, the search for answers to the essence of humanity, is directly connected to the realization/enactment of Kant's reasonable world. It takes the form of *Star Trek*'s galaxy. *Star Trek* seeks the realization of a reasoned and represented galaxy like Kant sought the realization of a knowable world. The project to know the galaxy acts as the space for humanity's universal realization. *Star Trek* manages the human condition in a reasonable galaxy.

The problem of humanity, however, requires more for its actualization than missions, excursions, and episodes. If *Star Trek* is to entertain the problem of humanity by creating knowledge beyond the world, the beyond must be geopolitically captured, transformed, and *prepared* as the world. It is through the political management of the beyond that it is possible to be human beyond the world. *Star Trek* must reproduce how Kant made philosophy and politics mutually constitutive in order to make the will to map and actualization of humanity possible. What makes *Star Trek* itself possible, as a metaphysical resolution of "the problem of the world and beyond," is the perpetual managing, policing, and reifying of the philosophical line between the world/beyond. The distinction between a sensible subject and the subject of non-sense (self and alien) is politically managed in two ways: through a galaxy of sovereign planets and an assumed future history of humanity.

The possibility for knowledge collection, securing meaning, and actualizing humanity within *Star Trek*'s missions requires the simultaneous political securing of a galaxy of sovereign planets. Although the United Federation of Planets seeks to spread perpetual peace, negotiate difference, and promote security throughout the galaxy, violence is never eliminated from the galaxy. On the contrary, it is simply managed, relocated, renamed, and represented. The result is emphasized in Michael Shapiro's statement that "the world in which (Kant) imagines the possibility of hospitality and peace is predicated on various forms of radical non-peace" (1999: 88). The Federation (like the discipline of International Relations), creates both places of peace, justice, and reason inside and zones of violence and uncertainty outside (Walker, 1993). Hence, although every contact on the frontier has the possibility of becoming dangerous, a prior matrix of sovereign relations between M-class planets secures a galaxy for the missionary search for knowledge and peace. True, *Star Trek* is always involved in negotiating differences and dangers; yet, these dangerous differences have always already been resolved and pacified in and through the spatial galaxy represented by the Federation.

Whereas this pacification of danger takes place via sovereignty in modern politics, *Star Trek* uses the Prime Directive. The Prime Directive produces an assumed galactic frame of reference for the *Enterprise* to pursue its missionary quest (its foreign policy) as if it was epistemologically and ontologically secure. The Prime Directive spatially reifies planets in the same way that state sovereignty reifies nation-states. Every culture/race is defined by some essential quality and spatially contained in a home planet, and, in effect, produces unitary alien planets/cultures. In this way the galaxy has always already been secured. Against a heterogeneous beyond, *Star Trek* reproduces an a priori galaxy that negates the possibility of alien complexity, diversity, and encounters (Romulans are from Romulus as earthlings are from Earth). The galaxy is divided between hermetically sealed planets. The beyond, the excess, and the different, meanwhile, are compressed into the performance of the line between world/beyond. Management occurs in this perpetual encounter between "Humanity" and "Alien": *Star Trek* has therefore always already limited the available political possibilities available to the *Enterprise* (i.e., declarations of enmity [die in war] or friendship [become like us]).

In addition to the Prime Directive's spatial order, the beyond is also temporally managed within an anthropological development of human progress. The Federation is also the political embodiment of Kant's cosmopolitan purpose. This teleological horizon of human development simultaneously founds and transcends the cultural divisions between reified planets. *Star Trek* founds a representational hierarchy of time between cultures called the Richter Scale of Culture and secures any temporal uncertainty. The Richter Scale classifies the evolutionary status of each species world.[1] Each alien world is judged against its ability to attain warp speed technology. Thus all species are set in relation to a universal conception of being—galactic humanity. One community dons the normalized title "human," others are left to develop in a shadowy dusk of underdevelopment's galactic dustbin—alien. The result is an "assumed future history" for all life forms (Wentland, 1980: 35). The West has used time to construct a singular direction to history into forms of progress, development, and modernity while negating other directions as stagnation, underdevelopment, and tradition (Fabian, 1983). An assumed future history presents itself as a natural and inevitable path of socio-political (and biological) development. *Star Trek* plots the past-present and future-present of a united singular and unproblematic culture called "humanity." A (Western) version of humanity stands as the measure of humanity, and all others. Through its search for the truth, its will to map the galaxy, humanity will become like "Q" (or are "Q" already humanity in the future?) and emerge as master of the galaxy. The beyond, in terms of unknown but possible futures, is therefore secured in a linear and teleological development toward human potential.

As in the disciplines of International Relations and International Development, in *Star Trek* any encounter with the beyond is always already managed within a prior geo-political system of spatial and temporal representation. The Prime Directive and the Richter Scale secure a Kantian galaxy for *Star Trek*'s missionary will to map and know humanity. The galaxy transcends and grounds all horizons of alien difference. *Star Trek* never comes face to face with an alien. It only encounters itself as alien. It effaces the beyond and as such the beyond is faced with humanity's self-image. This is the modern eternal resolution of "the problem of the world and beyond." *Star Trek* erases different voices, and different ways of being and different political possibilities are precluded. *Start Trek* violates the beyond so as to manage difference and reproduce the normalcy of its own categorical world. However, the beyond need not be used this way. *Starship Troopers* mobilizes the beyond that is erased, silenced, managed in *Star*

*Trek* and puts this humanist project into crisis. *Starship Troopers* subverts what *Star Trek* replicates.

## IRONIC TROPES OF THE SECURE WORLD: *STARSHIP TROOPERS* MOBILIZES THE BEYOND

*Starship Troopers* appears to be conventional science fiction and mimics *Star Trek*'s resolution of "the problem of the world and beyond." Read in the manner of a major literature, *Starship Troopers'* dominant narrative, following Kant, secures a spatialized inter-planetary political galaxy that it then temporally drives, through conflict, toward a horizon of philosophical resolution—knowing the Other. Its political galaxy mirrors the dominant cold war narrative that casts an alien species (the Arachnids from the distant planet Klendathu) as a force that threatens the future of human civilization (as represented by the United Citizen Federation) in "the ultimate showdown between the species." To this end, and in order to secure a galaxy of reason and human progress, the movie casts a group of youth in terms reminiscent of military recruitment narratives (Shapiro, 1998). Fresh out of high school, in search of themselves through love, sex, and excitement, they join the Federal Service to fight the enemy, become true citizens, and "save the world." "Saving the world" results in an epic battle between good and evil in which ultimate violence and power is used to defeat the mindless alien tyranny in the name of human salvation, truth, and freedom.

Notwithstanding the dominance of this reading, *Starship Troopers* can also be re-read as a minor literature deeply invested in examining the politics of security in modernity and displacing the major literature it exemplifies. Instead of *managing* the beyond to justify a geo-political framework (i.e., a world united or divided), the film *mobilizes* the beyond as a creative literary space to disrupt the normalized practice of reading and writing world politics. Whereas *Star Trek* secures a specific representation of world politics, *Starship Troopers* uses the beyond to open world politics to political interpretation. *Starship Troopers,* as a minor literature, recognizes the impossibility of securing humanity's universal realization in the ways that major literatures like Kant and *Star Trek* desire. *Starship Troopers* examines what the political securing of an ontological and epistemological world politics conceals. The beyond can be used as a space through which it is possible critically to re-read and re-write "the problem of the world and beyond." It produces a play of insecurities. Against the over-determined narrative about securing the possibility of reason, humanity, and the world from the wrath of the Arachnids, *Starship Troopers* mobilizes an ironic interpretive strategy that makes unfamiliar modern political readings of security.

Through irony, *Starship Troopers* seeks to unsettle and contest the normalized practices of world politics. As a critical device, irony develops a different epistemological and ontological relationship to the beyond than does Kant's representational world. Instead of managing a philosophical and political matrix of intelligibility, irony puts such productions into question. Because irony targets the dominant structures of intelligibility, often any use of irony is cast as an anti-political, anti-social, and anti-public strategy (Conway and Seery, 1992:2). The typical reaction to *Starship Troopers* said it lacked authenticity and realism.[2] Ironic strategies always run the risk of being branded relativistic and solipsistic because irony operates on the limits of assumed political, social, and public sensibilities. Obviously, this is only a condemnation if the meanings associated with the political, the social, and the public are assumed themselves to be apolitical, asocial, and assumed by public consensus. If, however, these concepts are themselves to be opened to political, social, and public challenge, then irony can be championed as a device that works against the political, social, and public domination of one epistemological and ontological practice over all others.

A politics that uses irony to challenge this domination can take the form of what William Connolly calls a practice of projectional interpretation. As a critical use of the beyond, projectional interpretation (irony) operates "first, by affirming the contestable character of its own projections, second, by offering readings of particular features of contemporary life that compete with detailed accounts offered by others, and, third, by moving back and forth between these two levels as it introduces alternative interpretations onto the established field of discourse" (Connolly, 1992: 145). As a practice, projectional interpretation instills the beyond into spaces of closure. It therefore offers a critical propinquity to the subject being challenged. Grabbed from the unknown, from the space that exceeds Kantian sensibilities, irony forces the beyond into the ritualized practices that over-determine modern politics. It opens the naturalized secured world to a plurality of alternative interpretations.

The film's use of irony is most apparent in the United Citizen Federation's service announcements. The announcements are placed at crucial (and fearful) shifts in the development of the plot (i.e., when going to war). These projectional interpretations remove the viewer from the thick of the plot and, in effect, create moments of rupture in the master narratives of modern politics. In the service announcement "A World that Works," for example, the world political cliché of "good us" against "bad them" is targeted. Specifically, the representation of humanity as an ordered, just, and rational civilization, produced against a swarm of ugly, fearless, and mindless Arachnid warriors, is placed in ironic distance to itself. Playing on the relationship between security and insecurity, soldiers are shown "making a better tomorrow" by teaching children to shoot automatic weapons, laughing at violent behavior, and supplying live ammunition with which children can play. A society obsessed with the illusion of securing external threats in the name of peace is shown steeped in the glorification of deadly weapons, trained killers, and ritualistic violence. The production, containment, and enactment of barbarism are revealed to be central to a system that claims to produce a just and civilized society. Titled "Doing Their Part," another service announcement's voice-over affirms the need for vigilance at home. Human peace, reason, and justice must be secured against the external Arachnid threat. "Doing their part," the viewer watches kids tenaciously squish neighborhood insects on the pavement, their mothers cheering psychotically behind them. Just as the mothers' psychosis reveals that in a rational state lunacy prevails, the service announcement uses irony to open the closed performances of socio-political life to reveal that the politics of security is founded upon the production of insecurity (Dillon, 1996).

Since the service announcements arrive at critical shifts in the film's narrative, irony is used to make the dominant cold war narrative of securing representation in world politics a political problem. This use of the beyond creates a different conception of world politics. Irony is used to implicate *Starship Troopers'* apparently conventional narrative within a politics of critical interpretation. A Kantian world, in which humanity and knowledge are deemed apolitical, becomes the target of critique instead of the model to be reproduced. Where *Star Trek* reproduced a modern world politics, *Starship Troopers* uses the beyond to displace reified world political performances by revealing their contingency. Through the radical phenomenological stance, a pluralist world politics is opened. The meaning of world politics shifts from the conventional reproduction of politics taking place in the world toward a critical engagement with the political productions of worlds.

This radical phenomenological world politics is best introduced through Martin Heidegger's notion of "being in the world." In his essay "Age of the World Picture," Heidegger charts a critical reversal (against Kant's world and the courage to use his own understanding) where the world's structure of involvement becomes that which is targeted for exploration. Heidegger states that

> Metaphysics grounds an age, in that through a specific interpretation of what is and through a specific comprehension of truth it gives to that age the basis upon which it is essentially formed (i.e., the world). This basis holds complete dominion over all the phenomena that distinguish the age. Conversely, in order that there may be an adequate reflection upon these phenomena themselves, the metaphysical basis for them must itself be apprehended in them. Reflection is the courage to make the truth of our own presuppositions and the realm of our own goals into the things that must deserve to be called in question. (1977: 115–6)

By examining how humanity secures the truth of itself in modernity, a Kantian world of representation, that which holds complete dominion over all "things," is first put into question. Heidegger (1969) unpacks Kant's question: What is a thing? Heidegger shows how the question "What is a thing?" corresponds to a specific conception of "Who is human?" (i.e., rational-sensible beings). He argues that Kant's correspondence between a world of things and the human world ignores the political securing of being human in the world. Being human in the world is shown to be a process of "worlding," wherein a specific conception of humanity is made to correspond to a specific conception of the world. In other words, "how humans are" makes possible "how things are" (i.e., appearances). By asking the question "how are we human," instead of Kant's "what is a thing," *being human in the world* is re-made a political problem. The beyond is infused into the world instead of produced as an outer space to be secured through inter-stellar adventure.

Whereas the question "What is a thing?" merely requires *Star Trek*'s implementation of an inter-stellar *order of things* (i.e., humans, planets, and aliens), the question "How are we human?" requires *Starship Troopers* to reflect upon the presuppositions that ground an age (i.e., being human). Although reflecting on societal values often seems more familiar to critical philosophy than science fiction, aspects of both have the potential to take "nothing less than the totality of the human world or social field for its object. . . . that things are not what they seem to be and that things need not eternally be as they are" (Freedman, 2000: 8). With such discursive breadth, *Starship Troopers* seeks to reveal how the knowledge of things (the enemy, the self, the world) is secured.

*Starship Troopers* illuminates the political practices of being human in modernity and hence stresses the political limits associated with the qualifications of political citizenship. As such, *Starship Troopers* draws the viewer, and ultimately the practitioners of modern politics, into a self-critique of the project of being human in the modern world. At one level, as a critique of what it means to be human under modernity, *Starship Troopers* hinges on the successful production of a distant "them," as a threat, and to the production of the close at hand "us," as that which is ordered and good. *Starship Troopers* uses stark contrasts to reveal the production of threats. Presenting humanity with a civilized, intelligent, attractive, caring, and fearful identity, the film uses bugs, horrible disgusting bugs, to solidify sovereignty's ontological difference between friend and enemy (Schmitt, 1996).

On a second level, however, the film's use of irony makes clear that securing "us" is not simply a defensive reaction against pre-existing threats. Instead, security is shown to be intimately involved in the active production of threatening narratives that explain, as David Campbell argues, "who and what we are by highlighting who and what we are not..." (1993: 48). Against, yet within, its clichéd ontological galaxy, *Starship Troopers* mobilizes the beyond to critique this dominant us/them narrative. It seeks to reveal how identity/difference, a relation of fear, founds a political galaxy. Campbell argues that fear is the order word of a security discourse. Historically, a discourse of fear bridged what it meant to be human in the world under Christendom (seeking salvation) and the emergence of modernity (seeking security) as the dominant trope of political life in the sovereign state (ibid.: 51). The church relied on a discourse of fear to "establish its authority, discipline its followers and ward off its enemies," in effect creating a Christian world politics. Under modern world politics, similarly, the sovereign state relies on the creation of an external threat to author its foreign policy and establish the lofty category of citizenship as the only form of modern human qualification (ibid.: 51). The "subject of security (policing modern citizenship in the project to secure society from external threats) is the subject of security" (Walker, 1996: 68).

*Starship Troopers* thus highlights sites where fear is created and conquered as crucial loci of qualified citizenship. The film defines the citizen as someone having "the courage to make the safety of the human race their personal responsibility...." In showing individual fear harnessed in boot camp, war, life, and death, the film produces civic heroes of humanity (Shapiro, 1998; Ferguson and Turnbull, 1998). By identifying fear as citizenship's locus of enunciation, *Starship Troopers* challenges the epistemological and ontological privileges given to citizenship's political status. By

re-writing fear as a discursive production and not essential to human qualification, the dominant narrative of security is jeopardized.

The film also destabilizes the assumed understanding of what it
means to be human under modernity. Simply put, the assumed distance
between human and bug is collapsed. The Arachnid threat, once thought
to be fearless and senseless, is revealed (in the castration, capture, feminization, and probing of the "Brain Bug") to be afraid and intelligent,
just like our heroic human citizens. Finding out that the "Brain Bug" is
afraid does not mean that humanity is winning the war. On the contrary,
it symbolizes a progressive realization that "they" are just like "us." The
problem is, although the human viewer has been cheering for humanity's
conquest over the bugs through violence and science, the modern discourse of security secures for itself the inevitable destruction of both protagonists. At one level, for the film to be successful the audience must
accept that, if humanity is to be saved, some bugs must die. However, at
another level, the movie makes clear that the reverse is also true. Human
life is just as expendable as Arachnid life. Within a discourse of security
the only possible response to a threat is the further securing of security.
A security discourse is constructed as a mutually constituting system of
fear for which the ultimate logical end is the total annihilation of being
itself.

By mobilizing the beyond in the space between bug and human, and
making it a space of critical irony, the dualism between hyper-reified identities begins to collapse. For example, a recruitment officer at the beginning of the film states that our heroes are simply "fresh meat for the
grinder" and, by the end of the film, friends churn friends into "special"
forces to be sacrificed on the front lines. "We're in it for the species, boys
and girls, it's simple numbers" is sufficient to defend the decision of one
friend to send another on a mission with a "low survival probability." Humanity is no different than what it despises. Xander, right before his fearful and intelligent brains are sucked out, accurately articulates the logic of
a security discourses' genocidal ambition: "one day someone like me is
going to kill you and your whole fucking race." No doubt the bugs will be
just as articulate when they are dissected. Both humans and bugs fuel a
politics of security by producing threats that are to be feared. Viewing the
bugs in disgust, humanity fails to recognize its own monstrosity. The
movie dashes any hope of ending a cycle of destruction. The film ends
with the line "they'll keep fighting and they'll win." The viewer is left
without knowing who and what "they" means. The politics of security
leads to the ultimate insecurity of being in the world/galaxy.

By mobilizing this play of insecurities, other possible readings/writings of world politics are not only possible but also understood as radical phenomenological practices of *writing* world politics. For example, the film writes the will to truth as a dominant narrative of modernity. In the overall search for the Brain Bug, so humanity can "probe its secrets," the service announcements repeat the modern scientific mantra "Do you want to know more?" The viewer is always admonished that "once we understand the bug we will defeat the bug." The film also writes important social relations into the mix of high politics. The co-ed shower scene, the interchangeable gender roles of the heroes, and the emasculation and feminization of the Arachnids, interrogate the dominant gender relations in a secured society. The playing of "Dixie" by a Black soldier and the dominance of confederate memorabilia throughout the camp highlights the feeling that our Aryan youth from Argentina, in Nazi S.S. Trooper uniforms, are acknowledging the historical role of racism and anti-Semitism in the creation of secured empires and geo-political strategies. Furthermore, the film writes in class conflict and homoeroticism to round out a montage of pluralistic possibilities of world politics. In other words, by dislodging the dominance of a security discourse, alternative narratives emerge and intertwine to form a pluralistic practice of writing modern politics.

All in all, *Starship Troopers* mobilizes the beyond to unsettle the dominant use of the world/beyond in modern politics. *Starship Troopers* reveals modern productions of truth and humanity in the world. It reveals a structure of involvement that programs like *Star Trek* assume/promote. However, *Starship Troopers'* ironic use of the beyond also has its limitations: What is beyond critique? The politics of critique uses the beyond as if it were a lack, a negative. For example, by bringing the beyond back into the space of the world, humanity is revealed to be lacking its original meaning. The beyond is used to give a critical distance from what it is meant to displace. As a result of this contemporary spatial fetish, *Starship Troopers* also reifies the world/beyond distinction. The beyond remains the negative of the world; it is the external realm of untruth that does not have standing in the modern age. It depends upon prior maps and narratives to demonstrate what is excluded and Other. The world/beyond distinction remains; both seek viable maps of the world. The world is opened only for it to be read more accurately, and then closed. *Starship Troopers* and *Star Trek* use the beyond as a negative space in relation to the positive world to be secured/saved, conquered/liberated, and known/advocated. However, this does not mean that the beyond cannot be used still differently. *The*

*Martian Chronicles* imagines world politics as a temporal practice of encounter, not as a spatial project of displacement, and moves toward a politics of encounter.

## THE POLITICS OF ENCOUNTER: *MARTIAN CHRONICLES* AND THE AFFIRMATION OF THE BEYOND

Written in 1950, Ray Bradbury's *The Martian Chronicles* is obviously not a response to *Star Trek* or *Starship Troopers*. Nevertheless, where both *Star Trek* and *Starship Troopers* use Kant's boundary between the world and the beyond, *The Martian Chronicles* affirms the beyond in itself and, as a result, undermines the perpetual negation in "the problem of the world and beyond." Although a possible geo-political reading of *The Martian Chronicles* holds that it is a novel (as is stated on the back cover) about the conquest and colonization of Mars (or the New World), a different reading (while not denying others) seeks the political, not in a major or a minor literature, but in the virtual *meanwhile*. *The Martian Chronicles* does not manage or mobilize "the problem of the world and beyond" to produce a world or foster critique; instead, it is a temporal framework (a chronicle) that offers "time to encounter" the excessive, non-sensible and contingent beyond. Its temporal narrative structure evades the spatial dominance in *Star Trek* and *Starship Troopers*.

Sensitive to time, the structure of *The Martian Chronicles* demands that the beyond in itself be encountered in a way unfamiliar to geo-politics. Bradbury's temporal narrative denies the prior ontological fraternity (e.g., a world of things or state of affairs) and offers change, indeterminacy, and heterogeneity as a privileged sensibility instead. It is composed of twenty-six vignettes, each with a date starting in January 1999 and ending with October 2026. Each date is understood as an encounter. The encounter for Bradbury is not the meeting of two worlds; it is different from geo-political encounters. He does not depend on a spatialized here/there. Nor does the encounter depend on a linear time, since each encounter can be read on its own or in any order. The location of the encounter is as inconsequential as the year. The encounter needs to be understood with the Event.

Bradbury introduces the Event in his first vignette, "January 1999: Rocket Summer." Whereas, an event (un-capitalized) is an attribute of the material realm defined as a state of affairs, order of things, or world, an Event (capitalized) is expressed by means of language, perhaps about things, but belonging to the incorporeal realm of the proposition (Deleuze, 1990: 4–6). That January in Ohio, "the warm desert air changing the frost patterns on the windows, erasing the art work. The skis and sleds suddenly useless. . . . The Rocket stood in the cold winter morning, making summer with every breath of its mighty exhausts. The Rocket made climates, and summer lay for brief moment on the land. . . ." (Bradbury, 1950: 1). The Event is irreducible to a state of affairs. The Event is not a distribution of "things" in Kant's phenomenal "world"; it is different in kind from Kant's "world." The Event is of another order. It belongs to the temporal order of verbs and becomings. Winter becomes summer, snow becomes hot rain, and snowy fields become green lawns. The Event is the becoming of a "summer day" in an "Ohio winter"—a paradox. As such, the Event exceeds or precedes the Kantian world/beyond because the Event is the "part which eludes its own actualization in everything that happens" (Deleuze and Guattari, 1994: 157). The Event does not take place "within" *The Martian Chronicles,* since this would only be an event within a novel; *The Martian Chronicles* "is" the Event itself. This is not a novel about Earth meeting Mars or about Humans meeting Martians (although they do). To assume these kinds of encounters, with such clear names, identities, and signs, is to assume an a priori world/galaxy in which encounters take place and emerge as appearances. *The Marian Chronicles* chronicle the Events of these encounters.

Using the stoic distinction in kinds of being, the Event is different in kind from the present, past, or future time (Chronos) within which events take place; it is the time of the Event (Aion) (Deleuze 1990:61). Aion is always both infinite past and infinite future. The Event is infinitely divided into past and future possibilities; it is nothing more than a mathematical point, a meanwhile. Deleuze and Guattari explain:

> the event "doesn't care where it is, and moreover it doesn't care how long it's being going," . . . It is no longer time that exists between two instants; it is the event that is a meanwhile [un entre-temps]: the meanwhile is not a part of the eternal, but neither is it part of time—it belongs to becoming. The meanwhile, the event, is always dead time; it is there where nothing takes place, an infinite awaiting that is already infinitely past, awaiting and reserve. (Deleuze and Guattari, 1994: 158)

This meanwhile, this becoming of the Event is not a ground or a foundation—thought it is ontological. Time must not disappear to the dominance of space. The whole is not given; it is an open totality (Deleuze,

1988: 105). The Event is repeated through its different encounters. Molar individuals meet molar individuals (*Star Trek*), molar individuals meet molecular individuals (*Starship Troopers*) and molecular individuals meet molecular individuals. Worlds collide and expectations get "selves" destroyed or killed. Life worlds re-code, over-write, and re-new other life worlds. Whole worlds (both Earth and Mars) are destroyed and created. Worlds are critiqued, examined, held at a distance, and displaced.[3] Each vignette, each encounter, is not a piece of a larger puzzle. They are lines of flight. They do not add up a guiding set of rules, a moral theme, a framework of intelligibility or a structure of intimacy. In other words, *The Martian Chronicles* is a meditation on the beyond in itself. Instead of managing or mobilizing the beyond, *The Martian Chronicles,* as an Event, uses the beyond to affirm a politics of encounters.

The politics of encounter is not about boldly going where no one has gone before, nor is it solely about making old worlds new. Instead, it is about multiplying new worlds that, for a moment, become actual, have existence, and then slip back into the Event. "August 2002: Night Meeting" provides a meditation on encounters. In that chronicle, Tomás Gomez is joined on his way to a party in the blue hills on Mars. While on the road, to pass the time, Tomás reflects on time itself. In his reflection he makes time stand out from space, he demonstrates how to read the world in terms of time, not space. That night Aionic time, the time of the Event, both infinite future and infinite past, is given tangible sense. Tomás says,

> There was a smell of Time in the air tonight. He smiled and turned the fancy in his mind. There was a thought. What did Time smell like? Like dust and clocks and people. And if you wondered what Time sounded like it sounded like water running in a dark cave and voices crying and dirt dropping down on hollow box lids, and rain. And, going further, what did time look like? Time looked like snow dropping silently into a black room or it looked like a silent film in an ancient theatre, one hundred billion faces falling like those New York balloons, down and down into nothing. That was how Time smelled and looked and sounded. And tonight . . . tonight you could almost touch Time. (1950: 80)

Tomás' attention to the complexity of time leads to an appreciation of the Event. He recognizes time as something that exceeds the modern matrix of intelligibility, the spatial strategies of resolving "the problem of the world and beyond" so as to enable/found modern political practice. Fortuitously, as he explains how this night makes the impossible possible, an encounter emanates from beyond the horizon. The encounter emerges from the Event. Deleuze and Guattari explain such an encounter in the following terms: "There is, at some moment, a calm and restful world. Suddenly a frightened face looms up that looks at something out of the field. The other person appears here as neither subject nor object but as something that is very different: a possible world, the possibility of a frightening world" (1994: 17). Tomás had stopped his car to pour himself a cup of coffee and take in the night air. A strange object—jade colored, with red jewels, green diamonds, six legs, and making the sound of sparse rain—passed, carrying a Martian with bright gold eyes. Tomás, out of habit (minus his gun), said "hello." Affirming the Event, instead of containing it by mapping it or by forcing it in-between reified worlds, enables possible worlds to flourish and different worlds to be encountered. The Martian responded, "hello," but their different languages prohibited understanding. When the Martian, always a quick study, learns English, both are embarrassed at the nakedness of their newfound connection and hence their awkward silence. When passing coffee, a token of Kantian hospitality, "their hands met and—like mist—fell through each other." Cold and frightened they stood face to face. They each proclaimed that the other must be dead, a ghost—they both assured the other that they were real, alive, and could feel their own presence. How could they not connect? Again Deleuze and Guattari,

> This possible world is not real, or not yet, but it exists nonetheless: it is an expressed that exists only in its expression—the face, or an equivalent of the face. To begin with, the other person is this existence of a possible world. And this possible world also has a specific reality in itself, as possible. . . . The other is a possible world as it exists in a face that expresses it and takes shape in a language that gives it a reality. (1994: 17)

Accepting the linguistic encounter, the Martian asks where Tomás is from. Not knowing what Earth is, it becomes sufficient to ask when. Resorting to the Event, Tomás explains that the Martians are almost extinct now that humans have arrived two years ago. In disbelief, the Martian proclaims "I'm alive!" When confronted with similar statements by the Martian, Tomás proclaims the same: "I'm alive!" Words failing, they each point to their respective cities, which are full of life and beauty in their own eyes; but each sees the other's city as not there or in ruins. Faced with the question of truth, the Martian proposes that they retreat back to their limited encounter:

Let us agree to disagree. . . . What does it matter who is past or future, if we are both alive, for what follows will follow, tomorrow or in ten thousand years. How do you know that those temples are not the temples of your own civilization one hundred centuries from now, tumbled and broken? You do not know. Then don't ask. But the night is very short. There go the festival fires in the sky, and the birds. (85)

They wish each other well, each driving off to their respective parties, wondering how such a strange encounter could have happened. With both their material and linguistic proofs proving insufficient, all that was left was the beyond, they only had the Event. As Deleuze and Guattari explain, the Event "is a concept with three inseparable components: possible world, existing face, and real language or speech" (1994: 17). Attributing it to a dream or a vision, as a test of the possible worlds, existing faces, and real languages, this encounter has its limits, but the Event re-emerges so Human and Martian become different.

Within the context of the Event, "October 2026: The Million Year Picnic" offers the political possibility of becoming Other. Humanity is becoming meaningless, of the beyond, but because of Bradbury's politics of encounter, it is an affirmative, not a negative, change. Humanity's loss is humanity's gain. "The Million Year Picnic" takes an affirmative approach to what is a dreadful scenario: the Martian Holocaust is coupled with Earth's nuclear destruction. Only two human families are left and they have escaped to Mars. When the second rocket is spotted, the father of the first becomes the future of humanity. Timothy, the son, looks on as the father says,

"Now we are alone. We and a handful of others who'll land in a few days. Enough to start over. Enough to turn away from all that back on Earth and strike out a new line—" The fire leapt up to emphasize his talking. And then all the papers were gone except one. All the laws and beliefs of Earth were burnt into small hot ashes which soon would be carried off in the wind. Timothy looked at the last thing that Dad tossed in the fire. It was a map of the World, and it wrinkled and distorted itself hotly and went— flimphf—and was gone like a warm, black butterfly. (180)

Massumi suggests that the possibility of becoming Other does not involve re-defining, exaggerating, or inventing new identities and categories (1992: 88). Instead, it involves exceeding a grid of representation, a cartographic imaginary, the map, and "the problem of the world and beyond." The laws, the beliefs, the geo-graph are carried off in the wind, an imaginary that Tomás Gomez might refer to as time itself. Becoming-Other does not proceed analogically; it proceeds by potential (97–98). This is different from rejecting direction (103). Direction can only be understood in reactionary terms since it implies a bearing and a true north. A potential is a gathering of encounters from the Event and actualizing a change. It is a line of flight. The family heads to the canal near the ruins so that Michael can see the Martians that he so desperately wants to meet. The last lines of *The Martian Chronicles* read,

> They reached the Canal. It was long and straight and cool and wet and reflective in the night. "I've always wanted to see a Martian" said Michael "where are they, Dad? You promised." "There they are," said Dad, and he shifted Michael on his shoulder and pointed straight down. The Martians were there. Timothy began to shiver. The Martians were there—in the canal—reflected in the water. Timothy and Michael and Robert and Mom and Dad. The Martians stared back at them for a long, long silent time from the rippling water. . . .

Of course the family wanders on human beliefs; they are still a nuclear family. Burning laws and maps does not erase the life world from which they emerge. However, it is a turn away from the limits and direction of humanity and the world toward the limitlessness of the beyond. Instead of managing or mobilizing the beyond to reproduce a sensible world, they are willing to affirm that they exceed the category "human" and embrace its meaningless as the virtual condition under which new and creative possibilities emerge. *The Martian Chronicles* is engaged in creating a new "earth." Meaning is a limiting practice; a meaningless human, is limitless—the Event of becoming otherwise.

## ENCOUNTERING WORLD POLITICS AND THE BEYOND

Recent affairs in world politics suggest that a commitment to anything but the eternal reification and simulation of "the problem of the world and the beyond" is still difficult, if not unimaginable. The war on terrorism or the American missile defense program (among other examples) is representative of the severity of the crisis of thinking beyond the containment and securing of "the problem of the world and beyond." They are fanatical attempts to *manage* the beyond. Such a management would entomb the United States (and later "the world" via the Star Wars program) in an invisible, unaccountable, unintelligible, and unimaginable shield against potential threats from invisible, unaccountable, unintelligible, and unimaginable enemies. The Bush administration is protecting the American imagination from the epistemological and ontological slippage into contemporary indeterminacy. As a major literature, the containment of the beyond must produce a world of states, rogue states, and anti-state actors. If any other beyond is *mobilized* (like that of environmental collapse, global economic disparity, or a generalized malaise in modernity), the strategy of American isolation via missile shields, or a united front, ceases even to register on the scales of efficacy.

Furthermore, wiping traditional threats, terrorists, or even world summit protests off the map and wrapping cartographic security blankets around International Relations' injured tropes only stalls and intensifies impending crisis. Under these conditions, managing and mobilizing conventional maps of the world fail to produce the desired results of creating effective political decisions and affirming alternative political horizons. Instead, strategies of management and mobilization perpetuate universal insecurity and injustice. Negating the Event, they fundamentally miss the opportunity of exceeding "the problem of the world and beyond" in itself. The conditions that make these events possible are ignored, reproduced, reanimated, and reified.

Encountering the beyond as that which exceeds a resolution of "the problem of the world and beyond," first, acknowledges how maps of meaning are perpetually produced, imagined, and insufficient, and, second, affirms possible futures and pasts that evade current structures of intelligibility. To encounter the beyond, therefore, is to activate the political on a temporal horizon of becoming. Instead of assuming a world politics, it makes the world political. It recognizes how each action creates, encounters, and becomes different. An adequate conception of the political, one capable of dealing with this profound, yet cliché, condition of indeterminacy, contingency, and change, must be created instead of further denying and reifying the problematic. It is ironic that one must venture "way out" into the realm of science fiction in order to examine how the beyond is used in everyday life. Only when appreciated in these quotidian ways, in the radical multiplicity of actual encounters, can the practice of world politics be wrestled from the modern political imagination.

## NOTES

1. Debuted in the episode "Errand of Mercy" in the original *Star Trek* series, the Richter Scale contains 45 categories ranging from no intelligent life

form, through technocracy age (Earth), and to the nearly omnipotent (the Q continuum). As a species speeds up, it is deemed to be further up, more modern, on the Richter Scale.

2. See for instance, Edward Johnson-Ott or Jim VanFleet's review at http://www.all-reviews.com/videos/starship-troopers.htm
3. See the vignettes "February 1999: Ylla," "February 2002: the Locusts," or "April 2005: Usher II."

## BIBLIOGRAPHY

Ashley, Richard K., and R. B. J. Walker, "Reading Dissidence/Writing the Discipline: Crisis and the Question of Sovereignty in International Studies," *International Studies Quarterly,* 34(3): 367–416.
Baudrillard, Jean. 1988. *America,* translated by Chris Turner, London: Verso.
Bradbury, Ray. 1950. *The Martian Chronicles,* New York: Bantam Books.
Connolly, William. 1992. "The Irony of Interpretation," in Daniel W. Conway and John E. Seery, eds., *The Politics of Irony,* New York: St. Martin's Press, pp. 119–150.
Conway, Daniel W., and John E. Seery. 1992. "Introduction," in D. Conway and J. Seery, eds., *The Politics of Irony,* New York: St. Martin's Press, pp. 1–6.
Deleuze, Gilles. 1988. *Bersonism,* translated by Hugh Tomlinson and Barbara Habberjam, New York: Zone Books.
Deleuze, Gilles, and Félix Guattari. 1987. *A Thousand Plateaus,* translation and foreword by Brian Massumi, Minneapolis: University of Minnesota Press.
Deleuze, Gilles, and Félix Guattari. 1994. *What is Philosophy?* translated by Hugh Tomlinson and Graham Burchell, New York: Columbia University Press.
Dillon, Michael. 1996. *The Politics of Security,* London: Routledge.
Fabian, Johannes. 1983. *Time and the Other: How Anthropology Makes its Object,* New York: Columbia University Press.
Ferguson, Kathy E., and Phyllis Turnbull. 1998. *Oh, Say Can You See: The Semiotics of the Military in Hawaii,* Minneapolis: University of Minnesota Press.
Franke, Mark F. N. 2001. *Global Limits: Immanuel Kant, International Relations, and Critique of World Politics,* New York: State University of New York Press.
Freedman, Carl. 2000. *Critical Theory and Science Fiction,* London: Wesleyan University Press.
Greenberg, Martin H., and Joseph D. Olander, eds. 1978. *International Relations through Science Fiction,* New York: New Viewpoints.
Heidegger, Martin. 1969. *What is a Thing?* translated by W. B. Barton, Jr., and Vera Deutsch, with an analysis by Eugene T. Gendlin, Chicago: Regency.
Heidegger, Martin. 1977. "Age of the World Picture," in his *The Question Concerning Technology and Other Essays,* translated and with an introduction by William Lovitt, New York: Harper and Row, pp. 113–154.
Massumi, Brian. 1992. *A User's Guide to "Capitalism and Schizophrenia": Deviations from Deleuze and Guattari,* Cambridge, MA: MIT Press.

Matarese, Susan M. 2001. *American Foreign Policy and the Utopian Imagination,* Amherst: University of Massachusetts Press.

May, J. A. 1972. *Kant's Concept of Geography,* Toronto: University of Toronto Press.

Nancy, Jean-Luc. 1997. *The Sense of the World,* translated and with a foreword by Jeffrey S. Librett, Minneapolis: University of Minnesota Press.

Schmitt, Carl. 1996. *The Concept of the Political,* Chicago: University of Chicago Press.

Shapiro, Michael J. 1998. *Violent Cartographies: Mapping Cultures of War,* Minneapolis: University of Minnesota Press.

Shapiro, Michael J. 1999. *Cinematic Political Thought: Narrating Race, Nation, and Gender,* New York: New York University Press.

Suvin, Darko. 1988. *Positions and Presuppositions in Science Fiction,* Kent, OH: Kent State University Press.

Virilio, Paul. 1997. *Open Sky,* translated by Julie Rose, London: Verso.

Walker, R. B. J. 1993. *Inside/Outside: International Relations as Political Theory,* Cambridge: Cambridge University Press.

Walker, R. B. J. 1997. "The Subject of Security," in Keith Krause and Michael C. Williams, eds., *Critical Security Studies,* Minneapolis: University of Minnesota Press, pp. 61–81.

Weldes, Jutta. 1999. "Going Cultural: *Star Trek,* State Action and Popular Culture," *Millennium,* 28(1): 117–134.

Wentland, Albert. 1980. *Science, Myth, and the Fictional Creation of Alien Worlds,* Ann Arbor, MI: UMI Research Press.

# Chapter 9

## FEMINIST FUTURES

### Science Fiction, Utopia, and the Art of Possibilities in World Politics*

### *Neta C. Crawford*

*The function of art and politics is to make people dream, to fulfill their desires (but not to allow their realization), to transform the world, to change life, to offer a stage on which desire (the director) plays out its fantasmatical theatrics. The* operations *common to the dream (or to the symptom), to this art, to this politics must, therefore, be recovered and made manifest. One such manifestation is* critique, *which must now be applied to art and politics.*

—Lyotard, 1993: 41

*Truth is a matter of the imagination.*

—Le Guin, 1969a: 1

What would a world without war or antagonistic states look like? What if morality were the first principle of foreign policy? How could all humans have their basic needs met? These questions imply a frankly utopian agenda, yet utopianism in the study of international politics was dismissed in the 1930s and 1940s, the era when realism became the dominant perspective in the social sciences and public policy. Utopianism also declined in political philosophy to the point where Judith Shklar wrote, "To speak of justice has become intellectually hazardous" (1957: 271). Utopia's fallen place is perhaps well captured by the practice of calling liberal idealists unrealistic utopians, a charge intended to silence utopians. Radical reformers, recognizing the tactic, often take pains to distance themselves from a utopian imagination.

Marx and Engels, for example, called the utopian socialist schemes of Saint-Simon, Owen, and Fourier "fantastic pictures" or "castles in the air" invented by those with a "fanatical and superstitious belief in the miraculous effects of their social science" (1979: 41 and 42). These utopias "reject all political, and especially all revolutionary action; they wish to attain their ends by peaceful means, and endeavor, by small experiments necessarily doomed to failure, and by force of example, to pave the way for the new social gospel" (Marx and Engels, 1879: 40). As Marx and Engels say in *The German Ideology*, "Life is not determined by consciousness, but consciousness by life" (1978: 155). Using a parallel construction, E. H. Carr writes in *The Twenty Years' Crisis*, "theory does not (as the utopians assume) create practice, but practice theory" (1939: 63). And, as Carr says in a continuation of his rhetorical, if not analytic, confusion of idealism with utopianism: "Politics are made up of two elements—utopia and reality—belonging to two different planes which can never meet. There is no greater barrier to clear political thinking than failure to distinguish between ideals, which are utopia, and institutions, which are reality" (93). More recently, in a discussion of the possibilities of creating a just world order, Janna Thompson distances her intellectual program from utopianism even as she proposes a theory of justice: "a theory of justice has to start from where we are, and not with a utopian or abstract ideal of how human beings should live, and therefore it has to reckon with social conditions as they exist and the interests, values, ideas of the self that arise out of them" (1992: 190). Such an admonition suggests that utopias are *too* utopian—that they imply a static, already achieved perfect harmony, peace, and justice—rather than a project or an image of a better place and how to get there. Politicians also eschew utopian labels even as they articulate what might be understood as utopian goals. For example, President George W. Bush told West Point graduates that "America has no empire to extend or utopia to establish. We wish for others only what we wish for ourselves: safety from violence, the rewards of liberty and the hope for a better life. . . . America has a greater objective than controlling threats and containing resentment. We will work for a just and peaceful world beyond the war on terror" (2002).

Scholars of world politics, even those concerned with promoting peace and justice, tend to agree with Marx, Engels, Carr, and Thompson, that utopianism is out of order.[1] However, unwillingness to engage utopias—whether in science fiction or really existing communities—marks a triple hesitation and a deep fear. The fear is that world politics is already a science fiction dystopia, that the clear distinction between science fiction and our present world has dissolved altogether. Or as Donna Haraway argues, "the boundary between science fiction and social reality is an optical illusion" (1985: 66).[2] The science fiction writer J. G. Ballard proclaimed in 1971 that "Everything is becoming science fiction" (quoted in Landon 1991: 327). Writing about Ballard's work, Baudrillard claimed that the "sort of projection, the extrapolation, this sort of pantographic exuberance which made up the charm of SF are now no longer possible. It is no longer possible to manufacture the unreal from the real, to create the imaginary from the data of reality" (1991: 311). SF, Baudrillard argues, is "no longer an elsewhere, it is an everywhere" (312).

Unsurprisingly then, analysts sometimes use science fiction or fantasy images to emphasize the absurdity of political situations. For example, Carol Cohn refers readers to Alice in Lewis Carroll's *Through the Looking Glass* to evoke the character of the language of nuclear defense intellectuals (1987). Similarly, reporter Jane Perlez, writing about war in the former Yugoslavia, says Serbian-held Bajna Luka was filled with "suspicion among ordinary Serbs" in August 1995. "Sadly, one Serbian official said, Banja Luka has come to be like the society the popular science fiction writer Philip K. Dick described in the book *The Clans of the Alphane Moon*. The fictional society is modeled on a mental asylum. The paranoid personalities, being the most intelligent, are the political leaders; the maniacs, with all their energy, are the military leaders, and the schizophrenics are the shapers of ideology" (Perlez, 1995: A8).[3]

Whether or not we live in dystopia, unwillingness to grapple with utopian science fictions signals three hesitations. First, it is a hesitation and failure of analytical imagination. Science fiction, as Weldes suggests in the introduction, may illustrate key concepts of realist and idealist international relations theory, such as the uses of nationalism, balance of power, organizational routines and bias, diversionary theories of war, misperception, and inadvertant escalation (e.g., Greenberg and Olander, 1978). Feminist utopian science fiction explores the ways politics is gendered and how roles, whether in households or between colonizer and colonized, constrain and dispose political actors and facilitate exploitation. It also illustrates how other elements of culture and belief, especially ethno-centrism, militarism, and pacifism, constrain and dispose societies toward war or peace.

But, it is possible to find more than illustrations of existing theories and practices of politics. Utopian and dystopian science fiction can stimulate new perspectives on existing theories, and even fresh insights into the processes and possibilities of world politics. Feminist utopias, like other science fiction, imagine the consequences of present social and technological trends. It goes further, however, by mapping a distinctly different terrain in its analysis of gender and other political and cultural questions. These novels take the givens of our social world(s) and use them as mirror, foil, and canvas. Through the imagining of possible worlds, we may come to understand our own world better, to recognize its historical construction, and to imagine new configurations, possibilities that are not constrained by pre-existing ideas and precedent logics of what is past and considered politically feasible in the here and now.[4] In sum, an out-of-hand dismissal of utopian fiction signals a failure to understand the aims and role of classic and science fiction utopias: they do not project a perfect world only attainable in our imagination, or at the cost of the loss of individual autonomy. Rather, they are a specific form of critique and ethical argument whose purposes are both analytic and emancipatory.

Second, a reluctance to engage the utopian imagination marks an unwillingness to acknowledge that *all* political projects—from nationalism, to liberalism, to socialism—are about creating something their advocates believe is better. Political rhetoric often appeals to utopian possibilities. The question is whether advocates acknowledge their values and whether analysts admit that, implicit in their analysis, they too have an idea of a better world. If utopian aspirations are acknowledged, they can be discussed and debated on their merits; if analysis is always rooted in interests, we would be pushed to admit those interests and make explicit the relation of our work to power.

Finally, rooted in our fear of already existing dystopia, reluctance to engage utopias marks an understandable disillusionment with, and hesitation to engage in, politics. "Unless we admit that the very notion is senseless, it demands at least an ounce of utopianism even to consider justice, and this utopianism . . . is absent today" (Shklar, 1957: 272). After a brief resurgence at the end of the long cold war, optimism has faded. Indeed, the truth of early-twenty-first-century politics is stranger than fiction and concern for the environmental, social, and political future of the planet prompts despair that progress can be made in such circumstances. Rita Manning notes that social scientists are not alone in their abandonment of the utopian impulse: "Philosophers have given over the task of sketching utopias to novelists, but I want to return to it. We can and should offer alternative visions. Perhaps fiction is the best way to motivate the acceptance of such visions, but philosophers can do much to fill in the details" (1992: 29). Despite any injunction to be realist or pragmatic or efficient and eschew utopianism, the incisive analysis, critique, imagination, hope, and attention to emotion characteristic of feminist utopian science fiction may be just the right ingredients necessary to engage and overcome challenges to life and dignity and to fuel struggles for a better world. "The utopian is not a fantasist but a revolutionary" (Goodwin, 1978: 2).

## CHARACTERISTICS AND PREOCCUPATIONS

Utopian fiction portraying another, better place (*topos*) is widely said to originate with Thomas More's *Utopia* (1516), although utopian features are evident in prior literature (Moylan, 1986: 2). Feminist utopias in Western literature date back to the sixteenth and seventeenth centuries. Much younger than utopian literature, the first science fiction novel, Mary Shelley's *Frankenstein* (1818) mixed several genres—romance, horror, and the critical perspective on science and technology that has come to characterize much science fiction.

Discussing early feminist utopias, Jane Donawerth and Carol Kolmerten argue that "women's utopian and science fiction[s] . . . historically speak to one another and together amount to a literary tradition of women's writing about a better place" (1994: 1). What makes feminist utopian science fiction distinctly feminist, despite the genre's variety, is the character of the better place feminists imagine: one "where gender will not be so limiting as in their own experience" (4). The work is characterized by a persistent and insistent ruthless critique of everything—to borrow a phrase from Marx—from business practices, to mental health care, treatment of the environment, social and political hierarchy, and, of course, constructions of gender. Feminist utopian science fiction also offers a ruthless imaginative reconstruction of everything—or nearly everything—and often shares an embrace of anarchy, empathy, and egalitarianism. Not only does the future not necessarily follow from the past, the past could be other than it was—historicity, contingency, and immanent possibility are all emphasized at once in utopian literature. Ursula Le Guin described some of the spirit that motivates this work in an introduction to *The Left Hand of Darkness:*

Science fiction is not predictive; it is descriptive. . . . science fiction isn't about the future. I don't know any more about the future than you do, and very likely less. . . . I'm merely observing, in the peculiar, devious, and thought-experimental manner proper to science fiction, that if you look at us at certain odd times of day in certain weathers, we already are. I am not predicting, or prescribing. I am describing. I am describing certain aspects of psychological reality in the novelist's way, which is by inventing elaborately circumstantial lies. (1969b: E)

We can learn much about the preoccupations of the feminists of an era, and indeed about the preoccupations of a culture, by examining the content of these utopian lies. The preoccupations of feminist utopias have changed over the centuries of their production. Donawerth and Kolmerten, who focus on Europe and the United States, suggest that eighteenth-century feminist utopians were preoccupied with the education and community life of women, focusing in particular on alternatives to traditional married life. Nineteenth-century feminist utopias shifted focus to property rights, divorce, suffrage, and political equality. Non-feminist nineteenth-century utopian authors (Owen, St. Simon, Fourier, Godwin) often viewed science, technology, and industry as the allies of utopian social organization and stressed humanity's rationality and perfectibility (Goodwin, 1978; Donawerth and Kolmerten, 1994). Though *Frankenstein* certainly portrayed science as potentially dangerous, early feminist utopian writers generally held a neutral or benign view of the role of science and technology (e.g., Gilman's *Herland,* 1915). In the early twentieth century, technology was still portrayed as a potential source of liberation, though especially after World War II, when science fiction writers began to understand nuclear weapons and the potential of biological science to transform human bodies and the natural world, the literature became more critical of science and technology (Sargent, 1995).

Feminist utopian science fiction is consistently anti-realist. It persistently challenges core realist assumptions—e.g., that the social world is governed by objective laws of human behavior and that these "laws" are rooted in human nature—and offers alternatives to realist analysis and prescriptions.[5] In realism, human interests are defined as power, decision makers are self-interested rational utility maximizers, morality is basically irrelevant, and politics can be understood apart from economics, culture, and emotions. To the extent that emotions matter at all for realists, the most important emotion is fear. Social life is Hobbesian, characterized by constant insecurity and brutishness, which is only overcome through the imposition of hierarchy, and anarchy is necessarily associated with insecurity. By contrast, feminist utopian science fiction offers counter-narratives based on different assumptions, suggesting, for instance, that human interest is also loving and community oriented, that there is more to decision making than utility maximizing rationality, that while being deeply pre-programmed by their culture, humans are also capable of altering their beliefs, and that morality has a central role to play in domestic and international politics.

In this short chapter I cannot, of course, discuss all recent feminist utopian science fiction or the interesting critical literature on it.[6] I focus instead on four interrelated preoccupations of contemporary feminist utopian science fiction that may be of interest to scholars of world politics and that illustrate its anti-realism: conceptualizations of the political; the role of emotion; militarism and non-violence; and ways to re-make the world.

## CONCEPTUALIZING THE POLITICAL

Realists often conceptualize politics quite narrowly, apart from, for instance, economics, gender relations, and ethics (Tickner, 1988). By contrast, "A utopian typically presents a total social project, comprehensive in its description of social life and organization" (Goodwin, 1978: 7). Personal, family, and community relations, as well as arenas realists more typically consider political (e.g., inter-state diplomacy and war) are imagined in all of their complexity, including their sexuality. Feminist utopian science fiction broadens the understanding of politics by including women and by analyzing power relations in their lives and work. Specifically, the consequences of child-bearing and -rearing, and the potential freedoms of a more egalitarian reproductive social formation, are examined in several recent feminist utopias by positing separatist women's communities or by developing new ways of reproduction. In Mattapoissett, the utopian community in *Woman on the Edge of Time* (1976), gestation occurs outside the mother and child-rearing is a collective responsibility among three parents. In Gilman's *Herland* and Gearhart's *The Wanderground* (1979), men are not needed at all for conception since women have developed the ability to reproduce without men via "parthenogenesis."

Essentialist views of differences between sexes are problematized by positing androgyny, whether in humans, or aliens, or even cyborgs, as in Piercy's *He, She and It* (1991), in which a cyborg has a male form but was programmed to have the sensitivity and empathy often considered characteristic of women.[7] Le Guin's *The Left Hand of Darkness* (1969) is perhaps the most famous example of the use of androgyny or "ambisexuality." The inhabitants of Gethen may assume either male or female physiology randomly during the "kemmer" period, which occurs every 22nd or 23rd day: "Normal individuals have no predisposition to either sexual role in kemmer; they do not know whether they will be the male or the female, and have no choice in the matter" (1969a: 91). Le Guin thus explores "aspects of ambisexuality which we have only glimpsed or guessed at . . ." by imagining the consequences of androgyny. The narrator explains:

> Consider: Anyone can turn his hand to anything. This sounds very simple, but its psychological effects are incalculable. The fact that everyone between seventeen and thirty-five or so is liable to be (as Nim put it) "tied down to childbearing" implies that no one is quite so thoroughly "tied down" here as women, elsewhere, are likely to be—psychologically or physically. Burden and privilege are shared out pretty equally; everybody has the same risk to run or choice to make. Therefore nobody here is quite so free as a free male anywhere else. . . .
>
> Consider: There is no unconsenting sex, no rape. . . . coitus can be performed only by mutual invitation and consent. . . .
>
> Consider: There is no division of humanity into strong and weak halves, protective/protected, dominant/submissive, owner/chattel, active/passive. In fact the whole tendency to dualism that pervades human thinking may be found to be lessened or changed on Winter. (1969a: 93–94)

Humanness and gender are thus simultaneously destabilized. If "men" and "women" can be otherwise, how "natural" were they to begin with? If gender is a social construction, and can be otherwise, so can humans. By making strange the very categories of man, woman, mother, and father through a critique and examination of ideologies and practices of childbearing, child-care, and sex, these authors insist that we see our everyday practices as social constructions and as a performance that might be otherwise. As Le Guin's male protagonist in *The Left Hand of Darkness* comes to realize about his relations with the androgynous Other, such destabilization can, paradoxically, promote understanding. "I saw again, and for good, what I had always been afraid to see, and had pretended not to see in him: that he was a woman as well as a man. Any need to explain the sources of that fear vanished with the fear; what I was left with was, at last, acceptance of him as he was. Until then, I had rejected him, refused him his own reality" (1969a: 248). Conversely, by positing strong female, black, homosexual, or alien protagonists, who must still reckon with racism, sexism, and alienism many years into the future, these authors remind us of the resilience of beliefs and practices and the psychological and political uses of "othering." Politics, thus re-cast, includes the most intimate and routine aspects of relations between people.

## EMOTIONS

While realism ignores or under-theorizes emotion, feminist utopian science fiction suggests that emotional knowledge and feelings are sources of political power as much as rational analytical knowledge. In particular, love, sex, and empathy are a means by which alienation is analyzed and bridged.

While some feminist utopias, especially earlier works, avoid sexual passion—"*Herland* women seem simply uninterested in sex save for reproductive purposes" (Ferguson 1993: 5)—late-twentieth-century novels incorporate love and passion, as relations of power, into their understanding of the structure of politics and the motives for action. The bonds of affection and desire—passionate heterosexual, homosexual, erotic, and platonic love—move people to challenge oppressive social structures, resist exploitation, and create new orders. It is as if these writers had read the poet Audre Lorde's essay "The Uses of the Erotic: The Erotic as Power," in which Lorde argues that "recognizing the power of the erotic within our lives can give us the energy to pursue genuine change within our world, rather than merely settling for a shift of characters in the same weary drama" (1984: 59). Even in Octavia Butler's brutal dystopias *Kindred* (1988), about the American South during slavery, and *Parable of the Sower* (1993), a post-apocalypse California where slavery, robbery, rape, and racism are rampant, love motivates, mobilizes, and elevates.

The focus on empathy in several feminist utopias anticipates work on empathy and the ethics of care in feminist philosophy, politics, and economics that began in the 1980s and 1990s (e.g., Gilligan, 1993; Manning, 1992; Tronto, 1994, Folbre, 2000). For example, Sargent's *The Shore of Women* (1987) explores the emotional content of relations in two separate communities, male and female, where men are moved to tenderness by the sight of brutality and rape, and women have created a harsh society.[8] Butler, in *Parable of the Sower* and *Parable of the Talents* (1998) explicitly tackles the pain and restraint that come from "hyperempathy" through her main character, Lauren Olemina, who feels the physical pain she causes others nearly as acutely as the person she has hurt. "If hyperempathy syndrome were a more common complaint, . . . if everyone could feel everyone else's pain, who would torture? Who would cause anyone any unnecessary pain?" (Butler, 1993: 105). In a land of ecological and social chaos that certainly resembles the contemporary understanding of a Hobbesian world, Olemina's hyperempathy moves her to create a spiritual community that systematically incorporates heightened empathy. In Gearhart's *The Wanderground,* empathy develops into telepathy and a means for others to remember and share their experiences.

Feminist science fiction is not alone in considering the roles of love and empathy, or its absence. Orwell's protagonist in *1984,* Winston Smith, does not develop the courage to rebel against authoritarianism until he is in a passionate emotional and sexual relationship with someone as critical as he is of the state. In Card's *Ender's Game* (1977) ethno-centrism and militarism socialize Ender Wiggin, a child commander, to kill the Earth's enemy, the Buggers, to save it from invasion. Apart from Ender's nascent empathic relation with the enemy, there is no empathy for the Buggers. State and society are thoroughly militarized and militarization and ethno-centrism encourage the complete objectification and homicidal hate that allows Ender to lead Earth's armed forces in the war. Stoic bravery is encouraged and equated with masculinity and Ender's sole empathetic relationships are with the few females in his life. Ultimately, Ender not only defeats the Buggers, but war results in their complete annihilation or "xenocide." Later, in *Speaker for the Dead* (1987) and *Xenocide* (1991), Card explores Ender's developing empathy for the Buggers.

## MILITARISM AND NON-VIOLENCE

While realism accepts violence as natural, most feminist utopian science fiction directly confronts questions of violence and non-violence and many "use persuasion rather than force, to establish order" (Pearson 1981, 67). Feminist science fiction, for example, explores processes of militarization that recall Lasswell's (1941) garrison state hypothesis, Tilly's (1992) observations on war-making and state-making, and Stanley's (1996) articulation of the emergence of "protection-racket" states whose elites manufacture conflict to consolidate domestic power. Le Guin's *The Left Hand of Darkness,* for example, examines the construction of a national identity through war.

> On this basis of material stability Orgoreyn [one power] had gradually built up a unified and increasingly efficient centralized state. Now Karhide was

to pull herself together and do the same; and the way to make her do it was not by sparking her pride, or building up her trade, or improving her roads, farms, colleges and so on; none of that; that's all civilization, veneer, and Tibe [Karhide's leader] dismissed it with scorn. He was after something surer, the sure, quick, and lasting way to make people into a nation: war. . . . The only other means of mobilizing people rapidly and entirely is with a new religion; none was handy; he would make do with war. (Le Guin, 1969a, 103)

And, like post–World War II science fiction more generally, feminist utopian science fiction has dealt extensively with post-apocalypse society. But rather than detailing routes to apocalypse, these fictions often take nuclear holocaust, political disintegration, or environmental disaster as a given, as the background or starting point of their narratives, and emphasize how humans react and rebuild their societies in the wake of destruction.[9]

Feminist utopian science fiction also explores the uses and limits of non-violent resistance. In Slonczewski's *A Door into Ocean* (1986), non-violent Sharers of Shora resist imperialist occupation by Valadon, which seeks Shora's natural resources. Sharers engage in daily acts of non-violent resistance: "people mislaid their passes with disconcerting frequency, and the lower ranked soldiers grew increasingly tired of replacing or enforcing them. The job of soldiers was to besiege cities and bring home fortune and glory, not to issue summonses to barefoot villagers" (199). Many Sharers who choose non-violent resistance to Valadon die. "Each day, two or three natives from one of the Perelion rafts would swim out to Headquarters, from deep underwater to postpone detection until they climbed onto the deck to be gunned down" (348). The strategy is deliberate: "Their motive would have been opaque, except for . . . missives that spread their purpose everywhere. They intended, quite simply, to convince the soldiers to stop killing and go home" (348).

*A Door Into Ocean* thus juxtaposes two worldviews: one society believes that the way to change minds is to use force; the other is non-coercive, believing that only children use force. Each side questions the others' humanity, although most Sharers ultimately come to regard the Valans as mentally ill: "It was understood, now, that Valans suffered a terrible madness because the Death-spirit ruled their souls . . ." (221). Part of the Valan's violence was attributed to insecurity, specifically their fear of what they could not control. "Soldiers feared Sharers, as Sharers feared them. Yet the sickness of the soldiers must magnify their fear and twist it into something beyond imagining. Only this pattern could begin to account for [the violence] that Merwin saw" (320). Sharers debate among themselves whether it is better to resist violently, because the only thing Valans seem to respect is force, or if by doing so they risk acquiring the "sickness" of "deathhastening" (238 and 309). They ultimately, by consensus, choose to continue non-violent resistance.

These works explore other innovative possibilities for resistance to violence and oppressive social orders. Perhaps the most common subversive move is attention to and use of language.[10] In *The Left Hand of Darkness,* Le Guin used the universal pronoun "he" out of an utter refusal "to mangle English by inventing a pronoun for 'he/she.'" But Le Guin later wrote that, though she "still disliked the invented pronouns," she had come to "dislike them less than the so-called generic pronoun he/him/his, which does in fact exclude women from the discourse" (1989: 169). In *Woman on the Edge of Time,* Luciente, an androgynous woman from a utopian community, tells Connie: "To explain anything exotic, you have to convey at once the thing and the vocabulary with which to talk about the thing . . ." (Piercy, 1976: 42). Piercy then introduced the pronoun "per" for "person." In *A Door Into Ocean,* Sharer language uses "wordsharing." The male protagonist, Spinel, struggles to understand wordsharing and finally, out of frustration, asks the character Merwen:

> "What the devil is '*wordsharing*'? Does the word for 'speak' mean 'listen' just as well? If I said 'listen to me!' you might talk instead."
> "What use is the one without the other? It took me a long time to see this distinction in Valan speech."
> Spinel thought over the list of "share-forms": learnsharing, worksharing, lovesharing. "Do you say 'hitsharing,'" too? If I hit a rock with the chisel, does the rock hit me?"
> "I would think so. Don't you feel it in your arm?"
> He frowned and thought of a better example; it was so obvious, it was impossible to explain. "I've got it: if Beryl bears a child, does the child bear Beryl? That's ridiculous."
> "A mother is born when her child comes."
> "Or if I swim in the sea, does the sea swim in me?"
> "Does it not?"
> Helplessly he thought, She can't be that crazy. "Please, you do know the difference, don't you?"
> "Of course. What does it matter?" (Slonczewski, 1986: 36–37)

Suzette Haden Elgin's *Native Tongue* (1984) similarly takes a critical and constructivist perspective on language. In *Native Tongue* the only two jobs women of a certain class may perform are child-care or work as linguists translating between humans and the aliens with whom they trade. The women translators create their own language, Láadan, because the dominant language, constructed by males, does not capture "a chunk of the world . . . that has been around a long time but has never before impressed anyone as sufficiently important to *deserve* its own name" (1984: 22). They attempt to spread Láadan so that, by the second novel, *The Judas Rose* (1987), they may revolt against the patriarchal order. Elgin thus shows how language structures possibilities, and suggests how the creation of an alternative language emancipates women from their subservient roles. Thus, to focus on language is to make a shift from confrontation in the physical world to transformation of the ontological world of knowledge and belief.

## REMAKING THE WORLD

While realism regards the potential for fundamental change as low or non-existent, the characteristic feature of utopian fictions is both a belief that a better world is possible and an attempt to show what a better world would look like. Feminist utopias are often based on egalitarian models of social and political institutions; some are communal and anarchist, such as Le Guin's *The Dispossessed* (1974), and several are separatist.[11] Marion Zimmer Bradley's *The Shattered Chain* (1976) describes a utopian community composed of members of a mercenary guild known as the Free Amazons. As Lucy Freibert notes, even novels with divergent approaches to separatism, child-rearing, and political organization, such as Gearhart's *The Wanderground,* Piercy's *Women on the Edge of Time,* and Gilman's *Herland,* "dispense with private property but provide rooms of their own for everyone," "furnish food, clothing, education, medical care, travel and recreation at common expense," "provide community dining facilities and child-care centers, and extend parenting responsibilities to all community members," and also reduce the fear of rape and assault (1983: 68). Feminist utopian science fiction also often, in re-imagining the world, focuses on the relationship of humans to their environments. For example, in Slonczewski's *A Door Into Ocean,* "Sharers see themselves as part of the web. Every creature has its niche, its function . . ." (1986: 352). And in what could be seen as a post-structural analysis, one of Slonczewski's characters argues, "Power is a 'sharing' thing, even on Valedon. The more power you hold, the more power holds you" (110).

Alternative decision-making procedures are often depicted in these utopias. Feminist philosopher Ann Ferguson describes one decision-making procedure in Gearhart's *The Wanderground* in which "there is a moment when the hill women, who live in a country separated from the urban patriarchal cultures are contacted by the network of 'gentles,' men who are fighting patriarchy from within who want to ally with them." Ferguson notes:

> This causes a huge disagreement in the telepathically connected women's community, and there occurs a town meeting in which both sides mind-stretch their views and feelings to each other but can come up with no consensus. What finally emerges is an agreement that some individual non-separatist women can go to meet with the gentles to form a communication network, but not as representatives of the women's community. This anarchist solution illustrates a creative ethical compromise characteristic of the contemporary women's movements' negotiation of the autonomy for the minority vs. the rights of the community, as represented by the majority. (1993: 12–13)

Alternative forms of decision making are also imagined for the international/inter-world community. An egalitarian international–inter-world organization is developed in *The Left Hand of Darkness* in which the history of inter-world interaction in previous centuries, the "Age of the Enemy," was war and eventually utter devastation. In its aftermath, 84 surviving worlds create an "Ekumen" or household arrangement to manage their affairs.

> "But the Ekumen is not essentially a government at all. It is an attempt to reunify the mystical with the political, and as such is of course mostly a failure; but its failure has done more good for humanity so far than the successes of its predecessors. It is a society and it has, at least potentially, a culture. It is a form of education; in one aspect, it's a sort of very large school. . . . The motives of communication and cooperation are its essence, and therefore in another aspect it's a league or union of worlds, possessing some degree of centralized conventional organization. It's this aspect, the League, that I now represent. The Ekumen as a political entity functions through coordination, not by rule. It does not enforce laws; decisions are reached by council and consent, not by consensus or command. As an economic entity it is immensely active, looking after interworld communication, keeping a balance of trade among the Eighty worlds. . . ."
> "What do you mean, it doesn't enforce its laws?" . . .

"It hasn't any. Member states follow their own laws; when they clash the Ekumen mediates, attempts to make a legal or ethical adjustment or collation or choice. . . ." (Le Guin, 1969a: 137)

## THE OPERATIONS COMMON TO THESE LIES

The operations of feminist utopian science fiction, and other science fiction, that enable its critique and vision are similar to the operations of critical theory and post-structural analysis. As with critical theory, the reader's present is deconstructed or destabilized through utopian science fiction's narrative techniques of extrapolation and estrangement (Suvin, 1979; Moylan, 1986; Wolmark, 1994; Freedman, 2000). Feminist utopian science fiction goes beyond critical theory, however, when new possibilities are imagined and new worlds institutionalized or "realized" so that we can see how they work (and fail) in the long run. Feminist utopian science fiction is thus similar to other forms of ethical argument that engage in deconstruction, reconstruction, and institutionalization (Crawford, 2002).

Extrapolation, one central tool of science fiction, is a crucial tool for deconstruction. David Brin's *Earth* (1991) is a brilliant example. Post-greenhouse effect environmental change has altered human life, ecological disasters loom, alienation is profound, and the communication revolution is exemplified in a global computer "net" that enables radical grassroots organizing. In *Earth,* authoritarian governments are less the dangerous entities than are multi-national corporations and mercenary organizations. Brin poses the possibilities of Earth being destroyed by humans through reckless disregard for the planet, or humans destroying themselves, and Earth long outlasting humans. Piercy's *He, She and It* also extrapolates environmental disaster and dangerous multi-national corporations as the setting for an examination of what it means to be human. Sheri Tepper's *The Gate to Women's Country* (1988) accepts traditional conceptions of women as nurturers and men as warriors and, through extrapolation, imagines the consequences of these characteristics if men and women live in separate communities. Le Guin agrees that "Science fiction is often described, and even defined as extrapolative." She says:

The science fiction writer is supposed to take a trend or phenomenon of the here-and-now, purify and intensify it for dramatic effect, and extend it into the future. "If this goes on, this is what will happen." A prediction is made. Method and result much resemble those of a scientist who feeds large doses of a purified and concentrated food additive to mice, in order to predict what may happen to people who eat it in small quantities for a long time. The outcome seems almost inevitably to be cancer. So does the outcome of extrapolation. Strict extrapolative works of science fiction generally arrive about where the Club of Rome arrives: somewhere between the gradual extinction of human liberty and the total extinction of terrestrial life. (1969b: A)

Extrapolation is the critique of a mirror. It is diagnosis through intensive magnification and examination of the likely consequences of present practices and policies. "We see in fiction what we refuse to see in the real world" (Miller, 1998: 352).

Estrangement is another operation of critique. Much of feminist utopian writing uses, for example, the literary device of a stranger traveling to that better place.[12] The participant-observer, not uncommonly a male who stumbles onto the feminist utopia with little or no prior knowledge of the community, is displaced. Through fumbling comprehension, the participant-observer explains the better place to us. In seeing the Other, and admitting how hard that seeing is, the stranger sees himself (or herself) more clearly. This is the mirror, foil, and canvas of the Other. Self and Other are re-interpreted, as Cornell (2001) argues, through an encounter that both allows and requires change. Simultaneously, readers become participant-observers, and through estrangement our own world is defamiliarized and a new world imagined.

Patai, Suvin, and others argue that utopian science fiction's "extraordinary capacity for moving the reader to new awareness" (Patai, 1983: 151) comes from this defamiliarization, or estrangement. Defamiliarization and estrangement work by making norms—dominant practices and expectations—seem strange, less taken for granted, thereby unsettling both the present and future. This is how androgyny, for instance, works to decenter and destabilize our usual understandings of gender. Similarly, the problematization of language works to estrange in *Native Tongue* and *A Door into Ocean*. The estrangement is doubled in *utopian* science fiction—the place is not only other, but also better in important respects than we would hope for in our own world.

Holistic reconstruction is crucial to feminist utopian science fiction's insistently anti-realist perspective. Feminist utopias are not just interesting, then, because they are imaginative works by women, but because they might contribute to the making of the future. Here, the fixes are not militarist or solely technical and economic; they are about social practices and cultural meanings, helping activists devise new strategies and social relations. For instance, Ann Ferguson derives the idea of oppositional communities from feminist utopias:

> to empower and change ourselves into effective social change agents we have to place ourselves in chosen oppositional communities or networks which oppose existing white supremacist capitalist patriarchal values. These should allow us to develop a concrete set of social practices in which we are supported for developing both autonomy and nurturance, both assertiveness and responsiveness, both analytical clarity or abstract argumentation and intuition where they are relevant. (1993: 19–20)

Thus, feminist utopian science fiction operates as ethical argument that, like most radical literature, stresses critique. Yet it also always offers an alternative practical and ethical argument in a thoroughly developed, if imagined, world. The sometimes explicit utopian versus dystopian contrasts, for example in *Woman on the Edge of Time, A Door Into Ocean,* and *The Dispossessed,* are part of this dialogue of critique and possibility that form the core of the ethical arguments of these works. "Liberation rests on the construction of the consciousness, the imaginative apprehension of oppression, and so of possibility" (Haraway, 1985: 66).

These ethical arguments are not always conclusive. Feminist utopian science fiction writers do not, as a group, share the nineteenth-century post-enlightenment utopians' belief in the perfectibility and rationality of humanity (see Goodwin, 1978: 4). They do not always, in their imagined institutionalization of the better place, neatly resolve dilemmas, such as reconciling "the value of liberty or autonomy with the value of community" (Ferguson, 1993: 7). Nor do they always tell readers how to get from the here and now to the better there and then. The utopias are not entirely pastoral and harmonious; almost all include conflict, dilemmas of conformity within community, and mechanisms for dispute resolution in the recognition that there will be disputes.[13] Octavia Butler's novels often, for example, lean more on the side of dystopia. But feminist science fiction does articulate the dilemmas of the here and now and give hope—often humorous and imaginative—for their solution. Science fiction, especially feminist utopian science fiction, is still a topos—a place that is elsewhere, still Other, still alien—and this is the source of the power of its critique and vision. These are better places, not perfect places. In sum, the operations common to these dreams are extrapolation, estrangement, and defamiliarization—operations of critique that probably could not move us without their emotional engagement, passion, and hopeful reconstruction.

They are ethical arguments that provide the impetus for and content of a better place.

## LOOKING FORWARD

> *Consistent realism excludes four things which appear to be essential ingredients of all effective political thinking: a finite goal, an emotional appeal, a right of moral judgment and a ground for action. . . . any sound political thought must be based on elements of both utopia and reality. (Carr, 1939: 89 and 93)*

International relations theorists are, with rare exceptions, rightly obsessed with analysis of the present order. Realists tend to take too much for granted, to stop speculating after invoking the constraints of "human nature" or the structural condition of anarchy. Despite moves by some theorists to take holistic approaches, there is still a tendency to reify divisions between domestic and international politics or to engage in simple extrapolation. Even feminist social scientists too rarely focus on the concrete levers and opportunities for change. If Alker (1996), Khong (1992), May (1973), and others who have stressed the role of precedent logics, analogy, and lessons of history are correct, it is unlikely that, given our present understanding of human history, humans will construct systems of peace unless they take a fresh look at the past for examples of peaceful institutions, or unless we look at the possible systems of peace and justice created by those who have imagined alternative institutions in all their detail. "Our task as philosophers requires that we try to imagine new, better political structures and different, better moral sentiments. Yes we must be realistic, but not to the point of presenting . . . the essentials of the status quo as unalterable facts" (Pogge, 1994: 224).

Feminist utopian and dystopian science fictions take little for granted and do the hard work of showing the interconnections of politics in one sphere with politics in another. It thus suggests new perspectives and avenues for research in areas previously neglected or under-studied by scholars of world politics. The "what if" questions of world politics are probably not answerable without considering agency, structure, and process at multiple "levels of analysis." Feminist scholars long ago abandoned the pretense of disinterested objectivity, and feminist utopian science fiction is unashamedly interested in creating institutions that work to yield peace and social justice. "Our reconstructive task," as Carol Cohn suggests, is "creating compelling alternative visions of possible futures, a task of recognizing and developing alternative conceptions of rationality, a task of creating rich and imaginative alternative voices—diverse voices whose conversations with each other will invent those futures" (1987: 718). At least four routes forward are suggested by feminist utopian science fiction. One route is by more thoroughly understanding the roles of emotion. Scholars incorporating psychology into the study of world politics have usefully shown how misperception and cognitive limits may affect decision-making.[14] Students of groupthink and nationalism have emphasized the importance of self-esteem and belonging in foreign policy. Yet with few exceptions, such as Lasswell (1965), most international relations theory assumes essentially emotionless rationality, or that if emotions do matter, fear is the crucial one. Yet, despite its central, if under-theorized, role, there is no a priori reason to believe that fear is the most important emotion in international politics, or that we understand how fear works (Crawford, 2000). Nor is it necessarily clear that the neat divide between affective and cognitive psychology should be preserved in social psychology and the study of domestic or world politics. We are thinking *and* feeling, self-interested *and* other-regarding. More work on other emotions, in particular anger, empathy, hope, and love, may yield interesting insights, for example, about when and why humanitarian interventions occur, when crises yield to war, and how identities and aspirations are formed and modified.

Second, attention to emotion thus inevitably brings us to the crucial role of emotional relationships between Self and Other. In feminist utopian science fiction, these relations are sometimes extremely problematic. But alienation is also bridged, often through communicative practices that rely less on arguments intended to persuade the Other and more on truly listening with an aim of understanding (Delrosso, 1999). Such an approach is characteristic of Habermasian discourse ethics, itself often derided as too utopian for international politics (Habermas, 1996; Crawford, 2002). Yet discourse ethics could provide a process for resolving ostensibly intractable disputes.

Third, utopian imagination and the development of specific utopian visions is also probably a necessary first step for identifying the obstacles to social and political change. Hedley Bull recognized the importance of thought experimentation, the use of imaginary orders as a heuristic, in a brief exploration of the requirements for "realisation of the vision of a disarmed world." Bull argues that "merely to have imagined a world in which states have disarmed to low quantitative and qualitative levels is not to give an account of how order in such a world would be maintained" (1977: 237). Bull goes on to suggest some of the material and institutional preconditions and conditions for such a world, and how disarmament could affect the possibility of just social change. Even deeper critique, and the articulation of goals and models for a more peaceful and just world, would be possible if utopian (and dystopian) imaginations were more explicitly part of the tool kit of scholar-activists.

Fourth, feminist utopian science fiction's reconstructive impulse shows how values can explicitly be articulated and realized. All utopias are ethical arguments; all ethical arguments are utopian. Consistent utopianism, which concerns itself with process as much or more than with outcome, thus includes the essential ingredients of effective political thinking: an infinite and desirable goal, an emotional grounding, a concern for justice understood as fair process and outcomes, and a sense of hope as the wellspring for action.

When E. H. Carr, paraphrasing Machiavelli, said "theory does not (as the utopians assume) create practice, but practice theory" (1939: 63) he was articulating the realist view that social scientists (objectively) observe facts on the ground and theorize from them about the objective qualities of the social world. Feminist utopian science fiction does not assume that the relation between social practices and our theories is so linear or one-way. Feminist utopian science fiction offers an implicit rejection of the ontology and epistemology of realism and substitutes an emancipatory and constructivist view of social science and social practice. In positing, for example, that it is possible for a world of "sharers" successfully to oppose an imperialist and militarist society bent on their exploitation, feminist utopians are suggesting not only critique but the power of our imagination to make the social world better. No social change we value has occurred without critique, struggle, and ethical arguments fueled by a utopian impulse. We are thus challenged by feminist utopian science fiction to be more ambitious.

## NOTES

* I thank Amy Nash for research assistance, Cynthia Enloe for encouraging me to teach science fiction and international relations at Clark University in 1993, and Ann Ferguson for sharing an unpublished manuscript. Ann Tickner inspired. Jutta Weldes and Iver Neumann provided excellent comments.

1. Exceptions include North (1976), Alker (1989) and Falk (1992). International relations theory avoids fiction more generally. Exceptions include Alker's (1996) exploration of story grammars in fairy tales, tragedies, and world histories and O'Neill's (1999) game theory analysis of the fairy tale Sir Gawain and the Green Knight.

2. Haraway's *Primate Visions* (1989) was partly inspired by and uses science fiction to understand primatology. In turn, Haraway's essay on cyborgs partly inspired Marge Piercy's *He, She and It* novel about a cyborg. See Elkins (1991) and Booker (1994).

3. Though a slight misrepresentation of the society described in Dick's *The Clans of the Alphane Moon* (1964), it makes the point desired by the Serbian official.

4. On foreign policy decision-makers' uses of history, see May (1973) and Khong (1992). On precedent logic, see Alker (1996).

5. But is it a tautology to say that feminist utopian science fiction is anti-realist? Are there "realist" utopias? In fact, there are. Callenbach's *Ecotopia* (1975) is one example. Skinner's *Walden Two* (1948) explores community organized on the basis of behaviorist theories. In Walden Two, only positive and negative reinforcement, not beliefs or communal affinities, structure relations among the group. Of course there is no shortage of primarily realist dystopias, such as Orwell's *1984*.

6. Good introductions include Barr (1981), McKenna (2001), Moylan (1986, 2000), and Wolmark (1994).

7. Scott's slightly dystopic *Shadow Man* (1995) posits five sexes and nine sexual preferences. Delany's *Triton* (1976) posits more than forty genders.

8. Sargent's *Venus of Dreams* (1986), *Venus of Shadows* (1988), and *Child of Venus* (2001) are more explicitly utopian.

9. For example, Sargent, *The Shore of Women* (1987) and *Venus of Dreams* (1986); Butler, *Parable of the Sower* (1993); Slonszewski, *The Wall Around Eden* (1989); Gearhart, *The Wanderground;* Charnas, *Walk to the End of the World* (1974); and Tepper, *The Gate to Women's Country* (1988).

10. The focus on language parallels arguments salient in feminist communities during the 1970s and 1980s. Orwell is also preoccupied by uses of history and the role of language in thought and political control.

11. During the 1980s women protesting nuclear weapons at Greenham Common, England, and in upstate New York at the Seneca Women's Peace Encampment constructed anti-nuclear activist communities. These separatist peace camps emphasized egalitarianism, non-hierarchical decision-making, and community responsibility for child-care, cooking, and housing construction. While at least some encampment participants were inspired by feminist utopias, the communities were far from perfect and their inhabitants recognized this, often spending hours in auto-criticism and planning in an effort to solve problems ranging from garbage disposal, to wheel-chair accessibility, to the use of language.

12. For example: Bryant, *The Kin of Ata Are Waiting For You* (1976); Piercy's *Woman on the Edge of Time;* Slonczewski's *A Door Into Ocean,* and Le Guin's *The Left Hand of Darkness.* Le Guin's *The Dispossessed,* often read as a commentary on the cold war, uses this device. There is little contact between two worlds, socialist anarchist utopia Anares, and more troubled

capitalist Uras, resulting in inhabitants holding uncorrected stereotypes about the other world. Economic relationships between the two planets are unequal, with Uras exploiting Anares. Readers learn of both worlds through the protagonist Shevek's unofficial function as ambassador to Uras and through his musings about Anares culture after he becomes estranged from it.

13. Tronto notes that "there is no ethnic, cultural, or even genetic diversity in the *Herland* population." By positing a homogenous society where there is no resource scarcity, Gilman removes "all possible source of conflict and of strife." Tronto argues that this is one of the novel's fatal flaws. In the single-minded pursuit of an ethic of care, "Gilman must posit a degree of social harmony and an absence of conflict that almost permits no individuation among people" (1994: 159–160).

14. See Jervis (1976); Lebow (1981); Jervis, Lebow, and Stein (1985); Larson (1985); Stein (1988); Vertzberger (1990).

## BIBLIOGRAPHY

Alker, Hayward R. 1989. "An Orwellian Lasswell for Today," in Robert L. Savage, James Combs, and Dan Nimmo, eds., *The Orwellian Moment: Hindsight and Foresight in the Post-1984 World,* Fayetteville: The University of Arkansas Press, pp. 131–155.

Alker, Hayward R. 1996. *Rediscoveries and Reformulations: Humanistic Methodologies for International Studies,* Cambridge: Cambridge University Press.

Barr, Marlene S., ed. 1981. *Future Females: A Critical Anthology,* Bowling Green, OH: Bowling Green State University Press.

Baudrillard, Jean. 1991."Simulacra and Science Fiction," *Science-Fiction Studies,* 18(3): 309–313.

Booker, M. Keith. 1994. "Woman on the Edge of a Genre," *Science-Fiction Studies,* 21(3): 337–350.

Bradley, Marion Zimmer. 1976. *The Shattered Chain,* New York: Daw Books.

Brin, David. 1991. *Earth,* New York: Bantam Books.

Bryant, Dorothy. 1976. *The Kin of Ata are Waiting For You,* New York: Random House.

Bull, Hedley, 1977. *The Anarchical Society: A Study of World Order in Politics,* New York: Columbia University Press.

Bush, George W. 2002. "Remarks at Graduation Exercise at the United States Military Academy," West Point, New York, June 1. White House transcript. http://www.whitehouse.gov/news/releases/2002.

Butler, Octavia. 1988. *Kindred,* Boston: Beacon Press.

Butler, Octavia. 1993. *Parable of the Sower,* New York: Four Walls Eight Windows.

Butler, Octavia. 1998. *Parable of the Talents,* New York: Seven Stories Press.

Callenbach, Ernest. 1975. *Ecotopia,* New York: Bantam.

Card, Orson Scott. 1977. *Ender's Game,* New York: Tom Doherty Associates.

Card, Orson Scott. 1987. *Speaker for the Dead,* New York: Tom Doherty Associates.

Card, Orson Scott. 1991. *Xenoxide,* New York: Tom Doherty Associates.

Carr, E. H. 1939. *The Twenty Years' Crisis, 1919–1939,* New York: Harper.

Charnas, Suzy McKee. 1974. *Walk to the End of the World,* New York: Ballentine.

Cohn, Carol. 1987. "Sex and Death in the Rational World of Defense Intellectuals," *Signs: Journal of Women in Culture and Society,* 12(4): 687–718.

Cornell, Christine. 2001. "The Interpretive Journey in Ursula K. Le Guin's *The Left Hand of Darkness,*" *Extrapolation,* 42(4): 317–327.

Crawford, Neta C. 2000. "The Passion of World Politics: Propositions on Emotion and Emotional Relationships," *International Security,* 24(4): 116–156.

Crawford, Neta C. 2002. *Argument and Change in World Politics: Ethics, Decolonization and Humanitarian Intervention,* Cambridge: Cambridge University Press.

Delany, Samuel. 1976. *Triton,* New York: Bantam.

Delrosso, Jeana. 1999. "The Womanization of Utopias: Sally Miller Gearhart's Rhetorical Fiction," *Extrapolation,* 40(3): 213–233.

Dick, Philip K. 1964. *The Clans of the Alphane Moon,* New York: Carroll & Graf.

Donawerth, Jane L., and Carol A. Kolmerten, 1994. "Introduction," in Jane L. Donawerth and Carol A. Kolmerten eds., *Utopian and Science Fiction by Women.* Syracuse, NY: Syracuse University Press, pp. 1–14.

Elgin, Suzette Haden. 1984. *Native Tongue,* New York: Daw Books.

Elgin, Suzette Haden. 1987. *The Judas Rose: Native Tongue II,* New York: Daw Books.

Elkins, Charles. 1991. "The Uses of Science Fiction," *Science-Fiction Studies,* 17(2): 269–272.

Falk, Richard. 1992. *Explorations at the Edge of Time: The Prospects for World Order,* Philadelphia: Temple University Press.

Ferguson, Ann. 1993. "Herland or Ourland: Feminist Utopias as Models for Social Change," unpublished paper given at the Harvard Divinity School.

Folbre, Nancy. 2000. *The Invisible Heart: Economics and Family Values,* New York: The New Press.

Freedman, Carl. 2000. *Political Theory and Science Fiction,* Hanover, NH: University Press of New England.

Freibert, Lucy. 1983. "World Views in Utopian Novels by Women," in Marleen S. Barr and Nicholas D. Smith, eds., *Women and Utopia: Critical Interpretations,* New York: University Press of America, pp. 67–84.

Gearhart, Sally Miller. 1979. *The Wanderground: Stories of the Hill Women,* Watertown, MA: Persephone Press.

Gilligan, Carol. 1993. *In a Different Voice: Psychological Theory and Women's Development,* 2nd ed., Cambridge, MA: Harvard University Press.

Gilman, Charlotte Perkins. 1979 [1915]. *Herland,* New York: Pantheon Books.

Goodwin, Barbara. 1978. *Social Science and Utopia: Nineteenth Century Models of Social Harmony,* Atlantic Highlands, NJ: Humanities Press.

Greenberg, Martin Harry, and Joseph D. Olander, eds. 1978. *International Relations Through Science Fiction,* New York: New Viewpoints.

Habermas, Jürgen. 1996. *Between Facts and Norms: Contributions to a Discourse Theory of Law and Democracy,* Cambridge, MA: MIT Press.

Haraway, Donna. 1985. "A Manifesto for Cyborgs: Science, Technology, and Socialist Feminism in the 1980s," *Socialist Review,* 15(2): 65–107.

Haraway, Donna. 1989. *Primate Visions: Gender, Race, and Nature in the World of Modern Science,* New York: Routledge.

Jervis, Robert. 1976. *Perception and Misperception in International Politics,* Princeton, NJ: Princeton University Press.

Jervis, Robert, Richard Ned Lebow, and Janice Stein, with contributions by Patrick Morgan and Jack Snyder. 1985. *Psychology and Deterrence,* Baltimore: Johns Hopkins University Press.

Khong, Yuen Foong. 1992. *Analogies at War: Korea, Munich, Dien Bien Phu, and the Vietnam Decision of 1965,* Princeton, NJ: Princeton University Press.

Landon, Brooks. 1991. "Responding to the Killer B's," *Science-Fiction Studies,* 18(3): 326–327.

Larson, Deborah Welch. 1985. *Origins of Containment: A Psychological Explanation,* Princeton, NJ: Princeton University Press.

Lasswell, Harold. 1941. "The Garrison State," *The American Journal of Sociology,* 46(4): 455–468.

Lasswell, Harold. 1965 [1935]. *World Politics and Personal Insecurity,* New York: Free Press.

Le Guin, Ursula. 1969a. *The Left Hand of Darkness,* New York: Ace Science Fiction.

Le Guin, Ursula. 1969b. "Introduction," in her *The Left Hand of Darkness,* New York: Ace Science Fiction.

Le Guin, Ursula. 1974. *The Dispossessed,* New York: Harper and Row.

Le Guin, Ursula. 1989. "Is Gender Necessary? Redux," in her *The Language of the Night,* New York: Harper Perrenial, pp. 155–172.

Lebow, Richard Ned. 1981. *Between Peace and War: The Nature of International Crises,* Baltimore: Johns Hopkins University Press.

Lorde, Audre. 1984. "The Uses of the Erotic: The Erotic as Power" in her *Sister Outsider,* Trumansberg, NY: The Crossing Press, pp. 53–59.

Lyotard, Jean Francois. 1993. "A Few Words to Sing," in *Toward the Postmodern,* Atlantic Highlands, NJ: Humanities Press International, pp. 41–59.

Manning, Rita. 1992. *Speaking from the Heart: A Feminist Perspective on Ethics,* Lanham, MD: Rowman & Littlefield.

Marx, Karl and Frederick Engels. 1979 [1879]. *The Communist Manifesto,* NY: International Publishers.

Marx, Karl, and Frederick Engels. 1978. "The German Ideology," in Robert Taylor, ed., *The Marx-Engels Reader,* 2nd edition, New York: W.W. Norton, pp. 146–200.

May, Ernest. 1973. *"Lessons" of the Past: The Use and Misuse of History in American Foreign Policy,* New York: Oxford University Press.

McKenna, Erin. 2001. *The Task of Utopia: A Pragmatist and Feminist Perspective,* New York: Rowman & Littlefield.

Miller, Jim. 1998. "Post-Apocalyptic Hoping: Octavia Butler's Dystopian/Utopian Vision," *Science-Fiction Studies,* 25(2): 226–360.

More, Thomas. 1992 [1516]. *The Common-Wealth of Utopia: containing a learned and pleasant discourse of the best state of a publike weale, as it is found in the government of the new ile called Utopia,* translated by Robert Adams, New York: Norton.

Moylan, Tom, 1986. *Demand the Impossible: Science Fiction and the Utopian Imagination,* New York: Methuen.

Moylan, Tom. 2000. *Scraps of Untainted Sky: Science Fiction, Utopia, Distopia,* Boulder, CO: Westview Press.

North, Robert C. 1976. *The World that Could Be,* New York: W.W. Norton.

O'Neill, Barry. 1999. *Honor, Symbols and War,* Ann Arbor: University of Michigan Press.

Orwell, George. 1983 [1949]. *1984,* New York: New American Library.

Patai, Daphne. 1983. "Beyond Defensiveness: Feminist Research Strategies," in Marleen S. Barr and Nicholas D. Smith, eds., *Women and Utopia: Critical Interpretations,* New York: University Press of America, pp. 148–169.

Pearson, Carol. 1981. "Coming Home: Four Feminist Utopias and Patriarchal Experience," in Marleen S. Barr, ed., *Future Females: A Critical Anthology,* Bowling Green, OH: Bowling Green State University Popular Press, pp. 63–70.

Perlez, Jane. 1995. "News From Front Grips Bosnian Serb's Big City," *The New York Times,* August 16, p. A8.

Piercy, Marge. 1976. *Woman On the Edge of Time,* New York: Fawcett Crest.

Piercy, Marge. 1991. *He, She and It,* New York: Knopf.

Pogge, Thomas. 1994. "An Egalitarian Law of Peoples," *Philosophy and Public Affairs,* 23(3): 195–224.

Sargent, Pamela. 1986. *Venus of Dreams,* New York: Bantam.

Sargent, Pamela. 1987. *The Shore of Women,* New York: Bantam.

Sargent, Pamela. 1988. *Venus of Shadows,* New York: Doubleday.

Sargent, Pamela. 1995. "Introduction," in Pamela Sargent, ed., *Women of Wonder, The Classic Years: Science Fiction by Women from the 1940s to the 1970s,* New York: Harcourt Brace, pp. 1–20.

Sargent, Pamela. 2001. *Child of Venus,* New York: Avon.

Scott, Melissa. 1995. *Shadow Man,* New York: Tor.

Shelley, Mary W. 1965 [1818]. *Frankenstein,* New York: Dell.

Shklar, Judith. 1957. *After Utopia: The Decline of Political Faith,* Princeton, NJ: Princeton University Press.

Skinner, B. F. 1948. *Walden Two,* New York: MacMillan.

Slonszewski, Joan. 1986. *A Door Into Ocean,* New York: Avon.

Slonszewski, Joan. 1989. *The Wall Around Eden,* New York: Morrow.

Stanley, William. 1996. *The Protection Racket State: Elite Politics, Military Extortion, and Civil War in El Salvador,* Philadelphia: Temple University Press.

Stein, Janice Gross. 1988. "Building Politics into Psychology: The Misperception of Threat," *Political Psychology*, 9(2): 245–271.

Suvin, Darko. 1979. *Metamorphoses of Science Fiction: On the Poetics and History of a Literary Genre*, New Haven, CT: Yale University Press.

Tepper, Sheri. 1988. *The Gate to Women's Country*, New York: Bantam.

Thompson, Janna. 1992. *Justice and World Order: A Philosophical Inquiry*, New York: Routledge.

Tickner, J. Ann. 1988. "Hans Morgenthau's Principles of Political Realism: A Feminist Reformulation," *Millennium*, 17(3): 429–440.

Tilly, Charles. 1992. *Coercion, Capital, and European States, AD 990–1992*, Oxford: Blackwell.

Tronto, Joan. 1994. *Moral Boundaries: A Political Argument for an Ethic of Care*, New York: Routledge.

Vertzberger, Yaacov Y. I. 1990. *The World in Their Minds: Information Processing, Cognition and Perception in Foreign Policy Decisionmaking*, Stanford, CA: Stanford University Press.

Wolmark, Jenny. 1994. *Aliens and Others: Science Fiction, Feminism and Postmodernism*, Iowa City: University of Iowa Press.

# CONTRIBUTORS

NETA C. CRAWFORD is Associate Professor (Research) at the Thomas J. Watson Jr. Institute for International Studies at Brown University. She is the author of *Argument and Change in World Politics: Ethics, Decolonization, and Humanitarian Intervention* (Cambridge University Press, 2002) and co-editor of *How Sanctions Work: Lessons from South Africa* (St. Martin's Press, 1999). She has also written articles for several books and for the journals *International Organization, International Security,* and *Ethics and International Affairs.*

AIDA A. HOZIC is Assistant Professor of International Relations in the Department of Political Science at the University of Florida. She is the author of *Hollywood: Space, Power and Fantasy in the American Economy* (Cornell University Press, 2001). Her articles have been published in *Review of International Political Economy, Review of Radical Political Economy, Afterimage,* and several edited volumes on the intersections between political economy, International Relations, and cultural studies.

NAEEM INAYATULLAH is Assistant Professor of Politics at Ithaca College. His current work is at the intersection of political economy and culture. He has published in *Alternatives, Review of International Studies, Review of International Political Economy, Millennium,* and *International Studies Review.* With David Blaney, he is working on a book titled *IR and the Problem of Difference.* He is a fan of *Star Trek: The Next Generation.*

PATRICK THADDEUS JACKSON is Assistant Professor of International Relations in the School of International Service, American University. He has previously published articles in the *European Journal of International Relations* and the *Journal of Political Philosophy,* and is a contributor to the edited volume *Constructivism and Comparative Politics* (M. E. Sharpe, 2002). He is presently working on a book entitled *Occidentalism: "Western Civilization" and Postwar German Reconstruction,* which explores the role of public rhetoric about transnational cultural community in legitimating policies after World War II. When push comes to shove, he prefers *Star Wars* to *Star Trek.*

RONNIE D. LIPSCHUTZ is Professor of Politics and Associate Director of the Center for Global, International, and Regional Studies at the University of California, Santa Cruz. His most recent books are *After Authority: War, Peace, and Global Politics in the 21st Century* (State University of New York Press, 2000), and *Cold War Fantasies—Film, Fiction, and Foreign Policy* (Rowman & Littlefield, 2001).

PATRICIA MOLLOY holds a Ph.D. in Education from the Ontario Institute for Studies in Education of the University of Toronto, where she teaches courses on war and cinema, art, and popular culture. She has written extensively on the cultural representation of international politics and has previously published in *Alternatives, Cultural Values, Afterimage,* and *Culture Machine.* Her book, *From the Strategic Self to the Ethical Relation: Pedagogies of War and Peace,* is forthcoming with the University of Minnesota Press in 2003.

IVER B. NEUMANN is Senior Researcher at the Norwegian Institute for International Affairs, Oslo. Among his English-language works in international relations are *Uses of the Other: "The East" in European Identity Formation* (University of Minnesota Press, 1999), *Russia and the Idea of Europe: A Study in Identity and International Relations* (Routledge, 1996), and, as co-editor with Ole Wæver, *The Future of International Relations* (Routledge, 1997). His many Norwegian-language publications include articles on popular culture.

DANIEL H. NEXON is currently a Visiting Assistant Professor of Government and Foreign Service at Georgetown University. He has published a number of articles on International Relations theory and is a contributor to the edited volume *Constructivism and Comparative Politics* (M. E. Sharpe, 2002). He is now working on turning his doctoral dissertation, "Contending Sovereignties: Religious Conflict and State Formation in Early Modern Europe," into a book.

JUTTA WELDES is a Senior Lecturer in International Relations at the University of Bristol. She is the author of *Constructing National Interests: The United States and the Cuban Missile Crisis* (University of Minnesota Press, 1999) and co-editor of *Cultures of Insecurity: States, Communities, and the Production of Danger* (University of Minnesota Press, 1999). She has published articles on popular culture and world politics in *Millennium,* as well as others in the *European Journal of International Relations, Mershon International Studies Review, Millennium,* and *Theory and Society.*

GEOFFREY WHITEHALL is a Lecturer at the University of Victoria, British Columbia and a Ph.D. Candidate in Political Science at the University of Hawai'i at Manoa. He has published "Wandering Grounds: Transversality, Identity, Territoriality, and Movement" (with Nevzat Soguk) in *Millennium.* His current research explores contemporary political theory in International Relations, geography, and political science through the themes of globalization, humanism, and popular culture. He is fond of the color orange.

# INDEX

Made in the USA
Middletown, DE
15 August 2017